GODFORSAKEN
SEA

GODFORSAKEN SEA

Racing the World's Most Dangerous Waters

Derek Lundy

YELLOW JERSEY PRESS
LONDON

Published by Yellow Jersey Press 1999

2 4 6 8 10 9 7 5 3 1

Copyright © Derek Lundy 1999

Derek Lundy has asserted his right under the Copyright, Designs
and Patents Act 1988 to be identified as the author of this work

First published in Canada in 1998 by
Alfred A. Knopf Canada

First published in Great Britain in 1999 by
Yellow Jersey Press
Random House, 20 Vauxhall Bridge Road,
London SW1V 2SA

Random House Australia (Pty) Limited
20 Alfred Street, Milsons Point, Sydney,
New South Wales 2061, Australia

Random House New Zealand Limited
18 Poland Road, Glenfield,
Auckland 10, New Zealand

Random House South Africa (Pty) Limited
Endulini, 5A Jubilee Road, Parktown 2193, South Africa

Random House UK Limited Reg. No. 954009

A CIP catalogue record for this book
is available from the British Library

ISBN 0 224 05970 X

Papers used by Random House UK Limited are natural,
recyclable products made from wood grown in sustainable forests;
the manufacturing processes conform to the environmental
regulations of the country of origin

Typeset by SX Composing DTP, Rayleigh, Essex
Printed and bound in Great Britain by
Creative Print and Design (Wales), Ebbw Vale

To Alexander Dickson Lundy (1921–1995)
Once a sailor

There is a poetry of sailing as old as the world.
– Antoine de Saint-Exupéry

Contents

Author's Note

All references to miles are nautical miles. A nautical mile equals 1.15 statute miles or 1.85 kilometres. Speeds and wind velocities are stated in knots, or nautical miles per hour (m.p.h.). So, for example, twenty-five knots is 29 m.p.h. ot 46 kilometres per hour (k.p.h.); fifty knots is almost 58 m.p.h. or 93 k.p.h. A wind officially becomes hurricane force when it blows at or above sixty-four knots – 73 m.p.h. or 118 k.p.h.

Dramatis Personae

The Vendée Globe, 1996–97 (sixteen starters)
Philippe Jeantot, race organiser and director

The Sailors
Christophe Auguin, *Géodis*
Isabelle Autissier, PRB
Tony Bullimore, *Exide Challenger*
Catherine Chabaud, *Whirlpool Europe 2*
Bertrand de Broc, *Votre nom autour du monde-Pommes Rhône Alpes*
Patrick de Radiguès, *Afibel*
Raphaël Dinelli, *Algimouss*
Thierry Dubois, *Pour Amnesty International*
Eric Dumont, *Café Legal le Goût*
Nandor Fa, *Budapest*
Pete Goss, *Aqua Quorum*
Hervé Laurent, *Groupe LG Traitmat*
Didier Munduteguy, *Club 60e Sud*
Yves Parlier, *Aquitaine Innovations*
Gerry Roufs, *Groupe LG2*
Marc Thiercelin, *Crédit Immobilier de France*

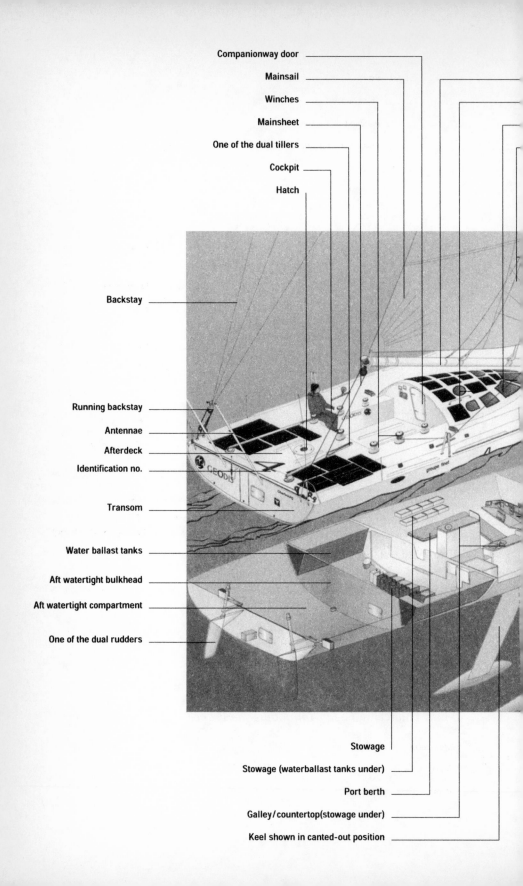

Companionway door

Mainsail

Winches

Mainsheet

One of the dual tillers

Cockpit

Hatch

Backstay

Running backstay

Antennae

Afterdeck

Identification no.

Transom

Water ballast tanks

Aft watertight bulkhead

Aft watertight compartment

One of the dual rudders

Stowage

Stowage (waterballast tanks under)

Port berth

Galley/countertop(stowage under)

Keel shown in canted-out position

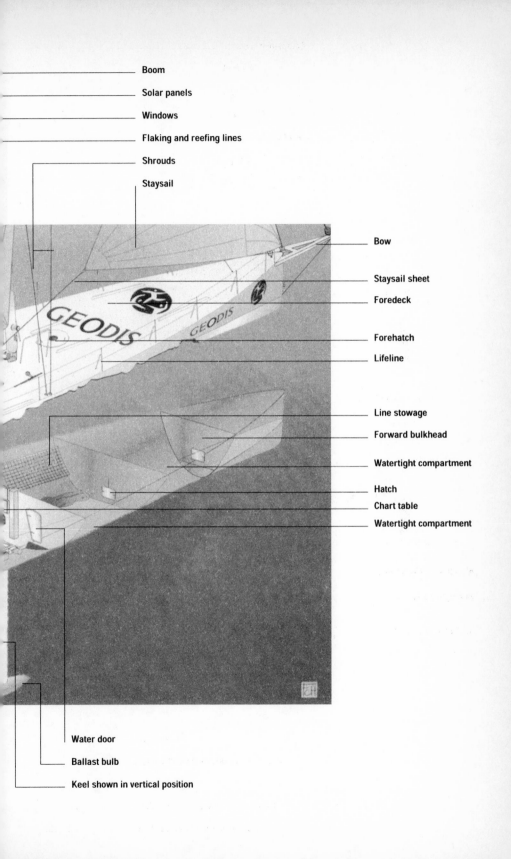

Boom

Solar panels

Windows

Flaking and reefing lines

Shrouds

Staysail

Bow

Staysail sheet

Foredeck

Forehatch

Lifeline

Line stowage

Forward bulkhead

Watertight compartment

Hatch

Chart table

Watertight compartment

Water door

Ballast bulb

Keel shown in vertical position

Prologue

Signatures of all things I am here to read,
seaspawn and seawrack . . .

– James Joyce, *Ulysses*

Each time I looked astern, I jumped. The dark shape on the stern rail seemed human – a squat little man crouching there malevolently, ready to leap at me. I looked back every ten seconds or so to try to gauge the height and speed of the following waves. Working the tiller with both hands, I tried to keep the boat square to the wind and seas. To maintain my bearings in the dark, I had to feel the wind on my face, try to catch the phosphorescent flash of the breaking crests. Every time I looked, the man-shape startled me. During each short interval, I forgot he was there. For half an hour, I'd been looking back, jumping, forgetting, looking back, jumping . . . On the horizon, five hundred miles from land, I imagined I glimpsed the skyline of a great city of lights.

The boat was driving hard to the south-east under a double-reefed staysail – about thirty square feet of drum-tight sail just forward of the mast. The wind was pushing us at almost six knots, as fast as our little boat could go. The resistance the bow wave created as the boat moved through the sea, and the fiction between the hull and the water, set a speed limit that, theoretically, we couldn't exceed. But sometimes we accelerated right through the immutable laws of hydrodynamics, as the boat surfed down the face of a twelve-foot Atlantic wave.

We were out on the open ocean for the first time in our lives – my wife and I – on a thirty-one-foot sailboat weighing five and a half tons. I'd sailed small boats for most of my life, but rarely out of sight of land. This passage was different – no Great Lakes slog to another marina, or coastal hop to the next homey anchorage. We'd crossed the Gulf Stream, and now we were aiming for the heart of the Bermuda Triangle, across the Sargasso Sea, south-east as hard as we could go, away from the dangerous December storm latitudes. We would keep this heading until we hit sixty-five degrees west longitude – nicknamed 'I–65', like an interstate highway, because of the flow of southbound boat traffic to the Caribbean. Then we would turn due south, looking for the steady north-east trade winds to ride into Charlotte Amalie or Jost van Dyke.

Leaving Charleston Bay, we had sailed on a gentle south-west breeze for several hours. Just before sunset, the land a dark line astern, we saw dolphins about fifty yards off our port side. They streaked towards us in a leaping joyful bunch. They did what dolphins do – chittered, dived, jumped, surfed our bow wave. Then, bored with our three knots, they sped off to bluer pastures. We were thrilled with the exuberance and insouciance of the wild dolphins, their sheer at-home-ness in the ocean. They soothed our fear of the thirteen hundred miles ahead. With such animals in it, the sea seemed friendly, benign, comprehensible. Everything would be all right after all.

Well, not exactly. Four days later, things were not all right. The sea, among its many qualities, is an unerring discoverer of weakness. And it had discovered one of ours. I hadn't properly sealed the engine ignition and gauges, which were set into one of the locker sides in the cockpit at about shin height. That night, on watch, I suddenly realised that the intermittent chugging noise I'd been hearing over the sounds of wind and sea was our auxiliary diesel engine trying to start itself. Sea water, scooped up by the bow's plunge, swept down the windward side-deck and into the cockpit, where it swirled out the drains in a luminous kaleidoscope. Some of the water had got into the ignition switch and shorted it out, creating the same effects as turning the ignition key. The engine, trying to start against the iron grip of the transmission – it was in gear to stop the propeller from free-wheeling as we sailed – soon wore down the batteries. I heard what was happening just as they were going dead flat. We used the engine to get in and out of ports and anchorages, to escape local calms and to charge our batteries for electricity. It could also come in handy sometimes in bad weather at sea, to help control the boat. But otherwise, when we were on a passage, the engine was a passive bystander.

We had spares or tools to replace or fix just about everything on board. But our ethos of self-sufficiency and redundancy was tailored for matter, not energy. Now we needed the two things we didn't have two of. To recharge the batteries, we needed the engine. The engine, which we could theoretically start with a hand crank in the absence of electricity, now refused to start that way. If we couldn't start the engine, we couldn't charge the batteries. Without the batteries, we had no electricity, and couldn't start the engine. No electricity meant no electric lights below (although we had kerosene spares), no log (to tell us speed and distance sailed), no compass light. No engine meant that we were truly a sailing vessel. We would have to wait for wind in the inevitable calms of the horse latitudes. The spare diesel fuel we'd carried to get us through them was now useless ballast.

A lot of people sail boats without engines, and even to me it had a theoretical appeal. Complete reliance on the wind took the sailor to the aesthetic heart of the process – the austere purity of air moving across the sail's airfoil and lifting the boat forward in a horizontal replication of an airplane's flight. But as a practical matter, out there on the corrugated sea, I wanted that damn engine. It was for more than electricity or breaking through calms. It represented the comfort and reassurance of technology. Without it, we were catapulted back a hundred years to the time of 'wooden ships and iron men'. We felt distinctly non-ferrous.

And if the engine could go – just like that, because I hadn't put ten cents' worth of plastic and caulking around a switch – what would be next? What other undiscovered oversight or carelessness might be lurking, ready to bring down the mast, destroy a sail, disable the self-steering wind vane, violate the first rule of sailing – keep the ocean out of the boat – by letting the ocean in?

For four days, we'd bumped and careened out to sea. I had hardly slept at all. Christine had done little better. I couldn't sleep partly because of the boat's wild motion, but mostly because of the noise. The waves sounded like battering-rams when they hit the hull. But worse, everything on the boat creaked and groaned. It was clear aural evidence, I was convinced, of wood and fibreglass molecules being torn apart. I lay in my bunk when I was off watch and waited for something to break. I'd beefed up the boat before we left – torn the insides out and reinforced everything in sight. But I had been desk-bound for most of my life, and it was the first time I'd done that sort of work. I wasn't sure I'd done it right. Was everything really strong enough? To me, it seemed merely rational to expect catastrophe.

To compensate for my disquiet, I spent a lot of time checking things. That was what I was supposed to be doing anyway. The sailor is an obsessive fusser about everything on board. The smallest oversight – like our unprotected engine controls – could make things uncomfortable at best, or begin a spiralling descent into disaster. Nothing can be left to chance; the sea exploits all weaknesses. On every watch, therefore (we alternated three hours on, three hours off, round the clock), I made my inspection.

On our fourth night out, the wind increased to a sustained thirty knots, gusting close to forty. It was on the cusp of being an official full gale. To us, new to the open ocean, it *was* a gale. The boat seemed barely under control. In the wave troughs, we strained to glimpse the foamy phosphorescence on the crests. Gauging wave heights from the deck of a small boat is like evaluating a referee's call against your own team: you're just a bit to involved with the action to be objective. With waves, honest errors result from the observer's angle of vision and the shape of the wave. The rule of thumb is to cut almost in half the height you think you see. I thought I saw waves that night that were twenty-five feet high, and, every so often, ones I couldn't bear to estimate.

We disconnected the wind vane. I began to steer by hand, trying to keep the waves more or less square to the stern. That was when I started to hallucinate that the dwarfish man on the stern rail was about to let me have it. There was something there, of course – the jerrycans with the now-useless diesel fuel, the man-overboard buoy container and the dinghy outboard clamped to the rail. Together, their shape in the black night was vaguely humanoid. I was so tired that I couldn't remember for more than a few seconds what it was that had startled me, or even that I'd been startled. When my hallucination expanded to include the full-fledged city skyline on the horizon, we realised we'd had it. We stopped the boat – hove to – to try to get some sleep.

Heaving-to is one of the pleasingly ancient and elegant manoeuvres that sailors have used for centuries to park a sailing vessel while they wait out bad weather, sleep, navigate or make repairs. In one typical method, two storm-sails are set and trimmed tightly, one to each side of the boat. The pull of one sail tends to cancel out the pull of the other, and the boat remains almost stationary. The rudder is then lashed so that the boat holds a fairly constant position, about forty-five to sixty degrees off the direction of wind and waves, drifting forward at a knot or so. The result is a tense equilibrium, with the boat's strongest point – the bow – presented to the gale. The transition from sailing to being hove-to is remarkable: the whipsaw motion subsides; there's much less noise (the most unnerving part of bad weather at sea); and the boat rises and falls on waves suddenly diminished, no longer carnivorous.

The wind seldom gusted past forty knots and for twelve hours, we rested, ate dried fruit and granola bars, and endured the racket of moderately heavy weather. But although we also slept a little, enough to get going again when our gale was over, the psychological pattern for the rest of our first open-ocean passage had been set: it was an ordeal to get through.

Later, we rolled and lurched for two days on smooth, slick swells, waiting for wind. I spent the time thinking up original insults for our recalcitrant engine. A few days after the wind filled in again, a low-pressure system began to form almost directly over our heads. It moved off to the north-east before it became a full gale. But the mass of cold air trailing down from the system's centre did cross over us. As the front – its leading edge – passed by, we got a second dose of thirty-five-knot wind and rough seas. This time we didn't hesitate, and hove-to for twenty-four hours until things improved.

As we worked our way south-east into the trade winds, there were periods of the poetry-in-motion we'd read about. Our boat weaved its way through deep blue, foam-tipped waves under a strengthening tropical sun. We were exhilarated by the swoop and dip of a vessel steering itself through a benign sea – the bright colours and shadows, the rhythmic swoosh of the bow wave, the sense of ancient harmony between a wind-driven boat and the sea. We saw flying fish break the surface and glide, wings flashing, for fifty yards or more. We watched sunrises and sunsets that – even through our fatigue – provoked momentary flashes of the seamless unity of the natural world, or a sense of that world as it used to be. Our fear diminished. We got a little sleep each day.

Still, I never stopped worrying that something might break. We had no long-range radio transmitter – only a short-wave receiver that got marine forecasts for the Atlantic Ocean, broadcast from landlocked Fort Collins, Colorado. If something went badly wrong, we couldn't get in touch with anyone who was more than about forty miles away, the range of our VHF radio. Neither of us had ever been so alone, so far from the rest of the world, so completely dependent on our own resources. While taking some pride in our self-sufficiency, we barely endured the isolation that made it necessary.

A few days after our gale, I noticed a bird flying by. It was a brown booby, a common-enough seabird. It was also the first form of life we'd seen for two days, since another seabird had flown by. I went below and made a note in our log that I'd seen a bird. And then it struck me what an empty place we were in – where one bird was worthy of note.

Braced in the cockpit, a city boy looking out over the unnervingly uncluttered aspect of the sea, I thought it looked as strange as the moon, or like some queasily heaving Sahara. It was a wilderness both fascinating and appalling. For us, our passage was a struggle through the empty and remote wilderness of the sea.

I always wanted to be a sailor who crossed oceans. I was sure that I would eventually sail around the world. In my heart, I sustained a boyhood vision of a single-handed circumnavigation: going around alone was the true test, the real accomplishment at sea. The voyage to the Virgin Islands seemed at the time a demonstration that robust dreams often grow sickly when they are bared to real life.

Our trip scared me to death. I felt that, at any moment, we could be overtaken by natural forces that would destroy us. It wasn't simply a matter of our crossing the ocean from Charleston to the Virgins. I didn't think the outcome was as certain as that. We would arrive only if the ocean let us through. Looking back, with experience, my attitude seems melodramatic. The dangers were not really so great, and the chances of cataclysm were actually very small. Still, whenever I've gone to sea in a small boat, some of the suspicion and fear has lingered. Even when the ocean's surface is tranquil, I, like Melville, can't forget 'the tiger heart that pants beneath it.'

I gave up my aspiration to sail alone around the world but I lost none of my fascination with the idea itself – not as practised by the casual tradewind cruisers, loafing through the tropics for years, but by the mavericks who go far south, below 40 degrees, into the ice and storms of the Southern Ocean. That kind of circumnavigation remains for me a passionate act of prolonged courage and endurance.

All this brought me, perhaps, inevitably, to the Vendée Globe round-the-world race. It encompasses the most difficult kind of single-handed sailing through the most dangerous waters in the world (the Southern Ocean), in the most extreme form possible (unassisted and non-stop). The bare facts: twenty-seven thousand miles, three and a half to five months alone at sea, chilling casualty rates, the unrelenting strain of handling sixty-foot boats day and night, the absolute certainty of weather and waves that could destroy them. Remembering my own fearful initiation into relatively safe bluewater sailing, it was impossible not to be intrigued by the race's audacity. I felt compelled to find out how the Vendée Globe skippers did it, why they did it.

I also felt a connection to the race because of Gerry Roufs. He was the first Canadian to have entered the Vendée Globe, and he had a good chance of winning. There was a small but significant affinity between us. Like me, he had trained to be a lawyer, and had then found something different to do with his life, though in his case, something precarious and uncertain, far removed from the affluent safety of the law. After a year, he left his law practice to become a professional sailor, and spent the next twenty years working towards his eventual membership in the single-handed, round-the-world elite.

Five hundred miles from the North Atlantic Ocean, sliding deeper into the Canadian winter, I followed the race. There was the occasional wire story in the Toronto newspapers. Nothing much on television. The Quebec media, especially the French-language side, provided more coverage because the race originated in France. More important, Gerry Roufs was from Quebec. He'd grown up in Montreal and had sailed at the Hudson Yacht Club, just outside the city. He'd been a junior sailing champion – a dinghy prodigy – and had sailed for several years as a member of the Canadian Olympic yachting team.

The traditional sources of information about sailing races – yachting magazines published in Europe, the U.S. and Canada – were always months out of date by the time they were available. The Internet was the real mother-lode. The Vendée Globe organisers had set up a web site. It contained good background information about the race, the sailors and the boats. The best part was the stream of bulletins posted by headquarters each day during the race, sometimes as many as five or six in a twenty-four-hour period. They were all in French, although a truncated English summary, often in an endearingly eccentric translation, was issued once a day or so. Periodically, the skippers themselves would send a few paragraphs about their daily experience from their boats via satellite fax, e-mail or single-sideband radio, and there were regular reports of latitude-longitude positions for each boat. Like several other competitors, Roufs set up his own web site as well, on which he posted intermittent journal entries, in both French and English, describing his activities.

Each day, I could read about the homely details of life on board these swiftest of ocean racers, the weather each boat was going through, its progress – through Biscay, the horse latitudes, the doldrums, the long swing around the South Atlantic High, and then to the south-east, below the Cape of Good Hope, and into the roaring forties of the Southern Ocean. It was an electronic feast of information.

'The sea is as near as we come to another world,' wrote the poet Anne Stevenson. She called it 'the planet ocean.' As the Vendée Globe boats made their hard, hazardous journey through the outlandish sea, I watched them from the haven of the planet earth.

1

In the Seas Entrall

The difference between a gale and what has become known as a 'survival' storm is that in the former, with winds of force 8, or perhaps 9 (say 30 to 45 knots mean velocity), the skipper and crew retain control and can take the measures which they think best, whereas in a survival gale of force 10 or over, perhaps gusting at hurricane strength, wind and sea become the masters.

– K. Adlard Coles, *Heavy Weather Sailing*

UNTIL CHRISTMAS Day, 1996, the race had been a typically robust version of previous Vendée Globe and BOC races. If anything, it had been easier on the competitors than most of the earlier events. None of the collisions with flotsam or ice in this Vendée Globe had put the sailors' lives on the line. It was true that the Southern Ocean had behaved as usual – its chain of low-pressure systems moving relentlessly along the racers' path. Storm- and often hurricane-force wind had piled waves up to heights of fifty or sixty feet. At times, the boats had surfed down wave faces at thirty knots, almost out of control. They had struggled through the dangerous and chaotic cross-seas that followed quick changes in wind direction and had been knocked down often. For several weeks, the skippers endured this trial by wind and cold, ice and breaking waves, skirting the edge of catastrophe as they threaded their way through the great wilderness of the southern seas.

True, it was still a long way to Cape Horn. The greater extent of the Southern Ocean still lay ahead for most of the boats. There was a lot of time left for something to happen. At some point in every one of these races, most often in the Southern Ocean, a sailor's life becomes problematic, hangs by a thread. Sometimes, a life is snuffed out: by inference at first, as contact is suddenly ended; later with certainty, as enough silent time goes by or the searchers find a boat, drifting and unmanned. Some names: Jacques de Roux (1986), Mike Plant (1992), Nigel Burgess (1992), Harry Mitchell (1995) – a few of the ones who have been wiped off the planet. Who knew exactly how? What were the circumstances? An unendurable rogue wave capsizing the boat? Ice? Or a sudden, treacherous slip over the side and into the sea, followed by a final minute or two treading the frigid water, watching the boat (with acceptance? anger? terror?) intermittently visible on the wave crests, surfing farther and farther away, its autopilot functioning perfectly.

There hadn't been any of that yet in this Vendée Globe. But the dragons were certainly there. The 'quakin' and shakin'' was about to begin. During the twelve days of Christmas, the race changed utterly.

The strength of the storm was a surprise. Catherine Chabaud, sailing four hundred miles behind Raphaël Dinelli, was getting the weather first as it swept from west to east. She radioed to him and the other sailors ahead of her a description of the strength and direction of the wind in the low-pressure systems that overtook her, one after the other. This time – seven weeks into the race, just before Christmas – she advised Dinelli to expect a low during the night, with the usual quick wind rotation from north-west to south-west, blowing at around forty to forty-five knots, as the cold front crossed over. It was nothing special – a typical Southern Ocean low of moderate intensity.

What happened instead was unusual and terrifying.

As the low-pressure system began its pass over Dinelli, a warmer high-pressure air mass crowded down from the north. The two systems squeezed together. The cold air of the low slid in under the warmer air of the high and pushed it up. The air already blowing into the centre of the low increased in velocity, shooting up and spiralling out higher in the atmosphere. As more air was displaced from the sea's surface, the air pressure there dropped even farther. Wind is the flow of air from areas of high to low pressure, down the pressure slope, or gradient. It's exactly the same process as water flowing from higher to lower elevations. The steeper the slope, the faster the air moves, and the stronger the wind. As the low approached, its pressure gradient grew ominously steeper.

When the system overtook Dinelli's position, the wind increased until it was blowing close to hurricane strength – sixty-four knots and over – and gusting to eighty knots. It quickly whipped up the constant swell of the Southern Ocean into huge seas. Dinelli's boat started surfing on waves that grew to between fifty-five and sixty-five feet – like fast-moving, always-toppling, six-storey concrete buildings. It was apocalyptic sailing.

Dinelli couldn't stay on deck because it was too dangerous. From inside the cabin, trying to make sense of the shape and steepness of the waves, he did his best to direct the onrushing boat by manipulating his autopilot. But control was impossible. *Algimouss* capsized, violently inverting in a few seconds. The tremendous shock compressed the mast so that it pierced the deck; the boom smashed through one of the large cabin windows and water flowed in. It was Christmas Day morning.

Dressed in a survival suit that had got torn in the capsize, Dinelli wedged himself into a corner of his upside-down cabin. Bit by bit, the water displaced the trapped air in the hull. During the capsize, the mast had snapped off a few feet above deck level. The standing rigging held it more or less in place, and it acted as a kind of keel, holding *Algimouss* stably inverted. After three hours or so, however, wrenched by the boat's furious rolling and pitching, the mast broke away completely. Freed of the resistance of mast and rigging, the three-ton bulb of ballast at the end of the keel regained its leverage, and the boat rolled upright again – sluggishly, because of the weight of water inside. As it did so, Dinelli, mostly underwater, half swam, half walked his way off the cabin top and down the sides until he was standing on the floor again. Now he could activate his satellite emergency radio beacons. He hadn't set them off sooner because the signal wouldn't have been able to penetrate the boat's upside-down carbon-fibre hull.

Within a couple of hours of righting itself, the boat had almost completely filled with water. The waves slammed in through the table-sized hole in the deck with such force that they broke the hull's watertight bulkheads. Each Vendée Globe sixty-footer was required to have three of these, dividing the boat's interior into compartments that could be sealed off, limiting the amount of inflowing water. But no material could withstand the force of these seas. Soon, the deck was at water level. Each enormous wave seemed determined to sink the boat.

Dinelli climbed on to the deck and tethered himself to the stump of the mast, struggling to stay on his feet as the boat lurched and plunged. The waves crashed over him continuously. His torn survival suit soon filled with water. The hull of *Algimouss* was completely submerged, its deck barely visible in the foam of breaking seas. Alternately soaked by waves of frigid Southern Ocean water and blasted by a wind-chill well below zero, Dinelli felt his body temperature begin to drop.

He stood on the deck of his boat for the rest of Christmas Day, through the high-latitude austral summer night and all the next day, the wind never dropping below gale force. Adrift in the Southern Ocean at almost fifty degrees latitude, twelve hundred miles south of Australia, closer to Antarctica, he was as alone and exposed as any human on earth could possibly be. As the second night approached, the twenty-eight-year-old sailor was exhausted and hypothermic. He knew without any doubt that he would not be able to survive until the next morning. Death was very close.

First, the Southern Ocean. To understand this story, you have to understand the Southern Ocean and what it means to sail through it in a small sailboat.

The vast sea area of the Southern Ocean is really the extreme southern portion of the Pacific, Indian and South Atlantic oceans. Its official demarcation is forty degrees south latitude. It includes the latitudes sailors long ago nicknamed the roaring forties, the furious fifties and the screaming sixties. It's an area of almost constant high wind and frequent gales, often exceeding hurricane strength. In storms, the waves build and build until they reach almost un-imaginable heights. The highest wave ever reliably recorded – 120 feet high – was encountered there. The waves of the Southern Ocean roll around the world unimpeded by land. Icebergs and smaller 'growlers' drift through the frigid water. Over the centuries, it has been a sailors' graveyard – square-rigger seamen called the Southern Ocean path to Cape Horn 'Dead Men's Road'. It embodies what Melville called 'that sense of the full awfulness of the sea'.

The Southern Ocean contains that point on earth that is farthest from any land. It's about 1,660 miles equidistant from Pitcairn Island, the *Bounty* mutineers' last refuge, and Cape Dart on Antarctica. Many of the Vendée Globe boats sail close by it, or even, by chance, right through it, as they make for Cape Horn. Only a few astronauts have ever been farther from land than a person on a vessel at that position. But that doesn't begin to describe the remoteness of this part of the planet. Some sailors call a large area of the Southern Ocean 'the hole'. It's too far away for even long-range aircraft to get to – assuming they want to return to land. On maps made when large chunks of territory had still not been penetrated by Europeans, cartographers would label the vast, unknown spaces *'Hic sunt dracones'* – 'Here are dragons'. This confident prophecy of un-predictable and fearsome dangers still applies to the Southern Ocean.

It's difficult for us to grasp the idea that parts of our planet remain in an almost primordial state of wildness and isolation. There are only a few places left on earth where merely getting across them is an achievement: Antarctica, whether on foot or snowmobile; the Sahara off its beaten and braided tracks; the Southern Ocean in a sailboat. The wildernesses of ice or sand or water are terrible places where nature retains power over humans to terrify and to diminish – a power it had everywhere until very recently in our history.

Two around-the-world races for single-handed sailors take competitors through the heart of the Southern Ocean. The Around Alone race (formerly the BOC Challenge) takes place in four separate legs. The boats make three scheduled stops along the way, and can also take unscheduled refuge, without disqualification, to make repairs or find replacements for broken gear. In the Vendée Globe, however, the competitors must sail non-stop and completely un-assisted. It is the most extreme of long-distance sailing races. According to the disarmingly simple rules, the race was created 'to answer the needs of sailors eager to reach their uttermost limits'. There are no complex handicaps or arcane racing rules like those in shorter competitions. In the Vendée Globe, the winner is the first to cross the finish line – one person, one boat, first home.

For the competing skippers, the Southern Ocean is the heart of the matter. It makes up almost half of the total race distance of twenty-seven thousand miles, and requires six to eight weeks of formidable effort to get through – if nothing goes wrong. The other sections of the race pose their own challenges and involve real dangers, but most are manageable. When they sail into the Southern Ocean, the sailors enter a realm of contingency: wind and sea conditions there can destroy even the best boat and the skipper unlucky enough to encounter them. The racers often find themselves in survival conditions – overpowering wind and sea become the master, and the sailor can only hang on and hope for the best. The race is really divided into three parts: the Atlantic, the Southern Ocean, the Atlantic. That middle section is the killer.

'After that, it's a holiday,' said one Vendée Globe skipper, Christophe Auguin.

In the Southern Ocean, the fragile lines that connect the sailor to humanity are stretched to the limit. Sometimes, they break. The sailors in these races depend for help on their connections with each other far more than on any remote and uncertain sources of aid from land. Some skippers have been lifted almost literally out of the sea by fellow racers. Most wouldn't have survived long enough to be picked up by diverted ships, or to be reprieved by life-saving equipment dropped from planes – if they happened to be within reach of them. And in some races, a boat and sailor have just disappeared – without word or trace.

Yet the racers are tied into the worldwide network of satellite and computer communication. On-board computers coordinate satellite-based navigation, communication and weather-forecasting systems. They can fax, e-mail, talk on long- or short-range radios, get detailed weatherfax charts whenever they want. Even in the Southern Ocean, where weather forecasts are sketchy and unreliable, the sailors can often see the weather that's on its way to clobber them. Sometimes, they can even avoid the worst of it.

Their navigation and safety equipment is sophisticated and powerful, and their systems are backed-up as if they were on Apollo flights to the moon. The boats' cabins look like electronics stores. The skippers are in constant contact with race headquarters in France or the US. The race directors, in turn, always know where each boat is, within a few miles or less – a constant radio signal (from an ARGOS transmitter) is broadcast from each boat to satellite receivers. When trouble comes – if a boat's rolled over by a Southern Ocean grey-beard, dismasted and waterlogged – the hypothermic and exhausted sailor can activate 'emergency position indicating radio beacons' (EPIRBs), which notify the satellites. The EPIRBs were the most revolutionary devices the boats carried, and they have changed dramatically the odds of rescue when a sailor gets into serious trouble. They are small and portable – one of the newer ones, for example, is the size of a large flashlight and weighs less than three pounds – and there are several different types. They were the devices the sailors hoped never to use, although in this race, they were destined to be used with some regularity. When an EPIRB is activated, race headquarters and marine-rescue centres know within a few minutes that the dragons have struck. Search-and-rescue operations begin right away.

But getting help to a boat's exact-known location can take days. If none of the other competitors can reach the spot, it may be impossible to get to an injured boat for a week or more – until a dispatched warship or diverted freighter can struggle through. Cargo ships make their regular way across the Southern Ocean – tankers, bulk cargo or container ships bound both ways round the Horn – but they stick to narrow routes, and are few and far between. And sometimes these big ships can't search properly because even they may be endangered by making search manoeuvres in heavy seas.

In any event, an EPIRB has to be on the sea surface for the transmission to work. It won't penetrate hull material or several feet of water. If the boat stays upside down – as Dinelli's did – the sailor must find a way of floating the beacon out of the cabin to the surface, while still keeping it attached to the boat. The newest, and most accurate, EPIRBs have a battery life of thirty-six to seventy-two hours or so, depending on the temperature. The colder it is, the shorter their operating time. After they quit, the boat's position becomes a matter of drift analysis – guesswork based on the vagaries of wind and wave action.

In early January 1997, thirteen Vendée Globe solo sailors were strung out across six thousand miles of the Southern Ocean, stretching from south of Australia almost to Cape Horn. The sailors had already been at sea for more than two months. Of the sixteen starters, only ten were still officially in the race. Three more kept sailing but had been disqualified for stopping in one port or another along the way to make repairs to their boats – strictly prohibited by the race rules.

Dinelli had been sailing as an unofficial entrant because he hadn't had time to make the two-thousand-mile sail required to qualify for the Vendée Globe. Two racers had withdrawn soon after the start on 3 November of the previous year because of damage suffered in a storm in the Bay of Biscay.

Deep in the Southern Ocean, the skippers had lived for weeks in wet foul-weather gear in cold cabins dripping with condensation or sea water that found a way in. The widely spaced boats were dealing with various weather conditions, none of them pleasant. At best, some were running uncomfortably, but not dangerously, before the gale-force depressions that travel unceasingly across the high southern latitudes. For other boats, there wasn't enough wind to enable them to handle the sea conditions – big seas persist for some time after the weather that created them has moderated. The boats were faltering in waves that struck anarchically from all directions without the governing discipline of strong wind.

Other skippers found themselves in particularly severe low-pressure systems – storms that made our Virgin Islands 'yachtsman's gale' seem like the briefest and most benign of squalls. They were struggling to control their boats as they surfed at breakneck speeds of twenty-five knots or more down waves like steep hills in winds of near-hurricane strength.

In just those conditions, during the night of 4 January, two of the sixty-foot-long Vendée Globe boats capsized. They were sailing fourteen hundred miles south-west of the Australian Cape Leeuwin at about fifty-one degrees south latitude – just inside the border of the furious fifties. The boats were within forty miles of each other, near the back of the strung-out fleet.

Aboard *Exide Challenger* (a sophisticated ketch – a two-masted rig), Tony Bullimore heard a loud bang. He could hear it even over the shrill tumult of his boat's rush through the storm. The carbon-fibre keel, fatally fatigued by the boat's unending motion, had suddenly snapped off, plunging down to the ocean floor – in this sea area, the relatively shallow south-east Indian Ridge – five hundred fathoms down. Suddenly deprived of its four and a half tons of ballast, the now top-heavy boat flipped over with shocking speed – two or three seconds. Just before it happened, the fifty-seven-year-old Bullimore had been standing wedged in his cabin, drinking a mug of tea he'd managed to brew up on his gimballed one-burner stove and smoking one of his roll-your-own cigarettes. As the boat flipped, he rolled around with it, and found himself standing on the cabin top, which was now the floor.

The abruptness of the event astonished him. He looked down through the big cabin windows, which were now acting as the bottom of the hull, and saw sea water rushing past, like a fast-flowing river under his feet. The howl of the wind passing at seventy knots around the boat's two masts and rigging had stopped. In fact, it was almost quiet – although the boat was still rocking and rolling.

His mug of tea had disappeared, but he still had his cigarette in hand. He stood on the inside cabin top of his upside-down boat, took a few draws on the cigarette and phlegmatically considered the situation. There wasn't much he could do, he thought. He went through the pluses and minuses of his position, trying to think through how he could survive. He had to try to get an EPIRB signal out to the world. Maybe he could use his tools to cut a hole in the hull. He became aware of the boat's heavy boom. It was mixed up with the tangle of mast and rigging below the boat. Swinging around in the underwater turbulence, it was tapping on one of the big cabin windows.

Suddenly, in one violent lurch, the boom smashed the window. The sea roared in like Niagara Falls. The electric lights, which had stayed on since the capsize, now went dead. Within seconds, the dark cabin filled with water whose temperature was close to zero degrees Celsius, leaving only a few feet of air near the top, which was really the cabin floor. Bullimore quickly became very cold. Now he waded through the chest-high water, found his survival suit, stripped off his foul-weather gear – it only protected him from rain, spray and the occasional breaking wave – and managed to pull the suit on over his cold and sodden underclothes. The insulated waterproof survival suit was designed to stave off hypothermia, but it was a model that left his hands and feet exposed, and all he could do was stuff his already frozen feet back into his soaked seaboots.

His food and drinking water were gone, except for some chocolate and several tiny sachets of water – a cup or so. Like most of the equipment in the cabin, his food and water had been sucked out through the smashed window by the powerful vacuum of departing waves.

There was no need now to cut a hole in the hull to release an EPIRB signal; the boom had done it for him. He activated one of his ARGOS-type EPIRBs and tied it to a piece of line. Plunging down into the freezing water in the cabin, he pushed it through the broken window and floated it up to what he hoped was the surface of the sea. But it could easily have become entangled in the mess of rigging and debris outside. Bullimore wasn't sure that his distress transmission was in fact getting out.

Whether *Exide Challenger* would stay afloat depended on his watertight bulkheads, in particular on the forward bulkhead, which was keeping water out of the boat's bow section. In case they didn't hold, he needed his life-raft, which was secured in the cockpit. Several times, his eyes and ears seared by the cold, he dived down and through the companionway hatch to cut it free. But it was too bulky to move, pinned against the bottom of the inverted cockpit by its own buoyancy. On his last dive, the hatch was caught by a surge of wave water and slammed shut on his hand. It chopped off his left index finger at the lower knuckle. In the icy water, the stub soon stopped bleeding and the cold numbed the fiery pain.

Bullimore crawled on to a narrow shelf high up under his new ceiling where it was relatively dry for now. But the water was rising and it soon began to wash over him periodically in this last refuge. He felt desperately cold and tired. He knew that the Australians were his best hope for rescue, but it would take them at least four or five days to get to him. That is, if the EPIRB had in fact made it to the surface – if its signal was getting through to anyone at all.

First, Thierry Dubois's *Pour Amnesty International* was dismasted. In wind that never fell below sixty-five knots (hurricane force) and in fifty-five- to sixty-foot-high seas, the boat capsized. It righted immediately but its mast had buckled and broken into three pieces Waves repeatedly smashed the two mast sections in the water up against the hull, threatening to hole it. Dubois had to use a hacksaw to cut through the rigging and free the remains of the mast from the boat. While he was below getting warm, getting his breath back, his boat was rolled again through 360 degrees by a huge, steep wave. Still Dubois did not activate an EPIRB. He would jury-rig (improvise from broken or spare material on board) a mast and a sail. In the tradition of the self-sufficient mariner, he was determined to reach an Australian port under his own power.

The following day, as he slept below, exhausted, and at almost the same time as Bullimore's capsize, another big wave turned the boat over. This time, it stayed upside down, drifting haphazardly among the long, wild Southern Ocean rollers. Now he set off his emergency beacon.

After two hours or so, the boat showed no sign of righting itself. In spite of its keel's weight, and even without the countervailing underwater resistance of its mast, Dubois's boat seemed comfortably stable upside down. Dressed in his survival suit, he squeezed through a small escape hatch in the transom (the vertical, or near-vertical, part of the stern). After several attempts at crawling up on to the slick, curved surface of the overturned hull, he managed to take advantage of a wave that washed him up on to it. He clung to one of the boat's two long, narrow rudders. The wind was still blowing at more than fifty knots. Enormous Southern Ocean seas, as high as the boat was long, towered over the exposed man and machine. The closest fellow-racer was twelve hundred miles to the east, and couldn't possibly sail back that far against gale-force winds and seas. At the tail end of the fleet, Dubois and Bullimore were particularly isolated. An Australian ship or a passing freighter were their only chances.

As he tried to balance himself on the overturned hull's rolling, slippery surface, in the high wind-chill of the storm-force winds, the waves periodically inundating him, Dubois believed that his life was over. The only uncertainty was how many hours, perhaps minutes, he had left.

In about 1805, Admiral Sir Francis Beaufort, of the British Royal Navy, drew up a scale that related wind strength to sea conditions. The navy adopted the Beaufort Wind Scale as part of its standard navigational repertoire in 1830. In modified form, it has since become a tool used almost universally by mariners. Its descriptions of wild weather are terse and clinical, but they provide a handy scale of relativity for appreciating what wind does to the sea. The sixty-five to seventy-knot winds that Bullimore and Dubois experienced were just above the sixty-four-knot (73 miles, or 118 kilometers, per hour) threshold of force 12 – hurricane force, the highest category on the scale. At sea, wrote Beaufort, 'Air filled with foam; sea completely white with driving spray; visibility greatly reduced.' Sea state is described as 'phenomenal', with mean wave heights of more than forty-four feet. Of the wind's effects as observed on land, the admiral noted, 'Very rarely experienced on land; usually accompanied by widespread damage.'

An adult human finds it very difficult to walk into a seventy-knot wind. It can blow over the unwary pedestrian. While one is facing the wind, breathing is difficult. At sea, water driven by a wind of that velocity is painful, and can damage an unprotected eye. In hurricane-force winds, sailors must often wear a diver's face mask, or goggles. On deck, the sailor must crawl from one handhold to the next.

If the wind seems bent on manslaughter, the waves generated by hurricane-force winds in the Southern Ocean are homicidal. That day, Bullimore and Dubois (and Dinelli ten days earlier) had fought seas that were the height of a five-storey building, with some as much as fifty per cent higher than that – almost an eight-storey building. But there's more to it than the height of the waves. Wave energy moves through water surprisingly fast. The speed at which a wave travels depends on its length – the distance between wave crests. The greater the length, the faster the wave. For example, waves whose crests are ten yards apart will move at eight knots; those one hundred yards apart, at twenty-five knots. But the Southern Ocean waves, with literally all the space in the world to form and build, are very long – the crests often two hundred yards apart or more. A wave of that length will travel at close to thirty-five knots.

To get an idea of the stresses that Bullimore and Dubois, and their boats, experienced, non-sailors might try to visualise a never-ending series of five-or six-storey buildings, with sloping sides of various angles and with occasional buildings half as high again, moving towards them at about forty miles an hour. Some of the time, the top one or two storeys of the buildings will collapse on top of them. The concussive effect of sea water isn't much different from that of concrete. Add the isolation, and the noise – the boom and roar of the waves, the deafening, unearthly, unnerving scream of wind around the obstructions of mast and rigging – and the picture should become clearer.

And now the Horn. To understand the Southern Ocean, you also have to understand Cape Horn.

In form and function, it serves the mundane purpose of capes everywhere: a promontory, or headland, dividing one body of water from another. But the Horn is unique. It's very far south, at fifty-seven degrees latitude. To go around it, vessels must plunge down, deep into the Southern Ocean. From Cape Horn, Antarctica is only six hundred miles away. Untrammelled in their progression around the globe, the Southern Ocean lows get squeezed together in the bellows of the Drake Passage between the Horn and Antarctica. Sometimes the systems get more complicated, and therefore more hazardous, as they meet the local weather coming off the nearby land masses. Williwaws sweep down the alpine valleys and far out to sea. The bottom comes up very quickly on the lip of the continental shelf. Waves shorten and steepen in the shallower water.

Cape Horn is the real, and certainly the psychological, turning-point of any voyage or race through the Southern Ocean. Actually a high rocky island just off the tip of the continent, it has a singular and mythological weight for sailors, as a symbol of pain, hardship and death. In the days of the square-riggers, ships would sometimes spend weeks trying to round it from east to west, against the prevailing wind, seas and current. Bligh's *Bounty* struggled to round the Horn for twenty-nine days before giving up and running off to the east. It eventually reached the South Pacific by way of the Indian Ocean and through the narrow straits off south-east Asia. Bligh's crew, with cruel and unconscious hypocrisy, never forgave him either for the hardships and terrors of that month, or for turning tail at the end of it.

In *Two Years before the Mast*, Richard Henry Dana describes his ship's ordeal in the frigid southern winter of 1836, as it tried to round the Horn from west to east with a cargo of California hides. This was supposed to be the easy way round, with its following winds. But it took them two weeks in head winds, uncharacteristic calms and easterly gales. They were often blocked by ice-fields. When they finally reached it, the Horn was a dismal and desolate sight, Dana wrote. But it was also a welcome vision to the frozen and exhausted crew. It was a signal that they might finally 'bid defiance to the Southern Ocean'.

My great-grandfather saw the Horn once as the grain-carrying square-rigger on which he was an able seaman surged past it on the way to Liverpool. He told my grandmother only that it looked to him like a small jagged mound in the sea, and that he hated and feared it.

For the pathologically adventurous sailor, rounding the Horn is the height of achievement. Although doing it may be a short-lived triumph – exactly because it means so much. The Argentine single-hander Vito Dumas sailed from Chile to Buenos Aires in 1934, and was welcomed as a hero. But Dumas's mind was not with the adoring crowds. His great moment had come and gone, he wrote later. All he could hope for was that somewhere, 'at another distant point in the sea, I could find another Cape Horn.'

Its ambiguous attractions are still potent. In 1985, father and son David and Daniel Hays sailed around Cape Horn in the smallest boat that any Americans had ever sailed there – an English-designed twenty-five-footer. They were lifelong sailors for whom the Horn was 'the big one'. In *My Old Man and the Sea*, David, the father, describes sailing as 'an incontrovertible act of truth'. Because the water had given him that gift, he thought he owed something back. To repay it, he had to take from the sea, not just the summertime pleasures of the coast, but all that it would give. And that, without question, was the Horn. When they rounded the cape months later, in a gale, of course, father and son thought simultaneously of the only possible toast for their finger each of Kahlua: 'To the men who died here.'

For sailors, Cape Horn has become a comprehensive metaphor – it's their Waterloo, Ithaca, Jerusalem, all bound together. Bernard Moitessier wrote: 'A sailor's geography is not always that of the cartographer, for whom a cape is a cape, with a latitude and longitude. For the sailor, a great cape is both a very simple and an extremely complicated whole of rocks, currents, breaking seas and huge waves, fair winds and gales, joys and fears, fatigue, dreams, painful hands, empty stomachs, wonderful moments, and suffering.'

The Vendée Globe sailors look ahead to Cape Horn as a marker of their return to the world, to civilisation. Christophe Auguin, a few days away from rounding the Horn in the Vendée Globe, exclaimed how much he was yearning for *'la sortie d'enfer'* – the 'exit from hell'.

On 6 January, two days after Bullimore and Dubois had capsized, Gerry Roufs sent one of his regular e-mail transmissions to his web site. He described the hurricane he had had to contend with a week earlier. Not just a Southern Ocean storm with hurricane-force wind, but an actual cyclonic storm, 'Fergus' had veered off the usual paths of South Pacific cyclones and ripped its way south past fifty-five degrees latitude. In the usual Southern Ocean storms out of the west, it's easy for the Vendée Globe boats to adopt storm tactics – running off before the wind, and keeping their sterns directly into the waves – as they race east towards Cape Horn. But caught in an area where Fergus's circling winds were blowing from the south, Roufs had had to turn *Groupe LG2's* tail to the ferocious seas and head off course to the north until the storm passed over. He was still sailing second in the race, but his forced diversion had lost him a lot of ground on the leader, Christophe Auguin.

'It's one thing to settle down comfortably to a series of depressions that move around between the 40s and 50s,' he wrote. 'But how do you avoid a strong depression coming from the north and whose centre falls smack-dab right on top of you? And then it's practically Noah's Ark. Fierce storm, sea very dangerous that could easily capsize the boat . . . I had to fly before 55 to 62 knot winds. For landlubbers: at this stage, children under 12 would fly away!'

In a storm like 'Fergus' 'the race's importance takes second place. You could say it's a question of survival,' he said.

He had heard about the other sailors' distress signals. It made him think again about how dangerous the Southern Ocean was. The longer you were there, the greater the chances of disaster. It was at once beautiful and terrifying.

'But I've been here long enough . . . At an average speed of ten knots, the Horn ought to appear on the horizon in a week and a half or less . . . As for the boat, it's my best friend because it's my ticket out of here . . . The only thing that bothers me is that a breaker filled the cockpit and washed away my two buckets even though they were secure.'

Roufs's boat was no different from the other racing machines, loaded down with technology but with rudimentary accommodation; he had lost his toilet and his sink in one cruel blow.

The day after this message, Roufs and the Frenchwoman Isabelle Autissier (the other woman in the race besides Catherine Chabaud), sailing about thirty miles apart, were overtaken by an extreme storm, this time just an intense version of the usual Southern Ocean low-pressure system. It developed very quickly, the wind rising from thirty-five to seventy knots in three hours or so. Because the wind had not had time to stretch out the forty- to fifty-foot-high waves, they were relatively steep and close together, particularly dangerous seas for small boats. For Autissier, the most impressive thing was that she couldn't distinguish the waves from the sky or clouds.

'The air was full of sea and the clouds were so close to the sea that everything was grey,' she told me. 'It was like a huge grey mass – white and grey because of the waves. It was very terrible, terrifying.'

During the course of the day, Autissier's boat was knocked down (flattened by a wave so that the mast was horizontal to the water) six times. Twice, the top of her eighty-foot mast was driven beneath the

water's surface. On one of those occasions, Autissier broke one of her
fingers as she was flung against the cabin top of the almost upside-
down boat.

It was during this severe storm, thirty hours after he sent his e-mail,
that the ARGOS radio position beacon on Roufs's boat suddenly
stopped transmitting. One second, it was beeping away, relaying his
constantly changing position. The next second, there was complete
silence. Perhaps it was only the ARGOS itself. Roufs might not notice
that it had shut down. He was far out in the Southern Ocean – in the
hole. No shore-based plane or ship could reach his position. Only
other vessels at sea might be within striking distance of him if something had in fact gone wrong.

The following day, Autissier, who was still sailing close to Roufs,
reported that she had not been able to make radio contact with him.
It might only be that his electrical system had failed and that he was
continuing to sail along, out of contact with the world. But winds in
the area were hurricane strength. Autissier herself was struggling to
survive. Roufs's boat remained silent. No EPIRB signals from
Groupe LG2 had been received by any of the monitoring satellites.
Nevertheless, at race headquarters in Brittany, a worried Philippe
Jeantot, the Vendée Globe director, ordered a search operation for
Roufs to begin.

2

A Solitude Supreme

*As for myself, the wonderful sea charmed
me from the first.*

– Joshua Slocum, *Sailing Alone Around the World*

*You can sail for one day, can't you?
That's all it is – one day after another.*

– Harry Pidgeon, Three-time single-handed circumnavigator.

'To young men contemplating a voyage I would say go.'
And go they did. With those words, and the rest of his unpretentious and understated story, *Sailing Alone Around the World*,
Joshua Slocum let loose generations of cruising sailors, and single-
handers in particular. Even today, Slocum and his classic book
remain the well-head of inspiration for solo sailing. Replicas of his
boat, the *Spray*, are built in fibreglass and steel, to run the downhill
passages of the world's trade-wind sailing routes. Slocum completed
his circumnavigation in 1898, and in the following ninety years,
eighty-three men and seven women sailed alone around the world.
That doesn't include another two dozen or so racing circumnavigations. Since 1988, there have been so many lone circumnavigators
that no one has been able to keep track of them. Most of the cruising
sailors have taken the traditional route: trade-wind reaches or runs

across the Atlantic and Pacific; through the Indian Ocean and south around the Cape of Good Hope and into the South Atlantic; or through Suez and the Mediterranean. The Panama Canal was the real reason so many people actually completed circumnavigations; it bypassed Cape Horn. In fact, the next solo circumnavigation after Slocum's wasn't completed until 1925 by the American Harry Pidgeon, who used the canal and avoided the Horn. If it were still necessary to sail around the dreaded cape, circumnavigators would be thin on the water.

Slocum, the tough, Nova Scotia-born, naturalised American sea captain was fifty-one when he began his voyage from the *Pequod*'s home port of New Bedford. As a boy, he ran away to sea and worked his way up to captain and owner of his own square-rigged barque, coming up 'over the bow', he liked to point out, and not 'through the cabin windows'. Slocum could do any job on any ship and sail it through any sea, but his fate is familiar to anyone in our time: he was bypassed and sidelined by technological change. As the cargo-carrying sailing ships became obsolete, so did many of their captains and officers. Slocum wound up 'on the beach'. He hated the noisome steamers that were replacing the beautiful, wind-driven clippers and freighters of the world. He couldn't bear working ashore in a boatyard, the only job open to him. He had been at sea in all the oceans for so long that living on land was strange and uncomfortable for him. Slocum's solution was to rebuild an old thirty-six-foot sloop and go to sea again. He decided to sail around the world.

His book about the voyage is a classic adventure story of the sea. Slocum matter-of-factly describes how he endured gales, loneliness, menacing chases by pirates, all the perils the sea could offer on the cusp of the twentieth century. With his lifetime of experience, Slocum really could deal with anything. But his book is remarkable in its placidity. The sea, benign, 'wonderful' and, above all, manageable, was merely a pleasant and bracing interlude between shoreside encounters that became more and more elaborate and celebratory as the single-hander's fame grew. A sailor could never trifle with the elements, to be sure; it was 'no light matter when the sea is in its grandest mood'. But the danger was really not all that great. The patient and prudent mariner could deal with anything. And it was a wonderful way to see the world.

This idea of the sea as a challenging yet yielding source of pleasure and satisfaction differed completely from Joseph Conrad's view of it as a menacing and destructive element. Or from Herman Melville's image of its 'remorseless fang'. English yachtsmen of the mid- to late-nineteenth century who wrote books about their coastal sailing adventures – John MacGregor, R. T. McMullen, E. E Middleton – agreed with Conrad. Going to sea, even in the narrow waters off the British Isles, was a harrowing excursion into the hostile wilderness. They wrote in the tradition of the Romantic poets, Byron and Shelley, for whom the sea was a lurid battleground between man and unruly nature.

On the contrary, Slocum's soothing narrative seemed inviting for anyone with a moderate amount of gumption: a good boat well handled, slipping purposefully through calms, roistering along in the sweet trade winds, riding out the odd gale with orderly storm tactics, coming to rest in a new port, at anchor in a palm-fringed, coral-studded lagoon in Paradise. With the building of the Panama Canal, Slocum's seductive future came true. Cruising sailors have been inspired by his unthreatening vision for a hundred years.

At a certain point in this evolution, however, the Slocum version breaks down. You could say that critical anomalies appear in his paradigm of the benign and pliable sea at the moment when small-boat sailors descend into the Southern Ocean and aim to pass south of the three stormy capes – Good Hope, Leeuwin, at the extreme south-western tip of Australia, and Cape Horn. Then the sailor is returned to the imagery of Conrad and Melville. South of forty degrees, the sea is neither benign nor manageable. Passing through it becomes a dangerous end in itself; there are no desirable ports of call at the ends of the earth. The sailor's experience of the sea in the high southern latitudes may thrill, but it can also kill. It certainly doesn't fit Slocum's story, his sea-view. The tough master mariner could have handled it in the *Spray* – as he did for a while in the vicinity of the Horn, as he had done many times in the fo'c's'les and on the quarterdecks of his obsolescent square-riggers. But if he had circumnavigated there, west to east about, deep in the Southern Ocean, both his tale and the inspiration it provided would have been completely different.

Today, countries like the United States, Britain, Australia and, especially, New Zealand contain large sailing constituencies, but public enthusiasm for single-handed, long-distance sailing is more widespread in France than in any other country. This fascination began in large part because of two men and their sailing exploits in the 1960s and 1970s: Bernard Moitessier and Eric Tabarly. When I asked the Vendée Globe skippers who had inspired them to start sailing, and to sail single-handed in particular, they always cited one or both of these legendary French sailors.

Moitessier and Tabarly went to sea for very different, though not mutually exclusive, reasons: Moitessier to save his soul; Tabarly to win races. But Tabarly also went cruising and Moitessier raced. Both men were superb technicians and innovators. Moitessier pioneered a radical new method of handling survival storms in small boats. This isn't an easy thing to test – he couldn't afford even one failed experiment. But his technique has become the most widely used practice of modern yachts in very heavy weather, and may well have saved lives. Tabarly, through his sophisticated racing designs and gear modifications, really began the process of professionalising sailboat racing. Moitessier appealed to the French because he was a skilled lyrical writer who could invest a sea passage with the solemn ecstasy of a mystical experience. Tabarly didn't write any books (until his autobiography, published in France in 1997). Instead, he inspired the French by example, and by beating the English at their own game.

In 1959, a retired English colonel of the Royal Marines called 'Blondie' Hasler bet Francis Chichester half a crown that he could beat him in a single-handed race across the Atlantic. Hasler had been one of the 'Cockleshell Heroes' – a group of Second World War British commandos who had quixotically, though successfully, paddled kayaks miles up the Gironde into Bordeaux harbour and attached limpet mines to the German warships moored there. He was the sort of person who needed danger to keep himself sane. Chichester, a pioneer aeroplane designer and pilot, would later make one of the great long-distance voyages – a record single-handed circumnavigation with only one stop. The eccentric bet developed into the first single-handed transatlantic race in the summer of 1960. It was very much an Anglo-Saxon race, although one of the five entrants was French (he sailed the smallest boat and came last).

In 1964, a second race was held (called the OSTAR, the *Observer* Single-handed Transatlantic Race, after its newspaper sponsor). Eric Tabarly, a young Breton lieutenant in the French navy, won the race handily in a novel boat of his own design. The French were delighted that their countryman had conquered *la transat anglaise*. In an explosion of national pride, they made Tabarly an instant hero, and he was awarded the *Légion d'honneur*. The old European dictum was that providence had given the empire of the land to the French, and to the English that of the sea. No more. It was as if the long history of English maritime dominance, which had rankled the French since well before the Royal Navy blockaded Napoleon's Europe for fifteen years, was finally over. One man in a home-made plywood sailboat had changed everything.*

Although he didn't win the OSTAR again until 1976, Tabarly's focused, almost fanatical, approach to the race set the tone for the future. To beat him, other sailors had to prepare in the same way he did: get a tailor-made boat and gear, practise sailing in all conditions, get physically fit, study the course and its weather. It was as if he was getting ready for the Olympics. It was a long way from Blondie Hasler's approach: give the boat a scrub, hop in after a few pints in the pub and shove off.

If Tabarly appealed to the hard edge of national pride, Moitessier had a more diffuse attraction. He was born in 1925 in Vietnam – then part of Indochina and the French overseas empire – where his father ran a small importing business. Moitessier always felt himself to be more Asian than French, and he subscribed to the colonial outsider's idea of the sea as a place in which to be solitary and at one with the natural world. He spent most of his life wandering oceans in sailboats and writing about his experiences. As Antoine de Saint-Exupéry wrote about flying and the desert, Moitessier wrote about sailing and the sea. His books are a mix of sea-going adventure, and descriptions and celebrations of his intense communion with nature.

Moitessier was one of nine starters in the first non-stop, single-handed, round-the world race, the 1968 Golden Globe. The Englishman Robin Knox-Johnston, sailing a leaky thirty-two-foot wooden ketch, eventually won by virtue of being the only one of nine starters to finish. The prohibitive attrition of the race – six withdrawals, one suicide after a long slide into madness, one later suicide – discouraged further attempts at non-stop racing until the first Vendée Globe in 1989.

After six months at sea, as he rounded Cape Horn, Moitessier, in

*In June 1998, the sixty-six-year-old Tarbarly was lost at sea off the coast of Wales when he was knocked overboard while reefing the mainsail at night on a voyage to Ireland. His four-man crew was unable to recover him.

his larger steel boat, was sure to overtake Knox-Johnston. But instead of turning north to the finish line in England, Moitessier abandoned the race and kept sailing east. He eventually reached Tahiti, after sailing more than one and a half times around the world, much of it through the Southern Ocean. Among other things, he didn't want to go back to the tumult of civilisation and give up the peaceful solitude he had found on his boat: 'It is all of life that I contemplate,' he wrote, '– sun, clouds, time that passes and abides.' His boat was a 'little red and white planet made of space, pure air, stars, clouds and freedom in its deepest, most natural sense'.

Philippe Jeantot was spurred by the epic 1968 Golden Globe race to create the Vendée Globe and has remained its director. He is one of the remarkable second-generation French racers, inspired by Moitessier and Tabarly, and inspires the third generation – like the current Vendée Globe skippers – in his turn. Jeantot has sailed alone through the Southern Ocean five times, winning two races. He can't go sailing without feeling the spirit of Moitessier, he told me. According to Jeantot, Moitessier's book about the Golden Globe, *The Long Way*, has changed the lives of so many people in France. It's a bible for many long-distance, single-handed sailors. In their regular e-mail reports from the Southern Ocean to race headquarters, two of the Vendée Globe racers mentioned that they were re-reading Moitessier. As if he were reading him aloud, late in the race, Christophe Auguin said, 'I will enjoy these last moments on the sea in communion with my boat.' And Marc Thiercelin, after he rounded the Horn, said, 'The thing I enjoyed most was the forties [the 'roaring forties' latitudes – challenging but not suicidal], this virgin territory where I was so serene.'

The inescapable problem of solo sailing, now or in Slocum's time, is that it's fundamentally unseamanlike, in both the traditional and legislative sense of the word. Traditionally, the ideal sailor has been the 'prudent mariner,' methodically and carefully working his way across the sea, taking what comes, avoiding risk as much as possible, getting his vessel and crew where they're supposed to go with minimum fuss. The eighteenth-century explorer and mariner James Cook comes to mind – sailing and charting unknown seas and coasts in all weather, in a ship inherently less seaworthy than any modern well-designed and built sailboat, with primitive navigational technology, lacking knowledge of large-scale weather patterns or cyclonic storm seasons, yet never losing his vessel to the perils of the sea. Contemporary cruising sailors by and large aspire to the same model: get across the sea as fast as you can with a minimum of trauma to boat or crew.

The essential elements of the modern mariner's prudence include having a skilled hand on the helm when necessary to avoid knockdown or capsize in heavy weather. A vessel also needs a strong crew to handle the boat's sails and gear in all conditions without undue fatigue and to keep a lookout – for large vessels that might run down small sailboats, and for ice or flotsam that might rip or smash open a hull, or tear off a keel or a rudder.

Most of the time, the single-hander can do none of these things. That's why single-handed sailing is unseamanlike. It also violates the international rules of the road, adopted at various conventions by the world's maritime nations. According to the Preliminary Statement to the Steering and Sailing Rules, sailors must manage their boats 'with due regard to the observance of good seamanship.' Good seamanship means taking all precautions required by the ordinary practice of seamen or the particular circumstances in which a vessel finds itself.

Often the collisions, knockdowns or dismastings suffered by the Vendée Globe single-handers occur when the skippers are below – sleeping or resting, cooking up some freeze-dried grub on their single-burner stoves or analysing weatherfax charts and trying to figure out how to handle the next Southern Ocean depression. Or they were down below in their cabins because it was just too unnerving or dangerous on deck: the psychological toll of the breakneck speed and the terrible noise of wind and sea; the intense discomfort of seas constantly sweeping over the boat, soaking the sailors in freezing water; the danger of being swept overboard by a breaking wave or of being on deck in a knockdown; the virtual death sentence of being outside in a capsize.

The image of sailors napping in their bunks as they barrel down thirty-foot waves at twenty knots under autopilot doesn't exactly suggest good seamanship. They're not keeping a lookout; there's no hand on the helm. Indeed, the race itself, the fact that the sailors are alone in the Southern Ocean, is outside the 'ordinary practice of seamen' contemplated by the rule. None of this legalistic cavilling matters to the racers, of course. In fact, the marginality of the enterprise is part of its appeal. One of the reasons the skippers go to sea is to get away from the excessive coddling and coercion of rules and regulations.

In round-the-world races, the intense competition and the boats' speed multiply the burdens and dangers of single-handed sailing. Both these factors encourage – or demand – behaviour that increases rather than minimises the usual risks of sailing alone. It's just a condition of solo sailing that the boat must be left to its own, and the self-steering system's, devices for long periods of time. Without a skilled human eye and hand to guide the boat through every wave of a storm, the single-hander must rely on the vessel's integrity, the uncertain vagaries of wave formation and shape, the attitude of the boat to the waves when they strike – and plain luck. When the 'hollow-bellower ocean' rolls, the single-hander is there along with the exhausting work of handling the boat, and with the fear.

3

The Baths of All the Western Stars

Long, long ago he gazed far out at sea in a sweet languor;
this was not he who'd fought with gods, embraced sea sprites,
laid out the grooms like slaughtered beasts and choked his
courts; his mind was now a virgin boy, his hands white roses,
and his old longings shone like mother-of-pearl deep down,
far down in the sea's depths as he, above it stooped,
smiled and with slow caresses combed his star-washed hair.

– Nikos Kazantzakis, *The Odyssey: A Modern Sequel.*

THE THIRD Vendée Globe race began on 3 November 1996, under a low, grey sky pierced occasionally by shafts of sunlight. Even though the North Atlantic winter gale season had begun, the wind was a moderate ten- to fifteen-knot south-westerly, left over from a depression that had raced across the Bay of Biscay and the Vendée coast the day before. The race organisers were lucky. The day of relative calm would make things easier for the large spectator fleet that always accompanied long-distance race starts. For the competitors, conditions were ideal. There was enough wind for them to manoeuvre handily at the start line. And they could get out to sea quickly, away from the dangers of the rocky coast and adoring fans in their clumsily handled boats; collisions between racers and spectators occurred all too often in the chaos of starts. But the good weather would last only one day. Another fast-moving low-pressure system was already sweeping in from the Atlantic. The forecast predicted gale-force winds and heavy seas on 4 November. No one got across the Bay of Biscay unscathed in November. The timing of the start is crucial, because it gets the competitors through the Southern Ocean during the southern hemisphere's summer. Sailing through in winter would be suicidal.

From Les Sables-d'Olonne, the race route runs south through the Bay of Biscay and down the Atlantic Ocean, swinging south-east around the Cape of Good Hope and farther south into the high latitudes of forty to sixty degrees – the Southern Ocean. The boats then begin the long dash for Cape Horn, keeping well south of Australia and New Zealand. In effect, the route is a circumnavigation of Antarctica. But sailors usually describe it as going 'south of the three stormy capes' – Good Hope, Leeuwin and Horn. Once around Cape Horn, the boats retrace their route north through the Atlantic and back to France.

According to the straightforward race rules: the course runs from Les Sables-d'Olonne to Les Sables-d'Olonne west to east by the three stormy capes without stopping. On the way, the boats must pass either side of the Canaries; keep Antarctica to starboard, Heard Island (a Southern Ocean speck about twenty-eight hundred miles south-west of the Cape of Good Hope) to starboard, and two southern Pacific waypoints (latitude–longitude coordinates) to starboard – these are designed to keep the boats north of the most dangerous Southern Ocean iceberg areas.

For sailboats, the shortest distance between two points is seldom a straight line, or a rhumb line, as navigators call it. Long-distance navigation under sail involves a complex calculation, varying with the season, the effects of wind and, sometimes, current. Wind and water are thrown into vast, regular curved or circular flows by the Coriolis effect – the consequence of the planet's rotation on its axis. The best course may be a delicately poised compromise – a line as short as possible that must, nevertheless, curve around windless centres of permanent high pressure, keeping the boats in the steady winds on the centres' broad peripheries. Sometimes, though, there's no alternative to a beeline across areas of calms and light, fluky wind: the doldrums, stretching across the equator, or the horse latitudes, centred at about thirty degrees north and south of the equator on the pole-ward sides of the trade-wind belts.

In the Vendée Globe, the sailors can expect gales as they leave the west coast of France in early November. As they sail south, they must skirt the constant high-pressure area of the North Atlantic High (also known as the Azores High) by keeping to the east, near the European coast. The boats get light and uncertain winds as they pass through the high-pressure zone of the horse latitudes, until they begin to pick up the north-east trade winds at twenty-two or so degrees north of the equator (a degree equals 60 nautical miles, 69 statute miles or 111 kilometres). They must take maximum advantage of the ideal sailing conditions provided by the trade winds, and then try to traverse the doldrums at their narrowest point. As they approach and cross the equator, they swing to the west, towards the coast of Brazil, to avoid the light winds of the South Atlantic (or St Helena) High. Then they curve back to the south-east, skirting the southern limits of the High. As they do so, the likelihood of gales increases again, and likelihood becomes certainty as the boats reach the latitudes of the Southern Ocean.

In this aqueous wilderness, vessels, and often a life, are lost in virtually every race that goes through. The danger of extreme weather lasts for many solitary weeks. The sailors must endure cold, snow, fog, ice and the unrelenting stress of storm after storm. During this stage of the race, many of the boats sail well within the northern limit of iceberg drift. They head as far south as they dare. The farther south they go, the shorter the distance to the Horn, but the greater the chance of catastrophic collision with ice. Usually, the skippers try to stay to the north of the stormy low-pressure systems to avoid the worst of the weather, and to ride the more favourable wind direction there. But sometimes, if a low tracks farther to the north than usual, the racers may have to avoid its worst wind by diving far south, almost to sixty degrees latitude, into the ice. It is in this part of the race that they have the greatest chance of encountering huge storm waves, and rogue waves, which are formed when two or more seas coalesce into a single monster, as much as twice the mean wave height.

Once the Vendée Globe boats round the Horn, they continue to experience typical high-latitude stormy weather. But for the first time in many weeks, they have some protection against the untrammelled waves – the continent shields them. However, they have a thousand miles to sail before they officially leave the Southern Ocean at forty degrees latitude. Dangers remain. Westerly gales still sweep this sea area, and even the relatively small waves close off the South American coast can be bone-jarringly dangerous. Because of local ocean currents, the northern limit of iceberg drift in the South Atlantic swings north close to the Falkland Islands. Racers may take some comfort from radar that works after two and a half hard months at sea, but such equipment has only a limited ability to detect ice. While radar may pick out large- and medium-sized icebergs from the surrounding sea clutter, it doesn't see the very small bergs, growlers and 'bergy bits'. Missing them, radar or not, is a matter of luck. On many of the boats, radars, or the electrical system that powers them, will have failed. When they round the cape, the skippers will have to continue their ice watch – and hope their luck holds as they race north out of the Southern Ocean and towards home.

Sailing back up the Atlantic, the boats repeat the calculations and tactics of their outbound course. They ride the westerlies up the coast of South America and work their way through the southern horse latitudes until roughly at the latitude of Rio de Janeiro, skirting the light-wind area of the South Atlantic High. Then they swing north-east, arcing across the south-east trade winds, which boost them almost to the equator. After ghosting through the calms of the doldrums, they pick up the north-east trades. Beating as closely as possible to the north-east, they try to enter the north-westerly wind belt to the east of the North Atlantic High. The final section of the race is a stormy winter slog back to their Vendée start point.

As they sail through the North Atlantic, the exhausted sailors have to muster their last reserves to watch for ships in the heavily travelled shipping lanes. And even here, far from the Southern Ocean, they can't stop watching the waves. While not as bad as the seas farther south, sea conditions in the eastern North Atlantic, and in the vicinity of the Bay of Biscay in particular, can be perilous. In westerly winter gales, seas that have travelled a thousand miles or more begin to steepen and break as they move into the shallower water over the European continental shelf in Biscay. Smaller steep waves can sometimes hurt a boat more than bigger, more gently sloped ones. After anywhere from 105 to 150 days alone at sea, the Vendée Globe sailors can breathe easy when they sail behind the sea wall at Les Sables-d'Olonne, but not before.

'The sea is still the sea,' said Moitessier. 'One must never forget.'

*

In the summer, holidaying French families pack the resort town of Les Sables-d'Olonne, drawn by the beaches and sunny weather of the Vendée coast. In winter, the town looks hollow and deserted. But on this cold, late-autumn Sunday, crowds numbering sixty thousand – some estimates said one hundred thousand – jammed the seaward fringes of the town along its sea walls and piers to witness the start of the Vendée Globe. They mobbed the docks and pontoons of Port Olona, the marina tucked away at the back of the harbour, where the race boats were docked. The town crackled with the hoopla of a big-money sporting event: bands, popcorn, media, cameras, autograph-hunters, applause and cheers, hero-worship.

The Vendée Globe boats perched themselves alongside the marina pontoons like impatient thoroughbreds, barely tolerating the last-minute tweaks and prods of their handlers. No one could afford even one weak point in their boat's complex armature. The sea is anything but benign; it finds the chinks. The Southern Ocean was on every skipper's mind. Even if they were as ready for it as it was possible to be, they knew it could still get them. But thorough preparation would improve the odds as much as possible. It would restrict the chances of disaster to the realm of freaky bad luck: a rogue wave; an invisible flaw in the rigging; a slip overboard off a slick, icy deck; an unseen growler ripping its way through the lightweight, inch-thick hull.

The skippers and their support teams swarmed the boats, trying to reach the purely theoretical end of the list of things to do before the imminent start. It is an axiom of long-distance sailboat racing (a kind of nautical Parkinson's Law) that the amount of work left to do always exceeds the time available in which to do it. There is always something else to attach to the boat, gear to stow, food to pack away, electronic devices to program. Weaknesses that had turned up here and there in the course of qualifying sails or sea trials – in a block (the pulleys on board a boat that assist in handling lines) or a sail, perhaps even in the structural solidity of the boat – still needed attending.

There were, however, a few exceptions to this method of preparation through crisis-management. Christophe Auguin, in particular, seemed to be smoothly immune to chaos. His technical team had been working on *Géodis* for months. They had fine-tuned a boat already seasoned in the 1994–95 BOC Challenge, the other single-handed round-the-world race, which Auguin had won. After fifty thousand miles, he knew his boat and its systems intimately, and had

had every opportunity to de-bug them. Unlike the other skippers, who worked alongside their support team members in the frantic months before departure, Auguin was able to leave the preparations to his team. He arrived ten days or so before the start, and stepped aboard his groomed boat, every inch the detached professional. The only thing he hadn't yet been able to test was *Géodis*'s new swinging keel.

A short, lean man with wiry dark hair, an intensely animated manner, gravelly voice and droll sense of humour, the thirty-six-year-old Auguin discharged purposeful energy. Like most of the skippers, he had been sailing for most of his life, in his case, from the age of five. As a boy, he had raced Optimist dinghies (ten-foot-long, blunt-bowed, wooden boats – a universal European training dinghy) for ten years on the coast of his native Normandy. Optimists are sailed alone, and Auguin liked single-handed sailing from the beginning. You're in charge of the boat. What kid could ask for more? He was good at it too. Winning races motivated him to keep racing – in longer events and bigger boats. It was his performance in the prestigious Figaro – a four-leg solo race in one-designs (each boat identical) around the French coast – that got him into the elite of French professional sailors. He came ninth in 1984 and fifth the next year. Then he won it. He gave up his technical teaching job and began the hunt for sponsors for bigger races.

Like most of the skippers as well, he was inspired by the twin icons of Bernard Moitessier and Eric Tabarly. He was part of the generation these two legends had pushed to sail. When he was young, Auguin closely followed the racing exploits of Tabarly and the far-flung voyages of Moitessier. He dreamed of sailing and racing like them.

Now Auguin seemed to be at his peak. If he won this Vendée Globe, he would become something of an icon himself. He had already shown the sailing world the right stuff – by winning the two previous BOC Challenge races. In the most recent BOC, he had set a speed record for a single-handed monohull (a boat with a single hull, like all the Vendée Globe and BOC racers). In the southern Indian Ocean, he had pushed *Géodis* (then named *Sceta Calberson*) 351 miles in twenty-four hours – an average speed of 14.6 knots. Inherently faster multihulls (that is, twin-hulled catamarans or triple-hulled trimarans), with full crews and a fresh helmsman every hour or half-hour, have set records for twenty-four-hour runs by averaging only four or five knots more over a day. The legendary clipper ship *Cutty Sark* managed 363 miles one day, a mere half-a-knot more an hour than the single-hander. Auguin's record was very impressive indeed, a triumph, really, of determination, courage and toughness – and, of course, some luck as well.

For a monohull, such sustained speed was possible only for the Vendée Globe or BOC designs (or the boats that sailed the various fully crewed circumnavigating races – the Whitbread or the BT Challenge, neither of which is non-stop). *Géodis* was designed by the naval architectural team of Jean-Marie Finot and Pascal Conq at Groupe Finot, outside Paris. There were eventually six Finot boats in this Vendée Globe, including all but two of the boats newly built for the race, as well as those for most of the skippers with a good chance of winning: Auguin, Yves Parlier, Autissier and Roufs. The Finot designs were among the most extreme of all the boats in the race; they were the ones with the greatest beam (width) – which increased their stability – the lightest construction, keels that could be canted to one side of the boat or the other for greater leverage, and the largest sail area. Together with a design by the firm of Joubert Nivelt – Thierry Dubois's *Pour Amnesty International* – they would also later raise the most serious questions about safety.

Auguin could luxuriate in a relatively tranquil lead-up to the race start because he had an experienced boat he was well familiar with, and a steady flow of sponsorship money. If anything, money was the more important factor. In these extreme races, preparation was everything, and thorough preparation was possible only if you didn't have to spend all or most of your time drumming up funds. Auguin's affluence and comparatively serene readiness, together with his impressive BOC results, had long created the perception of an advantage. He was the clear race favourite, the sailor to beat.

In fact, money was the real problem. It doesn't matter how much the French like solo sailboat racing, it is never easy to wheedle ten million francs out of a pack of companies or local governments. Sober and responsible potential sponsors have to be persuaded to spend large amounts of money to support an enterprise that is wildly irrational and risky. Sailors have to run sustained and focused campaigns. They're in the business of selling themselves as having just the right combination of buttoned-down reliability and lunatic courage to actually get one of the latest sailing speedboats around the world in one piece. Therefore, the skippers have to be organised and disciplined businesspeople. They have organisations to run, schedules to adhere to, presentations to make.

A former BOC and Vendée Globe competitor once said that the hardest part of these races wasn't sailing the Southern Ocean, but raising the money to get a boat and enter the race in the first place. Although seventy-five sailors had originally notified the race director, Philippe Jeantot, that they were trying to raise money to build or buy a vessel for this Vendée Globe, only sixteen entrants had shown up in Les Sables-d'Olonne. The rest had abandoned the effort for a variety of reasons, mostly financial.

The absent competitors included some of the best known single-handed sailors around: the unforgettably named Australian BOC veteran Kanga Birtles; the Italian Vittorio Malingri, whose rudder had broken in the southern Pacific during the 1992 Vendée Globe; Steve Pettengill, the American second-place finisher in the 1994 BOC; and Mike Birch, the legendary Canadian North Atlantic speed-record holder – and Gerry Roufs's mentor.

Jeantot had hoped that this edition of the Vendée Globe would include a healthy number of non-French entrants. He wanted a more balanced international event, one much more like the BOC. Early in 1996, he had optimistically predicted the inclusion of eleven 'foreign' sailors from eight countries. In the end, he got five sailors from four countries other than France, and two of those – the Canadian Roufs, a native of Montreal, and Patrick de Radiguès, a Belgian – spoke French and were French-sponsored.

Competition among the sailors was intense, sometimes bitter. It was a high-stakes game. The winner would achieve fame in the international sailing world and, in most of the countries represented, a certain amount of general public recognition. Anyone who simply finished the race would be famous among other sailors. In France, though, it's a little different. The Vendée Globe racers, and those who have competed in the various other long-distance single-handed races, are much more widely known and celebrated. When Titouan Lamazou won the 1989 Vendée Globe in the record time of 109 days, more than one hundred thousand people welcomed him back to Brittany on a chilly mid-winter day. This public attention isn't reserved only for French sailors. Gerry Roufs based his sailing career in France and, although he had to fight hard for it, won the same generous sponsorship money – if not the same unreserved acclaim – as any French sailor.

If Christophe Auguin was the primed and cool patrician among the competitors on the race start day in Les Sables-d'Olonne, Raphaël Dinelli occupied the other end of the preparation spectrum. His campaign had an air of tumultuous improvisation. He had been more than a million francs short until two weeks before the start, when the chemical company Prémac had agreed to sponsor him. He renamed his eight-year-old boat (the former *Crédit Agricole IV*, which Jeantot had sailed in one of his two BOC victories) *Algimouss*, after one of their products. Before that, Dinelli had tried unsuccessfully to raise money through public subscriptions and small company sponsorships.

But the twenty-eight-year-old native of the Aquitaine (he was the youngest skipper) had other serious problems. Without money, he hadn't been able to re-fit his boat, and that meant he hadn't been able to complete the Vendée Globe qualifying sail. According to the race rules, skippers had to have made 'an authenticated single-handed transoceanic voyage . . . of not less than 2,000 miles, without anchoring or putting into port'. Because time was short, the race committee gave Dinelli permission to sail one thousand miles instead. On 27 October, he sailed from his home port of Arcachon, near Bordeaux, bound for the Fastnet Rock Lighthouse off the south coast of Ireland. Even if he was lucky with the weather, he would get back to Les Sables less than three days before the Vendée Globe start.

Near Fastnet, he ran into a big storm – the relatively benign weather of summer had already ended in these northern waters. He couldn't adopt the storm tactics of the open ocean – running off before the wind – because he was in the narrow waters of the western approaches to the English Channel and had no sea room. He had to slug it out with the storm toe-to-toe. He hove-to in fifty-five knot wind. Perched right on the shipping lanes, he spent two harrowing days watching cargo ships plough by all around him. It was a matter of luck that he wasn't hit; while hove-to, he was almost completely unable to manoeuvre. The weather eased slightly, and then worsened again as a second depression bore down on him. It was crazy to stay there, he told himself. He could get run down by a ship at any moment. And surely getting through weather like this would be qualification enough for the race. He gave up on Fastnet and ran off for the Vendée coast.

The French Federation of Sailing and the National Offshore Racing Union weren't sympathetic to Dinelli's weather excuse and refused him official status in the race. Jeantot lobbied for Dinelli's inclusion; after all, the young man was sailing the veteran's old and beloved boat. And Jeantot knew what a winter storm in the northern shipping lanes was like. The day before the start, he announced at a press conference that Dinelli was in, only to reverse his decision, under official pressure, two hours later. Dinelli would begin the race as a kind of freelance entrant. The French press labelled him the 'pirate of the Vendée Globe'.

Dinelli is a little under six feet tall, with dark hair already receding, and a restless and animated intelligence. His grandparents were Italian immigrants to France, and some of his relatives live within a few miles of my home in Toronto. He's voluble and emphatic, talking in long, fast bursts of eloquent French. Over dinner and a Médoc, he defended his truncated qualifying sail and lamented the 'pirate' label the media had stuck him with. His boat adhered to the race rules, he insisted, and it had all the required safety gear. Although his qualifying sail had been cut short, he had dealt with a severe autumn storm in the narrow waters of the western approaches while some of the other competitors had qualified by summertime sailing in the open Atlantic. Who had been tested the most? Nevertheless, Dinelli crossed the start line on 3 November with his status as an unofficial entrant still under appeal to the French Federation of Sailing.

When they were asked before the race what they expected it to be like, several skippers responded with metaphors of war. They were pumped for action, like soldiers anticipating their defining moment of contact with the enemy. The square-jawed, mesomorphic Hungarian polymath Nandor Fa (he had designed and built his boat, *Budapest*) had sailed in both a previous BOC and another Vendée Globe. Being at sea under those conditions for so long was, for him, an intense philosophical experience. He wanted to test himself, to find out what he was worth. He wasn't going back to sea for pleasure, he said. It was truly combat. The Algerian-born Eric Dumont had crossed the Atlantic twenty-seven times under sail. In the Vendée Globe, he said, the sailors followed the road of the warrior. It was a tough three-and-a-half-month-long sprint. You couldn't delude yourself that you sailed the race as a kind of vacation.

Then he used a metaphor of conquest that many of the other sailors favoured to describe the race. At thirty-five years of age, he was sailing in his first Vendée Globe, he said, *'pour un Everest!'*

For one of the skippers, this martial imagery seemed a perfect fit. Pete Goss had spent nine years in the British Royal Marines. He'd joined when he was eighteen, and the soldier's virtues, absorbed over the years, still seemed to cling to him. They would be demonstrated in the race: under fire, a cool, methodical approach to problems; stoic patience in the face of physical danger and discomfort; a willingness to risk his life for a comrade. He saw himself as the point man for a unit composed of designers, builders, fund-raisers and all the technical specialists of the sailing trades – 'we' would muscle our way around the world through the Southern Ocean, not 'I'.

If you wanted to pick someone for an advertising campaign to promote the adventurous purity of sailing, you'd pick Pete Goss. When I first met Goss aboard *Aqua Quorum* in Southampton, I thought, 'Here is the sailor as hero'. Tall, handsome, modest, friendly, open, humorous, eloquent, he was the whole package. By the standards of these races, he got to the start line on a shoestring. His entire campaign cost less than US$600,000, maybe twenty per cent of the budget for some of the more flush French entrants such as Auguin, Autissier and Parlier (not coincidentally, all favourites to win). The Goss campaign had all the endearing earmarks of English amateurism. Goss sold his house and moved his wife and three children into a rented cottage in St Germans, Cornwall. When word got around about the project, complete strangers knocked on the boatyard door, volunteering to lick stamps or phone around to look for sponsorship money. An actor, 'a friend of a friend of a friend,' Joanna Lumley, offered to christen the boat, prompting wide media coverage. After an appeal over the radio for scrap lead for the boat's two-and-three-quarter-ton lead keel, people all over Devon and Cornwall donated fishing weights, organ weights from a church, old bathroom fittings and diving belts. Even so, Goss needed some big-time sponsorship money, and he managed to get £100,000 from Creative Fragrances (Aqua Quorum is one of its products) and a £50,000 grant from the Foundation for Sport and the Arts.

He kept saying that his fifty-footer (the only one in the race) could outsail the sixty-footers over the long haul. It weighed less and would surf sooner and faster in lighter winds. It was a simpler boat with a power-to-weight ratio as good as any of the sixty-footers. *Aqua Quorum* was a light, strong surfboard. Without its keel, it could float in eleven inches of water. When it was being built, six men could lift the bare hull from place to place in the workshop. But Goss, short of money, had built a fifty-footer because that was all he could afford, and he was making the best of it. He still had to carry the same amount of gear and stores as the bigger boats, and this weight made up a much higher percentage of his displacement than theirs. He saved weight every way he could – right down to slicing off half of his toothbrush. But every skipper could do that (and many did). There was no getting around the fact that Goss's higher gear-displacement ratio would affect his boat's performance more than the others. And unless they were surfing, shorter boats went more slowly than longer boats – speed is a function of waterline length. Goss would struggle to keep up from the beginning.

For the ex-soldier, there were no allusions to combat in explaining why he was doing this: 'I'm not going out to change myself, or dig deeper, or any of that shit.' He simply loved sailing. He was excited and challenged by the race, in the same way he'd been excited by his first Channel crossing with his father when he was twelve. It was 'bloody brilliant!'

Getting to the Vendé Globe is 'a kind of inevitable progression,' he said. 'You do one thing, which expands your horizons; so you take another step, and the next thing you do is a transatlantic race, and then another. If you're the kind of person that keeps taking those steps, ultimately you'll wind up doing the Vendée Globe.'

Sometimes he thought he was really an adventurer, and sailing was just the medium through which he took his chances. The Vendée Globe was almost pure adventure. It had next to no rules. He hated complex racing rules – like the ones for the America's Cup, for example – that almost required a lawyer to translate them. Like the French sailors and their public, Goss loved the simplicity of the Vendée Globe.

The only other Englishman to make it to the Port Olona marina docks for the 3 November start was Tony Bullimore, with his sixty-foot ketch, *Exide Challenger*. At first meeting, Bullimore seemed to be just a bloke. He still has the accent of his native Southend-on-Sea. Before he became a full-time professional sailor, he had run large night clubs, an exhibition centre and other businesses. When I met him at his home in Bristol, the short, stocky, bull-necked Bullimore presented himself as the friendly, down-to-earth, unpretentious antithesis of the stiff-upper-lipped, reserved Englishman. We went for lunch to a nearby café that was filled with tradesmen, lorry drivers and municipal road-repair crews. Everyone had huge plates of cottage pie with a veg and spuds, mounds of buttered white bread and mugs of tea. All seemed to inhale this stuff twice as fast as I could.

Bullimore's English bloke persona is deceptive. Indeed, he brings to mind the older usage of 'bloke': square-rigger seamen's slang for a respected ship's captain. He's an intelligent, discerning man, keenly attuned to the unspoken context of a conversation – body language, other people's emotional state. His answers to my questions were thoughtful and articulate. He is married to a Jamaican-born woman and uses his fame as leverage to promote kinder race relations in Bristol. His wife has never tried to stop him sailing, but she finds it all a strain. She'd especially like him to give up this solo, round-the-world stuff he's become so ardent about.

Bullimore entered his first single-handed transatlantic race in 1976. He was England's 'Yachtsman of the Year' in 1985. Prior to the Vendée Globe, he had sailed a quarter-million sea miles, and crossed the Atlantic nearly thirty times, mostly in fast multihulls of ground-breaking design. He has 150 sailing trophies in his living room. He likes sailing, and he likes yacht racing. But he has always had a passion for the sea itself – being at sea, especially alone. His wife described him, in a translated quote that was everywhere in the French press, as *'un bouledogue, un merveilleux bouledogue.'* He does have a bulldog look to him, and in this race, his human endurance would reflect the animal's mythic strength.

Getting to the start line of the Vendée Globe had involved the usual scrabble for money, although Bullimore eventually secured a generous corporate sponsor. But he had had other difficulties. Two weeks before the start, he was in a car accident and injured his wrist and shoulder. They still hurt as he began the race. Worse, before the accident, during his two-thousand-mile qualifying sail, he had collided with a fishing boat. The damage to *Exide Challenger* had to be repaired fast, and other fine-tuning work was set aside.

At sea, the devil was always in the details. When the race began, Bullimore wouldn't have to wait long to pay the price.

He saw the Vendée Globe as both the ultimate yacht-racing

challenge and the logical next step in his career as a professional racer. As it did for Goss, the Gallic style of the race appealed to him. He liked the way everything was defined simply and austerely: no stops, no help, no advice, no supplies. You stood on your own two feet. In spite of all his trophies, people could still say: 'Well, all well and good. But what about the Vendée Globe?' Bullimore agreed. This race would be his own last word on his ability as a sailor. It would be all the demonstration he would ever need of what sort of man he was.

The race rules prohibited the elegant yet spartan Vendée Globe thoroughbreds from using the auxiliary diesel engines that were part of almost every sailboat's repertoire. In the confined space of the Port Olona marina, and the long break-walled channel stretching out past the commercial basin to the sea, they had to be shunted around by attendant power boats. Inflatable Zodiac dinghies pushed the sleek machines into the channel. Volunteer trawlers from the local fishing fleet then towed them past the long piers that sheltered the port from the Biscay weather. The tens of thousands of people crowded along the bridges and sea walls lining the narrow channel, only a few yards away from the passing boats, cheered and applauded. A solitary trumpeter played 'Auld Lang Syne' over and over again, the notes rising clearly above the noise of the crowd. Several skippers – illegally – ignited hand-held emergency flares, which spurted and flamed like huge red and orange fireworks. As the racers cleared the port, the trawlers dropped their tows. Support team or family members who had gone along for last-minute help or comfort were taken off. The solo sailors hoisted their sails, and threaded their way out through the milling spectator fleet towards the start line, marked by two buoys three miles offshore.

The crowds noisily cheering on the Vendée Globe skippers were certainly celebrating the start of another extreme sporting adventure. They were acclaiming their famous, and favoured, heroes – the names Autissier, Auguin, Parlier were known to all of them. The knowledgeable French sailing public had a good idea of what these sailors would face over the next three or four months. They had every reason to believe that their country's dominion of the sea was about to be reasserted, albeit in its modern, diminished, single-handed yacht-racing form. The salute was an even-handed one, however. Secure in their confidence of a French sailor's victory, the crowds could afford to cheer for English, Canadian and Hungarian sailors as well. They were the champions through whom that public would vicariously sail the Southern Ocean south of the stormy capes.

But the crowds were doing more than sending off a group of specialised athletes. Their departure reverberated with the ancient dread of the sea.

Oh Lord, thy sea is so great and my ship is so small.

Even in our time, a vessel's putting out to sea is an occasion for ceremony and emotion. We haven't lost our shared remembrance of how hazardous it has always been for small ships on the open ocean. For only a hundred years or so have we been able to comfortably assume that a ship leaving port would actually get to its destination. Before that, people assumed only that things would probably be bad.

A thousand years ago, Viking fleets filled with traders or colonists heading west to Ireland, Iceland, Greenland and Newfoundland would set out with each boat undermanned. The Viking *hafskip*, or ocean-going ship, was, for its size, as seaworthy a vessel as existed until this century. Nevertheless, they often went down. As the boats were lost, their rescued survivors, when they could be picked up, gradually fleshed out the short-handed crews of the boats that were left. In a good expedition, half the fleet returned. According to the sagas, on Eric the Red's second voyage to Greenland, thirty-five ships of colonists set out; fourteen arrived. After the colonies had been established there, so many Viking *knarrs* were lost on Greenland's iron coast that a professional corpse-collector made regular trips up and down the coast salvaging bodies from the wrecked ships.

For centuries, before steam engines and the Suez and Panama canals changed the odds, the wrecks of sailing ships littered the coastlines of the maritime trading world by the thousands. They foundered or were overwhelmed at sea on a kind of loose and deadly schedule – in North Atlantic winter storms, in seasonal tropical cyclones, on the Southern Ocean route to the Horn and rounding the cape from east to west. As late as the early twentieth century, sailing ships and their beleaguered crews suffered in the seas around Cape Horn. In the 1905 sailing season, for example, of the 130 square-riggers that sailed from Europe for the US west coast by way of the Horn, only fifty-two reached port intact. One large Welsh shipping company owned thirty-six sailing vessels over the course of its business life; of those, twenty were declared wrecked or missing, nine of them ending their lives off the Horn. At twenty to thirty men per ship – crew members rarely survived – the numbers lost throughout the fleets mounted into the thousands and tens of thousands over the years. Even now, far from Cape Horn, storms cull the freighters and fishing boats of the world, much less often than before, but with regularity.

The Vendée Globe and BOC Challenge sailboat races are a throw-back. There's never been a race in which the whole fleet, or anything like the whole fleet, finished. Attrition rates have averaged, Viking-like, between twenty-five and fifty per cent. In this Vendée Globe, only nine of the sixteen starters would reach the finish line. Of those, six would officially complete the race.

Less extreme yacht races – the various transatlantic and coastal contests – are much safer. Boats or people are rarely lost in them. But there have been some startling exceptions. The Fastnet Race of 1979 was the worst disaster in the history of yacht racing. The 605 mile-long course runs from England to the Fastnet Rock lighthouse, eight miles off the south-west tip of Ireland, and back. It's a challenging race, but the contestants are never too far from land, and the distance can be covered in a few days. On 11 August 1979, a record 303 boats set off. When the fleet was in the open waters between Ireland and the English west coast, it was pounced on by a depression that had suddenly and dramatically deepened into a weather 'bomb'. For twenty hours, the boats were raked by wind gusting to hurricane force and steep seas as high as forty feet. Seventy-seven boats were completely capsized. Another hundred were knocked down at least once. Many boats lost rudders or suffered other serious damage. Several boats foundered. In spite of the largest peacetime rescue operation in British history, fifteen men died in the cold, rough water.

Perhaps in a North Atlantic port like Les Sables-d'Olonne, where some commercial fishing still went on, the inhabitants, if not the tourists who just came for the beaches, had never lost this vivid knowledge of the sea's perils. Fishing is, after all, the world's most hazardous peacetime occupation. These people knew that the Vendée Globe sailors were about to assume the most extreme risks. Saint-Exupéry called the Sahara 'the rind of the earth', a phrase that could describe where these sailors were going as well. What could be worse than a lone trek across the Southern Ocean – a scary slog around the fringe of the world? A circumnavigation of Antarctica: cold, remote, ice-threatened, wearying, a presumptuous provocation of nature. The spectators knew that the sailors would often suffer in much the same way as the 'iron men in wooden ships' had for centuries. They could also be sure some boats wouldn't return, maybe one or two of the skippers as well. No wonder there was a frisson at the Vendée Globe race start. It was the collective memory of danger and death on the ocean, sailors against the sea.

For most sailors, getting ready and then setting off on a voyage in a small boat is stress city, ulcer country. Even a lot of experience doesn't necessarily help. The English cruising sailor Eric Hiscock, who had sailed all his life and had three circumnavigations under his belt, always felt nervous before setting off. He couldn't sleep; he sweated and worried. On the one hand, knowing this should make less experienced sailors happy – even the great Hiscock suffered. On the other hand, it should give them pause. What the hell was someone like Hiscock worried about? If he was scared, they'd be damn fools not to be as well.

In two encyclopaedic sailing texts, the practical and unassuming Hiscocks – Eric and his wife – taught English-speaking sailors how to get a small sailboat ready for the sea, and to move it from A to B briskly and efficiently – to 'cruise without fuss'. Through his pages of technical detail – how to take sextant sights, how to tie knots, where to store the eggs – Hiscock, in a kind of orgy of unemotional didactic narrative, managed to inspire the English to go sailing, much as Moitessier did the French. But Moitessier, always at a slight emotional angle to the rest of the universe, never seemed to fear going to sea. In fact, it was always a relief for him. The sea was where he was happy. And like all mystics, he could be ruthless in his search for personal equilibrium. As he left on his one-and-a-half-times circumnavigation in the 1968 Golden Globe race, his weeping wife and thoughts of his neglected children upset him, but not for long. He abandoned them all when his voyage ended. As he watched the sun set on the first day, he inhaled the breath of the open sea. 'I feel my being blossoming and my joy soars so high that nothing can disturb it.'

For Moitessier, it was always a tranquil path to the open ocean.

For the Vendée Globe racers, contending with more than three thousand small spectator boats mobbing the start line, tranquillity was impossible. Even though there wasn't enough wind to create much of a sea, the wakes of so many boats had created a local patch of very rough water. There was supposed to be a security zone around the line, but it was mostly ignored by the enthusiastic watchers and well-wishers. Getting out on to the water was a relief for the skippers nevertheless. After the hectic months of preparation, the sea itself promised, at last, some time and space. In a few more hours, they could begin to settle into a routine, demanding and hard, but without the distractions of endless technical preparations and appeals for money. They could stop being fund-raisers and campaign administrators, and start being sailors again.

Now that they were finally on the water and approaching the start line, the Vendée Globe competitors had also finished with the dreaded moments of separation from their families, especially their children. They didn't seem to share Moitessier's emotional insouciance. Back on the Port Olona dock, Christophe Auguin held his thirteen-month-old son, Erwan, his hand tenderly cradling the back of the child's head for half a minute. Most of the skippers were leaving family behind – Laurent and Goss, their wives and three children; Parlier and Bullimore, their wives; Dinelli, his future wife and their sixteen-month-old daughter. Autissier and Chabaud were unmarried but remained close to their parents. Gerry Roufs's seven-year-old daughter, Emma, had given him a good-luck stuffed doll. Later, she cried and asked him not to leave her.

That kind of pain receded on the water with the excitement of the start and the concentration on not hitting anything before the whole enterprise actually began. Even in the relatively light winds, the racers moved fast, and reaction times were short.

In a long race full of crucial tactical decisions, the skippers had an immediate, though relatively minor, choice to make. They could treat the start as if it were the beginning of an afternoon race around the buoys: sail hard; jockey for position; try to hit the line right after the start gun; chance collisions with other competitors or the pesky spectator boats. The winner of this race would win it by sailing flat out all the time, by taking chances and hoping for the best. That was part of the spirit of the Vendée Globe, the argument went, and a skipper had to sail like the devil from the first moments of the race. Alternatively, they could take the long view. Why take any chances at the beginning of a twenty-seven-thousand-mile-long race? Better to hang back, stay away from everyone, if possible; look for clear air – free of the airflow disturbances created by other sailing vessels as they pierced the wind. Losing a mile or two didn't matter at this stage. It was better to be careful, and safe. Pour it on later.

In fact, maybe this wasn't such a minor decision after all. Perhaps an aggressive start was necessary to help set the psychological stage for the rest of the race. More important, maybe losing a mile or two now wasn't such a good idea. Often, less than a day, sometimes a few hours, had separated Vendée Globe, and BOC, finishing positions. Just a few hundred miles or less. In that case, losing a mile at the start might mean something, even with twenty-seven thousand miles to go. It might be a mile lost forever. A boat might never make it up.

There was also the matter of visibility. It made sense that at least some sponsors would insist on a dramatic start to get their company names and logos more prominently on television. The Vendée Globe was, after all, unique – an expensive sporting event that took place almost entirely out of sight of spectators, viewers and the media. True, some photos would be sent back electronically by the sailors themselves. Press planes, or boats, would have the chance to photograph the racers as they passed close to land – Cape Finisterre on the north-west point of Spain, the Canary Islands, the Cape of Good Hope or even, if the weather was good, Cape Horn. Rescue planes or ships might take a few pictures if they were called in to help wounded boats. Indeed, these often showed, more than any other images, how terrible conditions could be. But when things got hairy, the skippers themselves didn't fuss around with their cameras; they tended to concentrate on staying afloat and alive.

This was a sporting event, then, whose climax – the race south of forty degrees latitude through the Southern Ocean – remained obscure, veiled, remote. Its fans had to intuit and infer what was happening from faxes, e-mail or radio transmissions. As a result, the few hours before and after the race start were a rare and, from the point of view of media and sponsors, important opportunity to actually watch and record the boats sailing. The race organisers prolonged the moment by setting in front of the beaches of Les Sables two racing buoys which the racers had to round before heading out to sea. Paradoxically, after crossing the start line, boats in a round-the-world race headed back towards the shore, where spectators could get a last look at them. Skippers always felt some pressure to put on a good show at the start.

As always, making a tactical decision at sea was a matter of evaluating competing risks. Christophe Auguin and Gerry Roufs opted for as much tranquillity as they could get. Both reefed their mainsails and loafed along under reduced sail, planning to hang back and cross the line some distance behind the leading boats. Willingly they gave up the favoured end of the start line, which provided the best angle of sail towards the first buoy. If the Vendée Globe boats had simply been heading out into the Bay of Biscay, it wouldn't have mattered. But the spectator buoys off the beaches created a typical racing-start situation, with favoured angles and tacks (the direction of the boat relative to the wind) to consider. Auguin and Roufs decided to ignore all that.

The favoured Auguin didn't subscribe to the 'never lose a mile' theory. He thought it was much more important to avoid trouble around the crowded and chaotic start line. It was a very long race; he knew that he wasn't a patient man by nature, and impatience at the start could get him into trouble. He wanted to force himself to stay calm, to proceed methodically and carefully. He would have time later to use his depth of experience and well-tried boat to make up for a leisurely start.

The Canadian Gerry Roufs adopted the same tactic. This was surprising because he had the reputation for being an aggressive, very competitive sailor. He had 'a rage to win' according to his country-man Mike Birch, with whom Roufs sailed for years. His friends described him as tough, tenacious, very intense, confident of his ability to win any race and, even under great pressure, capable of staying completely focused on his goal. In spite of these 'type-A' characteristics, however, Roufs managed to win, and hold, close and admiring friends. A small, slight man of forty-three (his birthday was the day before the race start), with an impish face and black curly hair, he had a quick, intelligent humour and, on the water, was re-spected as a fair, if forceful, competitor. 'He had a great reputation,' said one friend. 'Everybody liked Gerry.'

He too began sailing in small dinghies as a child. Racing out of the Hudson Yacht Club near Montreal, he was Canadian junior champion in his boat class when he was eleven years old. This early success was where he went wrong, Roufs noted in his Vendée Globe media résumé. He really didn't want to do anything but sail from then on. Unlike most of his fellow skippers, however, Roufs stayed with dinghy racing well into adulthood. At twenty-three, he won a place on Canada's national Olympic sailing team, and remained a member for almost seven years. In 1978, he came second in the world championships in the 470 dinghy class (a very fast, sixteen-foot, two-man racer that requires an athlete's conditioning to sail). With this dinghy experience, Roufs became a consummate tactician and close-racing expert. If he had wanted to mix it up with the other boats at the Vendée Globe start, he would probably have been the best sailor in the field at doing so. He was used to the unnerving close calls and bravura manoeuvring of a high-speed battle for the favoured position on the line.

While he was sailing on the Canadian national team, he managed to graduate from the University of Montreal law school and even went into practice for a year. For Roufs, however, there was never any real contest between the strict, if lucrative, regime of law and mucking about in boats. And with dinghy racing becoming routine, his ambitions had grown: he wanted to sail bigger boats – across oceans.

The opportunity to do so appeared in 1983. Roufs joined Mike Birch as a crewman on the radically designed and constructed catamaran *Formule Tag*. Birch himself was a pioneer transatlantic sailor; he began racing in the early 1970s. He was also the first foreign long-distance sailor to base himself in France, where the willing sponsors were. After a string of transatlantic races, sailed mostly on boats he built and paid for himself, he had finally broken through with a victory in the first French-organised Route de Rhum transatlantic race, in which he was sponsored by the camera manu-facturer Olympus France. After his win, he found himself inducted into the small circle of fully sponsored, professional long-distance racing sailors, almost all based in France. Sailboat racers already knew that they needed multihulls to win races or set speed records. And multihull designs were becoming safer. They needed to be; in one single previous year, three of the four leading multihull naval architects in the world were lost at sea in boats they had drawn up themselves. Birch got the job of overseeing the building of *Formule Tag*, and then sailing it as its professional captain. (Later, demon-strating its staying power as a leading-edge machine, *Formule Tag* was bought by Knox-Johnston and the New Zealander Peter Blake, and, as a renamed and refitted *Enza*, made a record-setting 1994 dash around the world in seventy-four days, a record since broken.)

Designed by the Englishman Nigel Irens, *Formule Tag* was built in Quebec. Birch wanted at least some of the crew to be Canadian, so

Roufs, the skilled and intensely competitive dinghy sailor, signed on. It was a good symbiosis. Birch, who had lived in England for twenty-two years and hadn't started sailing until he was thirty, was conditioned by the early English view of sailboat racing. He still saw the whole thing as something of a lark, an adventure. With his cool and understated personality, he wanted to get the boat from A to B and back again, and not get too wet in the process. Roufs wanted to do it fast and first. He had the tactical experience, honed in the close-quarter maelstrom of fast dinghy racing, to bear down and win.

For three years, Birch and Roufs sailed together in the burgeoning number of transatlantic races: the Quebec–St Malo (fifth); the Transat Espagnole (third); the Monaco–New York (first). The older adventurer and the younger passionate technician became close friends. While Roufs was completely bilingual in French and English (trilingual, one friend said: he could speak French with a flawless Québecois or continental accent), Birch spoke very little French. He was happy to have the English-speaking Roufs close by in La Trinité-sur-Mer, the small sailing town in Brittany where they both settled. Their friendship grew into a kind of father-son relationship. For Birch, the younger man brought formidable energy and skills to their sailing partnership – as well as a gust of cold Canadian air into the life of the occasionally nostalgic expatriate. They got together frequently to gossip in English and to talk about hockey. In his turn, Birch inspired Roufs to extend his racing career farther afield. Growing up on the Canadian periphery of the American centre, Roufs wasn't influenced by the usual French or English role models: Tabarly, Moitessier, Chichester. Unlike the French and English sailors, who could only admire their heroes remotely, Roufs had the luck to actually sail with his mentor.

During the same period, in 1984, when *Formule Tag* was docked in Quebec City, Roufs met and fell in love with Michèle Cartier. Cartier, a petite, animated, beautiful, dark-eyed woman from a small village in Quebec, reciprocated. The two spent most of their time in La Trinité-sur-Mer, and bought a house in nearby Locmariaquer in 1989. Their daughter Emma was born that year.

Only an occasional recreational sailor herself, Cartier settled into a life that seemed conventional, but in an odd way, and that she shared with many of the Vendée Globe sailors' wives and companions. They stayed at home with the kids and helped with the business end of their husbands' lives, or worked at mundane jobs of one kind or another. Meanwhile, their husbands spent two-thirds of each year separated from their families, risking their lives crossing oceans under sail. There was no good reason why a Vendée Globe or BOC sailor shouldn't come home to a cosy hearth and adoring family after circumnavigating Antarctica in a sailing vessel. Square-rigger sailors did it for centuries. Perhaps a man who risked his life for a living needed the comforts of a traditional wife and home. But today, this seems somehow incongruous. Maybe it's only the discrepancy between the adrenalin-charged high adventure of the sea and the snug and predictable routines of home and children. It is also the contrast between, on the one hand, the men's companions and, on the other, Chabaud and Autissier – two women sailing alongside the men while the men's women stayed at home. The two female sailors and the male sailors' companions lived at both extremes of the domain of women's work, with its shifting and conflicting possibilities and demands.

Roufs flourished on the fast catamarans. He was a crewman on *Royale* when it set a transatlantic speed record in 1986. For three years, he crewed on *Jet Services V*. The cat twice won the Course de l'Europe (a race in stages around the coasts of north-western Europe), as well as two transatlantic races, both of which set speed records. And he sailed with Birch whenever possible: for a year in 1991–92; most recently in 1994, when the pair raced a forty-foot trimaran in that year's Quebec–St Malo race.

The year before that, however, Roufs took a first step towards his conversion to big monohull sailing, and the road to the Vendée Globe start line. He won a crew position on Isabelle Autissier's *EPC2*. His association with the highly regarded Autissier, his own growing experience and a bit of luck finally got Roufs what he really wanted – his own boat. He persuaded the French industrial-cleaning products company Groupe LG to let him take over as its skipper.

Groupe LG had sponsored the experienced single-hander Bertrand de Broc in the 1992-93 Vendée Globe. Sailing well in third place, de Broc had been ordered by the boat's designer, backed up by Groupe LG, to put into New Zealand because they suspected the boat might have keel problems. None was found when the boat was hauled out, and the mercurial de Broc, now disqualified because he'd gone into a port, reacted furiously. He loudly criticised his sponsor and the naval architect, and stormed back to France, leaving the boat stranded in

New Zealand. Groupe LG asked Roufs to sail it back to France for them. Roufs took the opportunity – made easier by a growing personal relationship with Franck Oppermann, the company's head, who had once run a business in Montreal – to take over as *Groupe LG*'s skipper.

He did well enough with the boat, finishing sixth and third in two single-handed transatlantic races. Then his sponsor decided to build a new boat for the 1996–97 Vendée Globe. The existing *Groupe LG* had been built in 1989, and a lot of changes had occurred in Open 60 design ideas since then. The old boat was now considered heavy and slow. Groupe LG commissioned the design from Groupe Finot.

The new boat, *Groupe LG2*, was launched in September 1995. Many of the other boats newly built for the race, or older ones in need of refitting and updating, got into the water barely in time for their skippers to make the two-thousand-mile qualifying sail required by the Vendée Globe rules. Roufs had the luxury of ample time to tune the boat and get rid of its bugs – the failures, misalignments, weaknesses, mysterious malfunctions and ghostly lapses – which were inevitable in any new and complex machine. But it was far from clear sailing for the Canadian. He was forced to deal with another problem that jeopardised his entry into the race as much as any technical difficulties, and that leached even more energy away from his race preparations.

Getting a sponsor to foot the bill for a Vendée Globe is a matter of somehow grabbing a piece of the pie when there aren't nearly enough pieces for everyone. As in any scramble by obsessed people for a share of scarce resources, the fight is bitter. Many of the aspiring newcomers, trying to break into the charmed circle of moneyed professionals hustle the sponsors of the established sailors. And sponsors aren't necessarily faithful either – perhaps they'll be able to get a louder bang for their franc with some other sailor. If they feel they're justified, as profit-seeking businesses, in handing out the money, then business considerations will dictate how, and to whom, the money is handed out. All this is a long way from the casual amateurism of Blondie Hasler's transatlantic innovation or the Golden Globe.

Roufs was a successful enough jungle-fighter to get a sponsor and enter the race. But it was a tough fight. He made the mistake of spending too much time on the building of *Groupe LG2*, and not enough time preparing for races. He didn't do well in the 1995 and

1996 Figaros. Groupe LG began to have doubts. Had it chosen the right skipper? It equivocated. There were lots of up-and-comers clamouring to replace the established sailors. The pressure on Roufs intensified. For months, he wasn't sure whether he would be able to sail the new boat in the Vendée Globe. One of his good friends watched him under the gun. 'Lots of people would have said, "Screw it, here's your boat, keep it. I don't want to hear any more about it".'

But Roufs had the qualities to win out: he was mentally tough and focused, confident he could keep the helm and win the Vendée Globe, too, in the end.

The turning-point was the 1996 Europe 1 Star transatlantic race (the French still called it *la transat anglaise*; it was the descendant of the original transatlantic race dreamed up by Hasler and Chichester), which started from Plymouth in June 1996. Most of the competitors whose boats were ready on time used the race to qualify for the Vendée Globe or the BOC. Roufs held firm with his sponsor: he was the best skipper for *Groupe LG2*. He proved it by finishing first. The win finally settled his credentials as skipper and, as the winner of the most prestigious transatlantic race, his status as one of the second-rank favourites for the Vendée Globe – behind Auguin, but level with Parlier, Autissier and Fa.

Yves Parlier had helped solve the sponsorship problem by getting an entire government in on his act. He persuaded the regional government of Aquitaine to put up the largest single chunk of the money for his expensive machines – forty per cent for this latest one. Isabelle Autissier had done the same thing with the region of Poitou-Charentes, which contained her home base, the old French naval port of La Rochelle. Both sailors had lined up other sponsors, but the governments provided the lion's share of the millions of francs needed to wage a Vendée Globe campaign.

I interviewed Parlier at his office on an elegant boulevard in Bordeaux, in the same walk-up, four-storey building as several medical specialists. He had three employees who helped him run the business of being a professional sailor in France – mainly fund-raising, and all the public relations and personal appearances that went with it. It was really a full-time communications enterprise, in which Parlier played the main role. The trick was to put together a professional package, with himself as the major selling feature, so that the sponsors would feel happy about linking their names to the project. As with all the sailors in their roles as highly organised business people, Parlier came to the office every day, made phone calls, went to meetings, organised the details of boat building, fitting-out and planning for his single-handed races.

In person, though, Parlier was anything but a typical businessman. If this race already had a hero, a bloke and a pirate, it had in Parlier the sailor as Olympian athlete. He was about six foot three, muscular in a visible sinewy way, with a classical profile, short, prematurely grey hair and, most remarkably, bright blue eyes that stared fiercely at me and everything he looked at. I'd read of people having a hunter's eyes, and I supposed that that was what Parlier's were – they had an unblinking, unyielding alertness. He answered my questions serenely, up to a point, with dry wit and a sardonic off-handedness about his set-backs and physical suffering. But after an hour or so, he got restless, his attention began to dissipate. This wasn't a man who sat still comfortably for long. His nickname among his fellow sailors was 'the extraterrestrial' because of his apparently inhuman skill for finding the right wind at the right time during races. But the name also seemed to fit his detached, watchful and, it seemed to me – travel-weary and struggling in rusty French – somehow superior persona.

Just short of his thirty-sixth birthday when the race began, Parlier had begun sailing young. His family, living in Paris, came to the little resort and sailing town of Arcachon each summer. Parlier began sailing one of the ubiquitous Optimist dinghies there when he was eight. As a teenager, he worked as an instructor in a cruising school, teaching armchair circumnavigators how to tie knots and use a sextant. He began sailing with a racing crew when he was eighteen and loved it. He was 'impassioned by everything that touched sailing'. He read all the books about it. Inspired by his idols, Tabarly and Moitessier once again, he also read about older single-handers like the First World War flying ace and French lawn tennis champion Alain Gerbault, who, forever haunted by the war and tired of his fame, sailed away to the then still remote and fabulous South Seas.

Parlier raced small, very fast catamarans called Hobie cats in the world championships in Toronto in 1976. His first single-handed race was the 1985 MiniTransat, an event for pocket racers up to twenty-two feet long from Brest to Point-à-Pitre on the French West Indian island of Guadeloupe. He not only won the race, but also demonstrated his enduring love of technical innovation. He built his boat himself, and it was remarkably ahead of its time. To a conventional fibreglass hull, he attached an unconventional honeycombed, carbon-kevlar deck and a carbon mast. He studied composite materials and worked for a while in the research department of the Yachting France shipyard.

His transformation to professional sailor and membership in the elite sixty-footer club began with his 1991 victory in the Figaro solo race. From then on, his résumé consistently reads *'vainqueur'* – 'victor'. He won four single-handed transatlantic races, including a record-setting Europe 1 Star in 1992. He also came fourth in that year's Vendée Globe, having used the 1 Star as his tune-up and qualifying sail.

Parlier's boat, *Aquitaine Innovations*, was the most revolutionary Groupe Finot design jockeying for space near the start line. Sculpted out of carbon fibre, its hull shape a synopsis of all the curves and proportions currently prescribed for maximum speed, the boat weighed only seven tons. This was slightly less than half the displacement of the boat that had won the Vendée Globe four years earlier. A cruising boat of, say, forty feet in length that weighed the same would be considered light displacement (a heavy displacement thirty-six-foot steel boat we owned recently weighed twelve tons). Parlier's boat would certainly go fast. But doubts hovered in everyone's minds about its durability. These reservations existed not only because of its unusually light construction, but also because of problems Parlier had already experienced.

Having launched the boat at his home port of Arcachon, on 1 June 1996, Parlier and his team had only two weeks to prepare it and get it to Plymouth for the Europe 1 Star, which Parlier would use as his qualifying voyage once again. During a short sail off Plymouth the day before the race, Parlier noticed some problems here and there. Most disquietingly, however, the mast itself seemed insecure. It was the boat's most unusual feature, and the only one of its kind in the Vendée Globe fleet. It pivoted to present its best aerodynamic profile to the wind in any conditions. Parlier had eschewed a canting keel in favour of the adjustable mast, which – in a display of technical hubris – he estimated would produce a three-day advantage over all the other boats by the time the race was over, while a movable keel would produce a one and a half day advantage, and only over the boats with fixed keels. However, keeping this sort of mast upright was a challenge. Parlier left the next day fearing that the boat's most crucial component, apart from the hull, wasn't solid.

His fear was justified. After a week of light weather, the Europe 1 Star fleet encountered a North Atlantic summer weather system with moderate winds – nothing Parlier's boat shouldn't have handled with ease. When the boat dropped off one moderate-sized wave into its adjoining trough, a spreader snapped. These paired struts on either side of the mast are butted against the shrouds – the sideways steel wire or rod mast supports – and they distribute and relieve the compression loads on the mast. When one of Parlier's spreaders broke, the complex web of countervailing tensions provided by the standing rigging to keep the mast in column was breached, and it collapsed. Parlier badly tore the ligaments of one of his fingers while he was dealing with the mess and getting a jury rig in place.

It took him three weeks to hobble back to France. There were problems getting money together for a new mast. Its manufacturer had financial difficulties and couldn't deliver on time. The replacement mast wasn't fitted until the beginning of October, and Parlier had time for only a few brief test sails in the Arcachon basin. As he manoeuvred *Aquitaine Innovations* close to the start line on 3 November, Parlier knew little more about his boat than when he had started the 1 Star five months earlier. And every time he used his hand, which was almost all the time, his finger hurt like hell.

None of this had any effect on Parlier's habitual aggressive sailing style. From the beginning, he took the no-quarter, never-give-up-a-mile approach to the race. Under full sail, dodging the milling spectator boats, he duelled in fast, zigzag tacks at ten knots with the like-minded Bertrand de Broc, the Belgian sailor Patrick de Radiguès and Hervé Laurent in Roufs's former boat, now *Groupe LG Traitmat*. They all wanted that magic spot on the line, the one true and favoured slant towards the first buoy. They threw the sixty-footers around like sixteen-foot dinghies. It was as if they were starting a quick three turns around the buoys, to be followed by a shower and a couple of drinks in the clubhouse. Like short-distance racing skippers, they tried to hit the start line a second after the gun. This requires the sort of eye, brain and limb coordination a quarter-back might employ to complete a long forward pass under pressure of a blitz. Or perhaps the fine judgement of the old Apollo space capsule pilots, who had to hit and penetrate the barrier of the planet's atmosphere at just the right angle – too steep and the spacecraft burned like a meteor; too shallow and it skipped off into deep space forever. The boat's speed and inertial momentum must be judged in relation to the distance to the line, the kind and size of wave action that might slow the boat down or speed it up, the constancy of wind direction and strength – all based on the skipper's snatched assimilation of data in the tumult of the minutes before the start. To spice things up a bit, the Vendée Globe sailors had to avoid slicing in two the weekend cruiser carrying monsieur and madame, 2.4 kids and a bottle of wine, eager to see the action close up.

Miraculously, no one was hit. Just as miraculously, de Broc managed to cross the line just three seconds after the start gun fired at two minutes past one in the afternoon. Parlier followed a few seconds later. De Broc couldn't see the first buoy the boats were supposed to round. It was obscured by spectator boats. He had to put his boat on autopilot and stand at the bow, peering through his binoculars and yelling at nearby boats for directions.

This was de Broc's brief moment in the sun. (Although, much later in the race, misfortune would spotlight him again.) He was sailing a 1989 vintage boat (as were de Radiguès and Laurent), a heavyweight of twelve tons called *Votre nom autour du monde* – 'Your Name Around the World'. In an ingenious fund-raising campaign, he had collected money from over six thousand private contributors – including the French president Jacques Chirac, and the builder responsible for three of the competing boats. In return, besides the prospect of some vicarious thrills, his sponsors got their names stencilled on de Broc's boat. Its hull was blanketed by the names, row after row, from deck to waterline.

By the time the buoy loomed up out of the spectator boats, Parlier's boat had shown its superiority in the lighter winds, and he had taken the lead away from de Broc. He rounded the Port Bourgenay marker and headed out into the open ocean at the front of the fleet. With his new and fast boat, his habit of winning and a willingness to push hard from the start, no one was surprised to see 'the extraterrestrial' in the lead as the Vendée Globe fleet disappeared over the horizon from Les Sables-d'Olonne out into the perilous Bay of Biscay.

4

———

Sea Dark, Sky Crying

Il y a les vivants, les morts et les marins.

– Victor Hugo

*The wind and waves are always on the
side of the ablest navigator.*

– Edward Gibbon, *The Decline and Fall of the Roman Empire*

THE VENDÉE Globe boats cleared the coast and began beating
to the south-west directly into the benign wind. But the good
weather was temporary. The forecast was for gale-force winds the
next day throughout the whole sea area into which they were
heading. On their weatherfax machines, which reproduced detailed
satellite weather maps, the skippers could see the front coming at
them. Nothing special, just another routine Biscay depression. They
could also see the systems behind it, jumping off the North American
coast and picking up steam over water, far out in the Atlantic, but
moving fast. With their speed, the racers could count on being out of
harm's way before the later fronts arrived. A slow cruising boat
would have been hammered several times before clearing Cape
Finisterre and getting out of the Bay.

The Bay of Biscay in any season outside languorous midsummer,
has a grim reputation. It's one of those relatively small bodies of

water, close to land, that can kill sailors. And it nearly always scares the hell out of them. It is defined by the French coast to the east and the peninsulas of Brittany to the north and Iberia to the south, with a notional line between the ends of the two peninsulas roughly defining its western boundary.

Any vessel leaving the west coast of France, and any sailing vessel heading south from any Western European port to find the trade winds to the west, must first cross Biscay. Biscay is often the worst place most tropics-bound European or British sailboats will encounter in years of cruising. It's not just the bad weather. The shallowing water of the continental shelf, which extends across half of the bay, creates the shorter, steeper waves that are particularly dangerous for small boats, as the depth suddenly decreases from several thousand fathoms to a hundred. Worse, there's no sea room. Often a boat can't run off before wind and waves. It must stand and fight. The westerly gales in the bay drive boats towards the French coast, a lee shore, and a boat running off before the wind soon finds itself running out of water.

Sailors hate lee shores. The term simply means a shoreline towards which the wind is blowing. The old square-rigged sailing vessels were especially vulnerable to getting trapped, or 'embayed', on lee shores. If the wind persisted, current and leeway (the sideways drift of the vessel under pressure of wind and waves) would eventually wear down their resistance and drive them ashore. They were unweatherly vessels – that is, they had a terrible time making progress to windward. At best, they could sail at little more than right angles to the wind direction. They were suited to do much the same thing as the Vendée Globe surfboards were designed for: run downwind at speed. A square-rigger captain would therefore do anything to avoid a lee shore. Leaving Europe, crossing Biscay to get south, with prevailing westerly winds blowing towards the French coast, however, the old barques, brigs, brigantines, barquentines, hermaphrodite brigs and ships had no choice but to chance it, work their way out to the west as the wind permitted and hope to avoid the storm that might be too much to stand up to.

Modern yachts are far more seaworthy, in every sense of the word. Our thirty-one-footer would have been safer in Biscay than most square-riggers ever were. The modern fore-and-aft rig (the familiar mainsail and jib configuration) can sail to windward on a course forty-five degrees off the wind direction or better. Deep keels reduce leeway. Most yachts these days can claw their way off lee shores – as long as the wind doesn't get too strong for a small boat; as long as nothing breaks; as long as the crew's nerves hold.

In reality, it's still the land that destroys most vessels, certainly those under sail. Moitessier called the coast – he meant the universal, generic coast – 'a great whore', presumably because it seduced weak seamen into their own destruction. Better the ascetic and pure safety of the open sea. The old adage applies: 'When in doubt, go out.' If a crew can't get its boat into harbour before conditions get bad, then they'd better get as far out to sea as possible. The deeper water means more manageable waves. Sea room allows for some flexibility in storm tactics. There's more time before a slowly moving boat may be driven ashore. Crews may well not survive a trip through surf on to a rocky coast. The waves quickly jackhammer the boat to pieces.

Sailing across Biscay, or anywhere in the North Atlantic above thirty degrees north latitude, in November was far from being anything like the Southern Ocean. But it was a sea area no sailor could ever trifle with either, a proposition the Vendée Globe skippers, a day out into the Bay of Biscay, were about to confirm.

Tony Bullimore was the first to go. On Monday afternoon, just over a day into the race, he turned back towards Les Sables-d'Olonne. His automatic-pilot system had failed. With the arrival of the expected storm, Bullimore and the rest of the fleet were forced to beat into full gale-force winds – never below force 8 on Admiral Beaufort's scale – and steep headseas right on their nose. The autopilot itself worked, but the potentiometers, which fed the pilot essential information about the angle of the rudders, hadn't been properly attached to the steering gear. The screws holding them came out as the boat slammed into the waves. The now-disconnected instruments fell off, rendering the entire system useless. Some form of self-steering is essential for any single-hander. And while Bullimore could have jury-rigged a form of the primitive sail-balancing methods used before wind vanes and autopilots, he didn't have a hope of staying in the race, or of making it through the Southern Ocean.

At the same time, all the diesel fuel in one of his two tanks leaked out on to his cabin sole (the floor). The tank hadn't been properly sealed off; once again, it was just a little bit of human error in the rush ashore before the race. But the consequences were critical. He needed fuel to run his generator, which charged the batteries, which powered all the instruments on board, including his autopilot when it worked.

He would lose five days and a thousand miles on the leaders by the time he got things fixed and put to sea again.

'I was in a good boat, but certainly nowhere near the fastest boat in the race,' said Bullimore. His chances of a placing in the race, something of a long shot to begin with, had completely disappeared in twenty-four hours. 'It was all really a bit of a pain.'

At least he wouldn't be disqualified. Under the rules, boats were permitted to put back to Les Sables-d'Olonne without penalty. Stopping or obtaining assistance anywhere else brought immediate disqualification.

The second to go was Didier Munduteguy, a forty-three-year-old veteran transatlantic sailor from the Basque country of southern France. This was his baptismal round-the-world race. He'd dreamed of circumnavigating under sail for decades, and sailing in the Vendée Globe would be the ultimate expression of his dream. His sailing apogee was short-lived, however. He had been kept up most of the first night by portholes that wouldn't close properly. Although a potential catastrophe farther south, they were simply an inconvenience now and could be fixed. Then, just after dark late Monday afternoon (night came early in November in these northern latitudes), Munduteguy's boat slammed violently into a wave during one particularly strong squall of over fifty knots. *Club 60e Sud* was dismasted. He had to get out on deck and hack through the standing-rigging steel wire still attaching the mast to the boat. As always when a mast comes down, the sailor had to move quickly to prevent it from smashing a hole in the boat's deck or hull as it careened around in the rough seas. He turned back towards Les Sables, running now with the wind and waves. It took him three days to jury-rig a sail and get back to the Port Olona docks. His Basque sponsors raised the money to fit the boat with a new mast and rigging, and Munduteguy sailed again on 16 November – right into another strong Biscay depression. *Club 60e Sud* suffered structural damage from pounding into the steep thirty-five-foot-high seas. A three-foot crack appeared where the cockpit joined the hull. The skipper didn't know what other unseen damage had occurred. The boat had to be examined from top to bottom, and Munduteguy withdrew from the race for good.

The third and fourth skippers to make the Vendée Globe U-turn were Thierry Dubois and Nandor Fa. Even in a group of people doing something as much out of the ordinary as racing alone around the world, these two stood out as unconventional. The twenty-nine-year-old Dubois had formed a symbolic partnership with Amnesty International in 1994, a year after he had established himself as an up-and-coming single-hander by winning the MiniTransat. The organisation had bought Dubois's idea that the single-handed sailor was an apt symbol of human rights. It endorsed his fund-raising campaign motto, 'So that the ocean will not be the only space for liberty and individual responsibility left to man on earth.' What could provide more of a contrast than the political prisoner confined in his cell for speaking or writing a few words against the murderers and torturers who kept him there, and the sailor in the cockpit of his boat, deciding everything himself, a model of exhilarating self-reliance, skimming across the sunlit sea?

The idea of contrasting jails and boats is a modern one. From an historical Anglo-Saxon perspective, at least, the two have often been considered more or less the same thing. 'What is a ship but a prison,' asked Robert Burton in *The Anatomy of Melancholy*. Samuel Johnson, tongue only half in-cheek, aphorised that the prisoner was, in fact, better off than the sailor. 'No man will be a sailor who has contrivance enough to get himself into a jail; for being in a ship is being in a jail, with the chance of being drowned . . . A man in a jail has more room, better food, and commonly better company.' Burton and Johnson were thinking mostly of the warships of their time, manned by sailors who were treated like slaves. Operating by what Winston Churchill described as the real traditions of the Royal Navy, rum, sodomy and the lash, these floating strict-regime gulags somehow managed to dominate the oceans of the world.

But things had changed. The prisoner and the long-distance sailor, although living in much-the-same-sized spaces, represented extremes of self-direction and powerlessness. In spite of the ironic historical echoes, Amnesty's instincts seemed right. Before the race, it put Dubois's boat on display in Paris, in the Trocadéro, the 'Rights of Man' square. Parisians flocked to see it.

Almost exactly two days after the race start, Dubois turned back towards Les Sables-d'Olonne. Sometime during the wild ride through the fleet's Biscay storm, his boat, *Pour Amnesty International*, had probably hit a piece of flotsam – a log perhaps, or a steel shipping container lost overboard from a container ship, or some other piece of sea-going junk. The ocean was full of this stuff now, and it posed one of the worst dangers for small vessels at sea – especially for fast-moving, light-skinned racers like the Open 60s. Dubois didn't want to consider the possibility that the hull had split just because it had hit a wave particularly hard, although that had certainly happened to Vendée Globe and BOC boats in the past. The skippers could never comfortably assume that their hulls would withstand pounding head-on into storm waves without the chemically bonded layers de-laminating – peeling apart under the repeated shocks. The hulls of most of the Vendée Globe boats were built out of layers of carbon fibre and fibreglass cloth saturated with epoxy resins; when the resin cured, the whole assembly hardened into a very tough and light shell. Whatever Dubois had hit, the collision had cracked the hull near the bow, and the carbon and fibreglass had begun to delaminate around the fissure. It wasn't too serious, but he was taking on a little water. There was no question of proceeding until the damage was fixed. The Southern Ocean, or indeed another Biscay depression, would eat him alive.

It took him another two days to nurse his boat back to the Port Olona docks. Considering that he had worked towards and planned for the Vendée Globe for three years, and that within forty-eight hours he had been effectively denied any chance of placing in the race, Dubois was surprisingly cheerful and optimistic. The split in the hull was only two feet long, and there was no structural damage. It could be repaired quickly. Even if he couldn't win the race now, he remained very much in the running. He could be out of the Bay of Biscay before the next depression arrived. Maybe he would avoid the light wind that the rest of the fleet had experienced off the coast of Portugal. He could make up some time on his competitors. Anyway, the important thing was to get out there and finish the job he had started. What he'd said before the race began still held: 'I have a boat for it; so I'll go.' He might yet meet his modest pre-race objective of finishing in the first five. Dubois sailed again on the morning of 9 November, six days after the official start. He would still make his rendezvous with the Southern Ocean.

For the Hungarian skipper, Nandor Fa, however, the path back to Les Sables-d'Olonne and re-entry into the race didn't work out so smoothly. From the beginning, his campaign reverberated with an air of tragic *Mittel-Europa* exhaustion. The forty-three-year-old Hungarian sailor seemed almost condemned to failure in this Vendée Globe, an echo of Sisyphus in his uphill struggles. It was almost as if his long, unlikely route – inspired by reading Francis Chichester when he was a young man – from gloomy, landlocked, Iron Curtain Hungary to the ecstatic individualism of the open sea, and his achievements there, had finally used up his formidable energy.

During the storm, Fa thought that the pivoting keel on his self-designed and -built boat, *Budapest*, was moving backwards and forwards with the violent motion. It was certainly supposed to move from side-to-side when he hauled on the block-and-tackle arrangement that powered it. But he thought that a fore-and-aft motion – even of an inch or so – was a signal that the keel might not be secure. He had launched his boat in June 1996 and, like so many of the other skippers, had had little time to get to know it. His qualifying sail was a relatively quiet affair, and he had never experienced weather like this Biscay storm in his new boat.

Back in Les Sables-d'Olonne, Fa was slow to find out if repairs were necessary. He seemed overtaken by weariness and indecision. He didn't haul the boat out of the water to look at the keel until the next day. It was fine: the slight movement was obviously normal in heavy weather. He had returned to port for nothing, and had destroyed his chance of winning the race. This self-inflicted set-back was devastating. He had worn himself out getting his boat ready on time. A consistent and skilled sailor, Fa had finished eleventh in the 1991–92 BOC and fifth in the previous Vendée Globe. He had been one of the favourites in this race, and wanted badly to win. That was out of the question now. On the one hand, he found it very difficult to contemplate enduring the trials of the race simply to finish it. On the other hand, he had gone through so much just to get to the start line that it seemed inconceivable not to go on. He relaunched his boat and sailed again on 9 November.

It was as if Fa was really looking for some sort of decisive intervention to relieve him of his ambivalence, something that would remove the responsibility of going on. Perhaps it was a weird example of willed self-destruction, or a simple coincidence, but he found his way out. Soon after restarting, while its skipper was below making some coffee, *Budapest* collided with a Panamanian freighter, damaging the mast and rigging and the starboard side of the hull. Fa returned to port, fixed everything and managed to sail for the third time near the end of November. But his heart wasn't in it. When his electrical system developed problems, Fa took the opportunity to call it quits. 'I'm exhausted,' he said. 'I can't find the strength to go again. It's wiser that I stay ashore.'

In spite of this Biscay attrition, three-quarters of the fleet got through their first bad-weather test in reasonably good condition. Among the boats remaining in the race, Parlier had suffered the most serious problem: he'd lost more than half his drinking water. As *Aquitaine Innovations* pounded into the force 8 wind and seas, the repeated shocks tore away the carbon-fibre cables holding some of the water drums stored forward of the boat's cabin. Even though he had been assured by his shore team that they would be strong enough, they broke quickly. The drums ruptured and emptied into the bilge. Most of the boats carried small desalinators to convert sea water into drinking water, but Parlier didn't have one on board. He had decided against it to save weight – in this case, ten or twelve pounds, a significant amount. Parlier now had to rely on the old methods of catching rain water to drink – rigging canvas as a water catchment or collecting water in buckets as it ran off the sails. He thought he could count on the usual heavy rain squalls as he passed through the doldrums. Later, in the Southern Ocean, there would be more than enough precipitation. Parlier would be all right if he got enough rain. But he began to ration his water consumption nevertheless. It was a long way to the South.

The boats remained tightly bunched together. By the end of the second day, after the storm had passed over, less than eighty miles separated the first ten boats. Dubois had taken the lead from Parlier, but gave it up as he turned back to Les Sables-d'Olonne to repair his damaged hull. The sea calmed down and, in the afternoon, the sun came out. The sailors began to get their boats back in order and dry things out. They were heading towards the Canary Islands. For now, there wasn't much to do in the way of weather routeing or making course decisions, it was simply a matter of boat speed – and of keeping a vigilant eye open for freighters as they crossed several heavily travelled shipping lanes. As the leading boats left Biscay behind and weathered Cape Finisterre in a moderate westerly wind, Parlier fell back into second place, fourteen miles ahead of Laurent, who was doing well in his old and heavy boat. At the head of the fleet, ten miles ahead of Parlier, Autissier had taken over the lead.

Isabelle Autissier had turned forty two just before the race start. I

interviewed her in English in her office in La Rochelle. Such is her
fame that she gives three or four interviews each week. However, she
enjoyed our talk, she said, because she had to think much harder to
answer questions in English – it was a challenge. A tall, solidly built
woman, with short, dark curly hair and blue eyes, Autissier shook
hands and made eye contact very firmly. She wore large, flamboyant
earrings, one of her trademarks. Otherwise, however, she appeared
to be a brisk, attractive, casually dressed businesswoman. She sat
behind her desk and answered questions completely but formally,
with a reserved manner. She spends most of her time there, behind
her desk, running her business – the marketing of Isabelle Autissier,
the professional ocean sailor. Apart from the various races themselves, she spends very little time actually sailing.

Later, when she drove us to the boat shed where her boat, *PRB*,
was being refitted, she piloted her dark blue Mercedes like a racer –
hard, fast and sure – then crash-bumped it up a foot-high kerb
without slowing down much, and half skidded into a small parking
space.

As she showed me around the deck of her boat, which was covered
with plastic and carbon-fibre dust, I could see the physical power in
her heavy shoulders and forearms, her somewhat clumsy walk. She
had an easy camaraderie with the workmen at the Pinta boatyard.
They reciprocated, but with obvious deference and admiration.
Autissier gives the impression of confidence, strength, modesty, self-
control, self-knowledge, self-containment.

Among other things, the boatyard workers were busy cutting holes
for escape hatches in the transom (the vertical part of the stern) of
Autissier's boat, one on each side. Several skippers mentioned to me
that they would make sure their boats had this safety feature for the
1998–99 Around Alone, or the millennium year Vendée Globe. The
news that several of the recent Open 60 designs remained upside
down indefinitely had hit home with the sailors, a new element in the
periodic table of hazards each skipper had to face. The escape hatches
were one of the necessary adaptations to this faster, but more deadly,
reality. They might be made mandatory for all the boats for the next
race, Jeantot told me.

Getting a boat with the speed to win the race now apparently
meant accepting the danger of permanent capsize. For Autissier, as
for all the other skippers, climbing out through one of the transom
hatches and up on to the overturned hull, clinging to a rudder or the

keel (assuming they were still attached) in a savage Southern Ocean storm, waiting for help from another boat or the Australians, hoping the boat wouldn't decide to flip right side up again, was now just another routine transaction that might become necessary in the course of her business.

Autissier began racing in 1988, when she was placed third overall in the MiniTransat. It was a wonderful experience, and she immediately decided to give up her job as a marine engineer and work towards becoming a professional sailor. She sailed the Figaro twice, and then two BOC Challenge races.

In 1994, she smashed the record for sailing from New York to San Francisco around Cape Horn by fourteen days. Now, in her first Vendée Globe, she was sailing one of the new Finot-Conq downhill sleds. She was the only skipper to have experience with a pivoting keel, and was considered a superb tactical sailor. She had been the first woman to break into the elite group of sixty-footer solo sailors. Autissier stood a very good chance of winning.

As with all the other Vendée Globe skippers I talked to, she loved the completeness of the experience of sailing alone. The unspoken passion underlying all of Autissier's remarks was the desire to completely control her own world. There was no sharing, no division of labour, no complex relationships to work out and endure. Just the childlike unity of self with the task at hand. The single-handed sailor at sea presided over a world of singular simplicity without much parallel anywhere else on earth.

Autissier's father was a Parisian architect who sailed as a hobby on holidays in Brittany. From the time Isabelle was six years old, he took her with him, in dinghies and, later, in the small cruising boats the family owned. He was a very good teacher. He taught the young girl the precise technical knowledge of the sailor – the careful, planned manoeuvres, vigilant attention to detail, prudent calculation of risk. She absorbed the creed that mistakes at sea are always dangerous, sometimes deadly. But her father, typical of recreational sailors, also had a romantic attachment to sailing. He told her his dreams of sailing west, with the trade winds at his back, to the remote green islands and blue seas of tropical archipelagos. The busy, big-city family man could never do it. But the girl was filled with the same yearning to be alone on a boat on the wide ocean. 'One person, one boat and the earth,' as she said.

And of course, she read Moitessier, read about Tabarly. They were her heroes. The idea of doing something alone, like them, entranced her. The French like solo heroes, she said. So do the Italians. Maybe it's a Latin characteristic. The Anglo-Saxons seem to prefer groups and teams. She had always been puzzled by the relatively few lone American long-distance racers, for example – even in the BOC races, which are organised in the US, and start and end there.

I recalled Philippe Ouhlen, a sailmaker and one of Gerry Roufs's close friends, commenting on his own experience with crewed racing in big Maxi and Whitbread boats. French crews, he said, were very tough and motivated, but they just couldn't get along together. They never gelled. He much preferred his experience with Anglo-Saxon crews: American, English, Canadian, Australian, New Zealander all mixed up together. There was a natural coalescence into a smoothly functioning group. Authority was asserted, acknowledged, deferred to with an easy and unresentful effortlessness. There was none of the prickly testiness of the French crews he had sailed with.

This was Autissier's observation as well. It was probably impossible to catalogue the exact reasons – they were inextricably immersed in the stew of experience, history and chance which induced people to behave one way and not another. But there wasn't any doubt: the French weren't particularly interested in team sailboat races. Autissier had been like countless other French girls and boys when she dreamed of one day sailing alone against everything. In France, even people who have never seen a boat or the sea are touched by the Vendée Globe. They're interested, in part, because of the nexus of journalists, sponsors and sailors that constitutes big news. But even that is just another manifestation of the French affinity for this sort of contest. It's a kind of release for them. On land, everything is organised, parsed and parcelled. At sea, nothing is certain or contained.

The Vendée Globe sailors 'face nature, as nature was years and years ago', said Autissier. 'So it's really fascinating, I think, for the French to imagine one lonely person against the wind.' Even someone who has never sailed can understand the simple equation of the Vendée Globe: the 'one person – one boat' idea; the simple rules. The boats just go around the earth. And there's always the chilling fascination of the Southern Ocean. For Autissier, it's a very lonely and primitive place. There are other wildernesses – high on Everest or other mountains, the desert, the rainforest – but none so far away and so huge. 'Very few people can understand that nobody can reach us.

We are too far from everything, for planes, for boats. Too far. In the twentieth century, it's hard to understand, to realise that.'

'It's like going to the moon,' I suggested.

'Something like that,' she said.

Autissier's technical training helped her when she began to build, sail and maintain her own sailboats. She could talk to the architects and the engineers in their own language. She understood the mathematics, the technical specifications of things. There was a precision in her discourse with designers, stress experts, builders of hulls and masts, electronics specialists. She knew why the carbon fibre went in such a direction and not another. She understood the mechanics of her canting keel, the stresses and forces acting on it as her boat swung along. Her engineering background helped her to interpret weather information, and to pick the best course, hour by hour, as she watched the eastward-moving patterns of undulating isobars unfold on weatherfax printouts.

Skill at weather and wind forecasting is particularly important in the Vendée Globe. In line with the view that the race should be sailed without assistance, outside 'weather routers' are forbidden by the rules. These are specialists – sometimes part of a boat's support team, sometimes hired on contract for the duration of the race – who have access to all conceivable information about the weather a boat is sailing in and heading towards. They are experts at interpreting the satellite pictures, and in translating their complex data into a specific course for the most favourable wind or away from bad weather.

Autissier accepted the principle that the Vendée Globe sailors should analyse their own weather data, without the help of professional routers. The skippers should win or lose on their own, not because one team's expert was better than the rest, but she thought that more complete weather information should be made available. The skippers received constant weather reports from the computers at Météo France, the French weather service, but sometimes this information was incomplete or inaccurate. She told me how astonished she had been by the ferocity of the Southern Ocean storm that assailed her and Roufs in early January with its seventy-knot wind and fifty-foot-high waves. The computer forecast had been for forty-knot wind – not much above average strength. Later, she read a newspaper article by a meteorologist who, two days before the storm hit, had predicted the much more severe conditions that

Autissier and Roufs actually experienced. He used more sophisticated weather-satellite information and was able to make an accurate
prediction. If Autissier and Roufs had had the same information, they
would have known what was really coming. Maybe they could have
diverted north or south and avoided the worst of the weather.
Whatever had happened to Gerry might not have happened. The
mystery at the heart of this Vendée Globe would never have arisen.

Two years earlier in the 1994–95 BOC Challenge, Autisssier demonstrated that she had what it took to win one of these races – if nothing
went wrong. By the beginning of December 1994, she was five days
ahead of the next boat as a result of her virtuoso weather-routeing
tactics during the first leg, a virtually insurmountable margin. On 2
December, twelve hundred miles south-east of Cape Town, loafing
along at thirteen knots in a relatively moderate twenty-five- to thirty-
knot wind, Autissier was dismasted. Without warning, a turnbuckle
gave way. A large double-ended screw that connects the rigging to the
hull and tightens it probably broke because of some inherent defect
in the material. Nothing is supposed to break in conditions like that.
While the help she subsequently received didn't disqualify her under
the less Draconian BOC rules, her chances of winning the race
disappeared at the moment her mast fell down. And it began a chain
of circumstances leading to her abandonment of the race.

  If capsizing or going overboard are the most brutal events a sailor
must deal with, losing the mast, while seldom fatal, is certainly more
common. A dismasting triggers an exhausting course of action:
moving fast to prevent further damage, setting up a jury-rigged substitute, nursing the boat to its destination. It can occur anytime. The
standing rigging and its attachments – the various tangs, toggles,
turnbuckles and chainplates – invisibly fatigue under the constant
stress of the mast's motion. The massive strength of sophisticated
carbon-fibre or aluminium masts and their supporting rigging is not
always enough to withstand the extreme destructive forces caused by
a knockdown or capsize. When the rig goes, the sailor's immediate
concern is that the broken mast and boom should not be driven by
wave action to smash holes in the hull or deck – exactly what
happened to both Dinelli and Bullimore after their boats capsized.

  The sailor must have powerful cutting equipment on board with
which to hack through the rigging so that the dangerous spars can be
jettisoned. Then, assuming the boat is still in one piece, the skipper

must set at least some jury-rigged sail and get moving in the direction of a port. For a single-hander, this requires extraordinary tenacity and effort, as well as a steady nerve. The boat, without the stabilising effect of mast and rigging, which increase resistance to rolling motion, is much more likely to be rolled over again. At the greatly reduced speed of a jury rig, with its much smaller sail area, shelter is even farther away.

For a desperate hour and a half after her mast came down, Autissier chopped and sawed at the rigging with pliers, a knife and a hacksaw. The boat rolled violently in the three-degree water. She tried to save her boom, which would have made a tolerable replacement mast, but it broke as well, weighed down by the weight of water in the mainsail.

'Thirty knots of wind, sea dark, sky crying,' she said in a message to her French home base. 'I'm working to clear off the deck and see what I can do. There is almost nothing left on deck. Nothing left of my dream. But I won't think about that now. I am safe . . .'

That night, David Adams, a close friend of Autissier's who had been sailing nearby, circled back to lend moral support. Adams had been one of Autissier's crewmen on *EPC2* during her first and unsuccessful attempt the previous winter to break the speed record for sailing a vessel from New York round the Horn to San Francisco. There wasn't much Adams could do. They shouted back and forth to each other for a while. Then, as night fell, and at Autissier's insistence, Adams sailed on, and left her to fend for herself.

It took twenty-four hours to jury-rig a mast out of one of the spinnaker poles. Autissier then headed for the French-owned Kerguelen Islands which were twelve hundred miles to the west and twenty-five hundred miles south-west of the Cape of Good Hope. Using a small storm jib as a mainsail, and another jib as a foresail, she managed to push her boat 100 to 160 miles a day and arrived in the Kerguelens in a blizzard two weeks later. Her shore team located a replacement mast and shipped it there by way of a French naval vessel. But it was almost forty feet shorter than the original and would severely restrict her speed during the rest of the leg to Sydney – the second stop in the BOC race.

In three days, Autissier set up her new mast and, for good measure; used her spinnaker pole as a mizen-mast so that she could set a little more sail. When she got back out to sea again, her rig didn't do badly. One day, she managed a twenty-four-hour run of almost 230 miles.

Two weeks later, however, she found out that the Southern Ocean had only given her a reprieve. A storm with sixty- to seventy-knot wind swept over her. As the front crossed over her position, the change in wind direction created the usual dangerous cross-seas. It became increasingly difficult to position the boat to take the waves on the stern. And a little later, while she was running under bare poles in the slightly moderating wind, the wave with her name on it found her. 'I could hear the big groan of a big wave, and I thought, This wave is dangerous. But of course, I could do nothing. '

The boat was pitchpoled end over end and rolled 360 degrees simultaneously. Autissier had been thinking of going on deck to put up a storm jib, but had delayed for a while. It saved her life. If she'd been on deck when the wave hit, she would have died – drowned immediately, swept off the deck into the roiling sea, perhaps crushed against the mast or rigging by the force of hundreds of tons of water. As it was, she was in a small passageway connecting the main cabin and the aft compartment when the boat capsized, and was able to roll with it without injury.

'I felt the boat going flat in the water. Then, I felt the boat's keel turning. I was just pushed on to the ceiling of the boat, and a lot of cold water came inside.'

When she crawled out of the passageway, she saw that both her jury-rigged masts were gone, and to her horror, that the cabin top had been torn away. Its immensely strong composite carbon-fibre construction, moulded as an integral part of the deck, had crumpled under the terrible assault of the wave. She saw only low grey sky where the cabin top had been. Autissier realised then that even if she'd been in the main cabin, at the chart table or in her bunk, she probably wouldn't have survived. Virtually everything that wasn't bolted down had been sucked out of the fifty-square-foot hole in the deck by the force of the wave. 'I was lucky,' she said later, with impressive understatement.

Nothing pumps water out of a boat faster than a frightened sailor with a bucket, or so goes the old saying. Autissier's boat was completely open to the waves that continued to roll over it, and *EPC2* was already dangerously waterlogged. She rigged a stopgap tent over the hole and bailed for two hours. Then, regretfully, Autissier activated her emergency radio beacons, the first time she had ever done so. She took refuge in the boat's forward watertight compartment and began to wait.

This time, there weren't any other competitors close by and in a position to help. Fortunately for Autissier, she wasn't completely off the beaten track – by Southern Ocean standards anyway – less than one thousand miles south-east of Adelaide. The Australian air force was presented with yet another of its apparently annual opportunities to conduct a remote-rescue operation. It dispatched a C-130 Hercules at first light the morning after Autissier's capsize. The missile frigate *Darwin* sailed from Fremantle, on the west coast of Australia, a few hours later. It would take over two and a half days to reach Autissier's shattered boat.

After the Hercules reached the search area defined by Autissier's emergency beacons, it still took almost three hours to find the boat, so difficult was it to pick out the white deck from the visual clutter of breaking waves.

On New Year's Eve, 1994, a helicopter from the *Darwin* lifted Autissier off the deck of her boat. New EPIRBs were dropped on to *EPC2* in the hope that it could be salvaged, but even with the relatively precise positions provided by the beacons, the salvage vessel just couldn't see Autissier's boat amid the Southern Ocean rollers. Her million-dollar racer drifted away for good.

5

To the Great South

Oh, who can tell, save he whose heart bath tried,
And danced in triumph o'er the waters wide,
The exulting sense – the pulse's maddening play,
That thrills the wanderer of that trackless way?

– Lord Byron, *The Corsair*

IT WAS still a close race as the Vendée Globe fleet, with Autissier at its head, bore down on the Canary Islands. Then Laurent, still surprising everyone with his veteran boat, took the lead, with Autissier, Parlier and Auguin exchanging the next three places as local conditions momentarily favoured them. The favourite, Auguin, had been steadily moving up through the fleet. He was still methodically working himself and his boat into the race – checking his gear, studying the weather ahead, getting into the rhythm of the boat and the sea. So was everyone. But Auguin had said he was holding back, not going flat out until he got himself and his boat's systems in order. This was different from the BOC Challenge races in which he had done so well. In those, racers had to go flat out from the beginning of each of the four legs. There wasn't time later to make up for ground lost early on. And damage to the boat could be repaired at the end of each stage, the degrading insults of sea and wind smoothed away by the ministering specialists on the support teams. The boats began each leg renewed, with a fresh armature against the sea's assault. In the Vendée Globe, the wise skipper was obliged to husband his strength and resources, to keep the expenditures of finite energy controlled to last for 120 days. That meant getting some sleep each day, a formidable problem for the single-handed sailor.

After three days without sleep on our passage to the Virgin Islands, I hallucinated that the dwarfish manlike shape on our stern rail had it in for me. Five hundred miles from land, I imagined I saw clearly the lights of a big-city skyline twinkling away just a few miles off our beam. These were vivid experiences. But at least I knew they weren't real. My brain told me to forget about trivialities like sailing our boat to the Virgin Islands. Instead, I had to do something really important right away: sleep. If I didn't, there would be trouble. Hallucinations are nature's way of telling us to get a little shut-eye.

'*Oh sleep! it is a gentle thing, / Beloved from pole to pole,*' said the Ancient Mariner.

Getting sufficient sleep is difficult enough for people living comfortably and stably ashore. Probably most of us are sleep-deprived to one degree or another. On a small boat at sea, it can be a struggle to get even the bare minimum of sleep required to stay psychologically healthy, and to retain enough smarts to remember how to light the propane stove without blowing yourself up, or how to accurately transfer the GPS position coordinates to a paper chart. With sailors relying on electronic navigation devices, it's no longer necessary to take sextant sights and go through the detailed arithmetic of a sight reduction with its many possibilities for errors. Sextant navigation is as obsolete today as the astrolabe, except for antiquarian enthusiasts who keep it up as a hobby, like riding on steam trains. The opportunity for sleep depends on the weather, the size and experience of the crew, and your own state of mind. For obvious reasons, it's even more difficult for a single-hander.

Many of the Vendée Globe skippers consulted sleep experts and underwent tests to find out about their individual circadian rhythms. Getting enough sleep in the course of a long, gruelling race was so tricky that the sailors treated it as another major technical problem to be solved through research and technical know-how. Both Auguin and Autissier, for example, underwent tests and developed a schedule of their best sleep times in the course of a day, as well as the optimum length of time for each sleep period. Ideally, Auguin would try to get between six and seven hours' sleep in every twenty-four, divided up into naps that were either one and a half hours long or less than half an hour. Autissier tried to sleep between three and six each morning, then from 11:00 a.m. to 12:30 p.m. and from four in the afternoon to five thirty, for a total of six hours a day. Her sleep specialists had established those times as her personal best-sleep periods. Laurent aimed for an optimum six hours of sleep a day as well, in naps of varying lengths: a half-hour, an hour or an hour and a half. He also tried to make his sleep time more efficient by practising yoga exercises. He took them up two years before the race expressly to be better able to calm himself and fall asleep almost right away. All the skippers had some sort of personal sleep routine designed to knit up their ravelled sleeves of care.

The timing of these extended naps may be the result of expert analysis of individual circadian rhythms, but the pattern differs completely from the traditional single-sleep period of most human societies – so-called monophasic sleep. The sailors have adopted what is really a polyphasic sleep cycle.

Some of the most important research conducted on the effect of polyphasic sleep on alertness and performance was based on studies of long-distance solo sailors by Claudio Stampi, a medical researcher and round-the-world racer. He correlated the various types of sleep patterns adopted by sailors to their performance in several shorter races, three to seven weeks in length. Many of the skippers fragmented their sleep periods down to less than two hours, some to an hour or so, others to between ten and thirty minutes. This pattern allowed for frequent checks on course and sailing performance. Most of the competitors adapted well to this episodic sleep schedule. Stampi concluded that each person had an individual best nap duration. The trick was to strike a balance between recuperation from fatigue on the one hand, and avoidance of sleep inertia on the other. The grogginess and bewilderment of sleep inertia is a consequence of waking up from the intensely recuperative, very deep slow-wave sleep. The effects may last for several minutes or more. Sailors had to avoid that if possible. A lot could go wrong in the time it took to come to their senses. Stampi also found that even when faced with hard physical work, difficult navigation and weather routing calculations, the competitive and hard-driving sailors could keep going for a long time on this splintered regime of four or five hours' total sleep in each twenty-four hours, even interspersed with periods of little or no sleep.

The Vendée Globe skippers had sleep plans but at sea, things were different. Almost anything could upset the schedule. In light or fluky wind, the sailors had to keep an eye on the course and sail trim. In the Atlantic, near shipping lanes or in areas where fishing fleets operated, they had to watch out for ships. At their speed, the Vendée Globe boats very quickly ate up the safe distance to the sailor's cramped horizon. In heavy weather, it could be difficult to sleep because of the noise, the motion, having to reef or furl sails, fear. In the high latitudes, the skippers felt at least some obligation to watch out for ice, even if they knew it wouldn't show up on radar or if visibility from deck was obscured by rain, snow, low cloud. If the boat was beating, the motion on board these downwind specialists could be so short and violent that it was hard to lie down, let alone sleep. Needless to say, wind and waves don't respect anyone's scientifically determined nap schedule. *But if you break the bloody glass you won't hold up the weather.* If the next Southern Ocean low slammed into Autissier at 4:30 p.m., she could forget about her afternoon snooze.

On top of handling the boat, the sailors had to analyse weather and choose their course tactics. Doing this well was so important in the competition that it ate up hours each day. They had to stay in touch with everyone. There was no point in having all those phones, radios, faxes, e-mail if you didn't use them. Sponsors and the public expected it. Then there was everything else: cooking food and eating it, carrying out personal hygiene, taking off and putting on salt-stiff and cumbersome foul-weather gear, each of these often a surprisingly long process in the rock-and-roll turmoil of the cramped cabins. In fact, everything took much longer because of the boat's motion. The most natural behaviour became studied. It took practice to learn how to keep some muscles taut so you could stay put, while at the same time relaxing the muscles that allowed a bowel movement to take place. Especially when you were shakily perched on a bucket. The sailors were continuously wedging themselves in here, bracing themselves there, hanging on for dear life in the big seas of the South. You could get exhausted on a boat, doing nothing all day except making sure you weren't suddenly flung, like a big-ring human cannonball, across the cabin on to some bruising piece of gear or malevolent carbon-fibre protrusion.

Finally, the skippers had to fix things. This is a continuous and time-consuming part of life on any boat – because the damp and salt are hostile to every piece of gear or equipment on board, because of the motion that invisibly fatigues material. On boats that often pushed their design and construction envelopes, fixing things could become a skipper's main pastime.

The Vendée Globe, in all its aspects more extreme than any other ocean race, is probably the ultimate laboratory for the effects on performance of reduced, fragmented sleep for long periods of time. On the one hand, the skippers appear to react well to their sleep deprivation. Most of them finish the race. They handle their boats competently and set new race records. They remain lucid and focused. Their motivation and competitiveness is fierce to the end. Yet no one knows but the skippers themselves the extent to which sleep deprivation contributes to the trouble they sometimes get into in heavy weather. Maybe dog-tired brains don't make good tactical decisions in the face of approaching weather systems, or perhaps they fudge or delay necessary course changes demanded at critical moments by a backing wind and the development of tricky cross-seas. There's no way of testing these propositions, of course. Anyway, even well-rested skippers can't prevent Southern Ocean broaches, knockdowns or capsizes if they're in the cards.

Auguin's methodical start was part of his prudent plan for this Vendée Globe. Now he served notice that his adjustments were just about complete. A lot would be decided over the next few days, he predicted, as the boats negotiated the relatively light winds of an almost stationary high-pressure system. Auguin was happy with the prospect. Like all the racers, he relished the exhilarating flat-out, downwind rush of Southern Ocean sledding. In the roaring forties and the furious fifties, you hung on, endured and hoped for the best. But he liked light-wind sailing as well, its delicate compromises and fine lines. In the mild and fickle breezes on the fringes of the North Atlantic High, you had to think things out, tweak the sheets (the lines controlling the sails' attitude to the wind when under way), watch halyard tension (the lines used to raise and lower the sails), adjust the outhauls and leech lines (sail-tensioning controls), carefully balance the water ballast, and keep the boat footing. Above all, you had to scrutinise the weatherfax maps for tell-tale isobar curves and bunchings, for hints of how the systems around you might move or change over the next day or so.

The leading skippers formed into two groups as they hunted for the best wind. Parlier, Autissier and de Broc (in fifth place) stayed closer to the Portuguese coast, looking for wind that might be generated by the temperature difference between land and water. Auguin and Laurent swung farther out into the open ocean, sniffing for steadier breezes away from the adulterating influence of the continent. As it converged on the Canary Islands in a few days, the fleet would discover who had made the best guess.

The differences were still small – the ninth-place Roufs was only forty-three miles behind the leader Laurent; de Broc and Eric Dumont would sail in sight of each other for the next three days. But slight displacements of one boat from another could be crucial in light and changeable conditions. Winds were often spasmodic and localised. One skipper might encounter a hole and wallow there for hours while a competitor a few miles away skips along before his own private wind. Anyone who has ever raced a sailboat in a light breeze knows the baffled frustration of watching boats a hundred yards off ghosting away from one's own becalmed and rocklike craft.

For the Vendée Globe sailors, only a week out, forty miles might mean nothing, or it might represent an already unbridgeable gap. These uncertainties would increase as the boats approached the fickle latitudes of the doldrums. Decisions made there, or just luck, could determine the outcome of the race. The skipper who broke through the calms and uncertain winds of the doldrums to the south-east trade winds a few miles (but in the light airs, a day) ahead of a rival could add three hundred miles to his lead before the other boat even tasted a breeze. The same thing could happen as the racers descended into the roaring forties of the Southern Ocean. The lead boat could pick up the low-pressure storm winds first and shoot ahead as, day by day, the strengthening wind drove it proportionately faster. While no one could predict the ultimate effect of a few miles in these early stages, in previous Vendée Globes the skippers' tactics in negotiating the doldrums during the southbound Atlantic leg had proven decisive in the final results. Everyone thought these minor early advantages were worth fighting for.

Roufs's ninth-place position was a surprise. Everyone had expected him to be up front with the lead boats, jostling aggressively for an advantage. Roufs seemed relaxed, the usual joker. He announced that everything was OK because he finally found his supply of jam, which someone had stowed in an unlikely corner. Now he could eat jam-flavoured yoghurt, one of his favourites, along with the big breakfasts he liked. But after that, his radio was uncharacteristically quiet. The 470 dinghy and Europe 1 Star champion didn't like being so far back – he wasn't used to it. He began to bear down harder to reduce the possibility of someone else getting that early jump south out of the doldrums and leaping ahead of the fleet.

Parlier, worried about his dwindling water supply, thought for a while about anchoring off one of the Canary Islands and filling his jerrycans with water from a mountain stream. The race rules allowed the sailors to anchor, as long as they didn't receive help from anyone ashore. And they themselves could not move beyond the boundary of land and sea, the high-tide waterline. They had committed themselves to the sea for the duration of the race and must stay within its domain. He gave up the idea, however, when he found out that the unusually dry weather had desiccated the islands' streams. It wouldn't be worth his while to land. In the meantime, he said, he was wearing a straw hat, keeping his sleeves rolled down and breathing through his nose.

Apart from the boats that had put back to Les Sables-d'Olonne for repairs, the rear of the fleet was occupied by Raphaël Dinelli. Like Bullimore's, his autopilot had broken down in the shocks of the Biscay storm, and he had almost turned back to port as well. But he had an old autopilot on board, and he managed to fit it and get it working. All this had cost him time. He was already a long 270 miles behind the leader. He had a good following wind now, however. Under full mainsail and boomed-out genoa (the large jib, held in position with a pole), he managed to surf at seventeen or eighteen knots on the modest waves.

All the skippers had experienced minor damage in the pounding of the Biscay storm, and they used the relatively calm weather to thoroughly inspect their boats. That usually included climbing the mast to check on the various fittings there. But Marc Thiercelin, in seventh place, just ahead of Pete Goss, couldn't bring himself to do it, not without an adrenalin-inducing emergency. The masts on the Open 60s were mostly around eighty-five feet high, and they tapered off alarmingly near the top. Thiercelin decided he would climb it some other time, when it was absolutely necessary, but not now. He had suffered an ear injury in an earlier accident and became dizzy when he climbed or dived underwater. Anyway, he didn't have the soul of a mountaineer, he said; not like Parlier, who liked to climb mountains in his spare time.

There are several ways for lone sailors to haul themselves up their masts. The traditional device is the bosun's chair – a plank of wood, nowadays swathed in padded nylon, with pockets for tools and spare shackles or a can of penetrating oil. This works better when there's crew on board to haul its occupant up using one of the powerful sheet winches or the anchor windlass. The single-hander can do it too, however, using his or her own muscle and a line-clamping arrangement to take the weight in between pulls. The advantage of the bosun's chair is that, once you actually get to the top of the mast, you can tie yourself off and work sitting down, in relative – very relative – comfort. Even in the calm water of an anchorage, a slight motion at the water level – from wind chop or powerboat wake – is translated into alarming swings and jerks at the mast top. In a seaway, the masthead's movement is grotesquely exaggerated, an aluminium bronco ready to buck the sailor to kingdom come. Some solo sailors use variations of the mountaineer's climbing gear – complex collections of lines, clamps, carabineers and slings – and walk upward using the mast as a guide and handhold. These are quick but more precarious than the bosun's chair, and it takes more effort to hang on while you're working. Cruising boats often have mast steps for going aloft. You put your feet in these aluminium brackets, which are screwed to the mast, and just climb up. They create a lot of windage, however – slowing a boat down in light winds, increasing the size of its profile to the wind in heavy weather. For that reason, racing boats never fit them. The cruising sailor, usually sailing with a spouse and sometimes children, accepts less efficiency in exchange for handiness.

Going up the mast used to be a routine part of the sailor's job. Almost all the sails on a square-rigger had to be reefed or furled by men who went aloft, up the windward ratlines on the standing rigging, and then out along the yard-arms, feet braced against the monkeylines, bellies and chests laid across the wildly rolling yards, wrestling with the recalcitrant, flogging canvas. A sailor who fell was a dead man if he hit the deck. Those working at the ends of the yard-arms stood a slightly better chance because they were more likely to fall into the sea. It was occasionally possible to recover a man overboard, though not often at night or in bad weather. In high latitudes, frostbite was routine. The hard, heavy sails had to be pounded into submission with fists that soon bled. Sails on square-riggers were always bloodstained. The men could spend most of a day or night at a time up there in cold and gale if many sails had to be reefed, furled or reset at the same time. The topsail or skysail yard-arms might be 150 feet above deck. The crew went up in all weather. There wasn't any choice – that was the only way the sails could be handled. Still, it was often exhilarating and a source of pride: who but real blue-water sailors – the iron men – could hand and reef aloft under any conditions?

We jolly sailorboys up, up aloft, and the landlubbers lying down below, below, below.

But nothing reckless. The goal was to survive.

One hand for yourself and one for the ship.

If you fell, you died.

Thiercelin was able to postpone a trip up his mast, but Autissier had been forced to climb hers. A halyard had broken. She had to go up eight storeys right to the top to fit another one, threading it through its sheave, hanging on against the snapping, whipping motion, magnified – think of the mast as an upside-down pendulum – seven or eight times from that at deck level.

One of the interesting aspects of this Vendée Globe was that Autissier wasn't the only woman in the race. Over the past six years and two BOCs, everyone had got used to the idea of the boys – and Isabelle. Now another woman, Catherine Chabaud, was making a serious bid to join the club.

Near the end of the first week at sea, she was sailing in next-to-last place among the skippers who hadn't turned back to Les Sables-d'Olonne. But at least she was still in the race. She had weathered the Biscay gale, although at the cost of losing some of her electronics, including the crucial autopilot. Since then, she had been steering by hand, or by the old method of balancing the sails against the lashed helm so that the boat steered a generally consistent course. It was easier to do that in her boat than in most of the others. Yawl-rigged, it had a smaller second, or mizen, mast near the stern (like the ketch rig, except the mizen on a yawl was smaller and set farther aft), and this allowed for more sail combinations, as well as sail area at both ends of the boat, to help balance it for self-steering. She was beginning her successful attempt to fix her electronic systems, although they would continue to cause her trouble.

She also added touches of civility to the race. In covered boxes of soil secured in a corner of her cockpit, she was growing little lentils and other green plants. She planned to harvest them and make salads full of vitamins. Her little garden corner couldn't survive the Southern Ocean weather, but the woman alone on the sea, tending her plants, making elegant fresh green salads to enliven her dehydrated, packaged meals, was an endearing image.

Her passion for racing was awakened as soon as she began to sail at the age of seventeen. She studied mathematics, but became a journalist. Committing herself to open-ocean professional racing in 1991, she gradually worked her way through the various races: two Figaros, two Round-Europes, a MiniTransat, the Europe 1 Star. It was the well-worn path to the Vendée Globe. Consumed by the professional sailor's dream to go round the world, she saw the Vendée Globe as its natural realisation.

'It's my Everest,' she told me after the race. 'When you like sailing, you want to go to its Everest – to sail in the South, to sail to Cape Horn.'

'Weren't you afraid?' I asked her. 'I sail, but I'm very sure I wouldn't want to enter the Vendée Globe, or even to sail in the Southern Ocean.'

'I'm afraid too, but I wanted to go there so much anyway. Because I like to sail alone very much. And also, sailing for me is a way of life. It's an adventure. And the Vendée Globe is the biggest human adventure in sailing.'

Having dreamed for many years of entering the Vendée Globe, she was ecstatic to be at sea. The Southern Ocean and Cape Horn were magnets drawing her south, to *le grand Sud*, where it was so beautiful and so remote – the outback of the world.

Much as she wanted to take part in the great adventure, Chabaud almost didn't make this one. She planned to enter the millennium Vendée Globe in 2000. But in early September 1996, just two months before the start, Philippe Jeantot, concerned about the number of no-shows with fund-raising problems, called her to ask if she could enter the race. Chabaud said no, it was too late. She had no boat and no money. But two weeks later, she happened to run into the BOC and Vendée Globe veteran Jean-Luc Van den Heede at a boat show in La Rochelle. He told her that his boat was available for charter – he had decided that he'd done enough of this sort of thing himself for a lifetime – and that there wasn't a lot to do to it to make it ready for sea. As she talked to Van den Heede, Chabaud realised that she had to do it, she had to sail this Vendée Globe. There was still a lot to learn about solo racing before she could hope to win, and this would be the opportunity. She wouldn't have a chance of winning in the older boat, but it was a proven strong and safe vessel.

It was 21 September when Chabaud decided to enter the race. In the next forty-three days, beating all the odds against it, she lined up sponsorship money from Whirlpool Europe, which had supported her in most of her previous single-handed races, fitted out the boat, and made her two-thousand-mile qualifying sail. She also got herself ready, as much as possible, for the abruptly assumed challenge. A dietician helped her prepare her meals in weekly packages, balancing her preferences and the need for high-energy food. She tried to ready herself for the Southern Ocean she both hungered for and feared, seeking the emotional equilibrium that would see her through months of lonely anxiety. She cut off her long blonde hair so it wouldn't get in her way or, more dangerously, get caught in a winch or the loop of a line. Her goal was to finish the race. Finishing without being disqualified would be 'the cherry on the cake'.

As I talked to Chabaud a few months after she finished the race, in a café in the Paris suburb of Suresnes, a few minutes from her parents' home, I was aware of a continuous susurration of recognition and homage by the people coming and going around us. We *did* stand out, with my paraphernalia of microphones, wires and a tape recorder. But there was no mistaking her fame. We were on her home ground, but I supposed it would have been the same almost anywhere in the country.

I hadn't interviewed any of the skippers in public before this, and I was surprised by Chabaud's obvious celebrity. The same thing happened a few days later when Tony Bullimore and I gorged on our bloke's lunch in Bristol.

'That's Tony Bullimore – It's Tony Bullimore – Bullimore – Tony – Capsized – Southern Ocean – Bullimore.'

The waves of discreet, pleased acknowledgement washed over us. I felt as if I was lunching with a hero – the inclusive glow of Bullimore's valour, absurdly, pervaded me as well. If I was with him, his associate, perhaps his intimate, his public might think well of me too. Perhaps they would take me, with my grey beard and weathered face, for a sailor who had also been brave at sea. It was a nice, if phoney, moment.

Sipping coffee with Chabaud was different. With all the electronic tools of my real trade strewn about the table, I was obviously a journalist of some sort. Just an ordinary person, like them, drawn to her by her great achievement.

Chabaud is almost six feet tall, blonde, big-boned, with a long Gallic nose. She is warm and direct, friendly. She reinforced the impression I'd had from all these sailors: confident energy, matter-of-fact modesty, intelligence. She had lived her dream, sailed the Southern Ocean and rounded the Horn. But like all the skippers, she understood how hazardous it was, and that you were just plain lucky if nothing truly bad happened to you.

Chabaud touched my arm sometimes as we spoke, just a light tap on the forearm or back of the hand. Of course, it didn't have the significance of a touch in an Anglo-Saxon business conversation between a man and a woman who had just met. That would have been strange, a mélange of subterranean messages. With Chabaud, the touches seemed to be extensions of her own intense desire to engage, connect, make solid contact with whomever she was addressing. There was a pattern to the contact. When she talked about Roufs, she touched my arm. When she described her near-capsize – watching the white water of the Southern Ocean submerge and almost overwhelm her boat as she clung to its nearly horizontal mast – she touched my hand. It was the same when she described how she felt as she finally rounded Cape Horn; when she told me about the albatross that stayed with her for a month, and that she named Bernard after Moitessier, whom she read for inspiration and for his detailed practical advice about how to survive high-latitude sailing; and as she recalled her enormous, tearful emotion when she saw the photos of Bullimore's and Dubois's boats, floating upside down, their sixty-foot hulls dwarfed by the beautiful but terrifying Southern Ocean waves forever curling above them. These were such difficult things to truly understand if you had never been there. I had forgotten that Chabaud had only been back three and a half months when we spoke. She was trying to assimilate the meaning of experiences that were still fresh in her mind. I think her touches were an attempt to make me feel what it had been like, and how a human being would feel there, doing almost unimaginable things. As if the enlightening knowledge, unintelligible in words, might instead flow through to me along some obscure synaptic pathway.

*

On 8 November, Parlier, still pushing harder than anyone else, forcing Auguin and Autissier to push harder than they wanted to at this early stage, took over the lead from Laurent. Parlier's decision, just a gamble really, to stay closer to the Portuguese coast had paid off. He found a little more wind there. By the end of the day, he was twenty-five miles ahead of Autissier, who had, in turn, put Laurent seven miles behind her. Auguin was forty-one miles behind the leader. These foremost boats shared similar conditions for the next two days as they closed with the Canaries – benign skies and a ten-knot northerly wind. The fleet had been lucky with the weather, apart from the Biscay depression the day after the start. The whole sea area down to the Canaries could have been rough going. But only the boats that had put back and then started again – Dubois, Bullimore, Fa and Munduteguy – suffered repeat performances from autumnal gales as they set out again to cross Biscay towards Cape Finisterre.

During the early part of the night of 10 November, with the race a week old, Parlier passed to the east of the main island of Gran Canaria in a slightly stronger fifteen-knot north-east wind. Having decided it wasn't worthwhile stopping for drinking water in the islands, he had only enough to last for another three weeks, even on reduced rations.

Autissier, still second, followed Parlier past the islands later the same night. Laurent and Auguin dropped farther behind – Auguin more than eighty miles back. By the end of the next day, Parlier had increased his lead over Auguin to 120 miles, emphasising the fragility of each boat's position. The race favourite feared he would be at least two hundred miles out of first place within another day because Parlier and Autissier had picked up more wind as they passed the Canaries. Laurent and Auguin, as well as de Broc and the other boats farther back, remained stuck within the high-pressure system and the light northerly winds that had dominated these latitudes for several days. The tail-end of the fleet enjoyed stronger wind like the leaders. Roufs, Thiercelin, Goss, Chabaud and de Radiguès were closing the gap, threatening to squeeze Auguin and the other boats in the middle. Auguin publicly wondered whether his strategy of a slow and cautious start had been the right one after all. He regretted not pushing harder to reduce Parlier's lead before the Canaries. If the last Vendée Globe was anything to go by, he might never be able to make up a gap of a few hundred miles, even one established at this very early stage in the race. But the variable winds, the violent squalls and, above all, the calms of the doldrums lay ahead, and anything could happen.

So far, nothing in the race was more surprising than Laurent's performance in the old *Groupe LG Traitmat*. It had been built for the inaugural Vendée Globe race in 1989 and, sailed by Titouan Lamazou, had won in a still-record time of 109 days. But so much had changed in Open 60 design ideas since then. Laurent's relatively narrow, under-canvassed and heavy boat (at twelve tons, it was almost twice as heavy as Parlier's lightweight) seemed an anomaly as it chugged along beside the other members of the leading group of four. Its speed so far held several lessons. The new designs were conceived as supreme downwind machines, stable at high speeds and able to squeeze as much advantage as possible out of the following winds and seas of the Southern Ocean. In what might be called normal sailing conditions – the storms, lighter winds and more moderate waves of the Atlantic – the new designs might not be much of an improvement. Nevertheless, all the other boats of the vintage of *Groupe LG Traitmat* were stuck much farther back in the fleet, together with several of the new-generation designs – Thiercelin's *Crédit Immobilier de France* and, especially, Roufs's *Groupe LG2*. The difference in position early in the race wasn't a matter of luck. The boats had, by and large, shared the same weather and winds. Laurent had certainly experienced conditions very similar to those of Parlier, Autissier and Auguin, with whom he was keeping pace, in their modern boats, two of them brand new. His performance so far was the result of his sheer technical skill as a sailor, and of his determination to make the endless fine-tune adjustments that were necessary to keep the boat moving at its best in light conditions.

If I were betting on anyone to win a Vendée Globe, or a BOC race, where differences in boat design were factored out, I'd bet on Laurent. With a state-of-the-art boat, and the money to run it properly, he had the stuff to win any race he entered. As long as bad luck was filtered out of the equation as well, I suppose. You can't win if you hit flotsam, or something vital breaks, or you meet one of those waves with your name on it. Laurent was a technician, the hard-headed, buttoned-down nerd of the Vendée Globe. Like the other skippers, the thirty-nine-year-old mechanical engineer was in this business to go fast and win. But unlike the others, he saw no other dimensions to the enterprise, so he claimed. No romance of the sea for him, or any of that other claptrap Moitessier wrote about. He wasn't about to name an albatross Bernard or talk about communing with his boat. Thin, six feet, bespectacled, bearded, with longish hair, a native of Lorient, on the south coast of Brittany, Laurent took a sardonic, detached view of his profession and of its hangers-on – journalists, for example, for ever going on about the danger and romance of solo sailing. As I interviewed him in the cramped cabin of *Groupe LG Traitmat* after the race, Laurent softened up a little when he realised that, although in a very inferior category, I had at least spent some time at sea, enough to appreciate the sailing he had just done. After our interview, he offered to lead me, in his modest Honda Accord with the Groupe LG logo on the door – he wasn't yet in Autissier's Mercedes category – through the maze of dockland streets in Lorient and back out to the autoroute south to Locmariaquer, where I had another appointment.

When he was seven, Laurent signed up for judo classes at a sports centre. But there was some sort of clerical error, and when he showed up on the first day, he discovered that he had been registered in a sailing class by mistake. No one else in his family has ever sailed, and even now he still fights with his parents and brothers about his occupation. They don't understand why he wants to do it for a living. It is not a real job they say. They think that it's just an excuse to do nothing, and that all he really does is have a good time.

'One of my brothers who lives in Bordeaux – not very far away – came to see the start of this Vendée Globe. That was the first time he had seen the start or finish of any of the races I've been in. And I've been doing this job for twenty years.'

Laurent claims that his reasons for sailing alone are equally pragmatic. He did it when he was young because he often couldn't find anyone to go out with him. Later, when he began to sail bigger boats, it was easier to find sponsors if he was sailing alone. And journalists, for their own obtuse reasons, were more interested in solo sailing. How can one person do everything for so long on such a big boat? they wondered. Single-handing was merely a logical response to the prevailing realities of his business.

There was certainly some ironic understatement in Laurent's account of his professional development. He was genuinely detached and analytical in how he went about sailing – the tactics and process of it all – and also about the need to market himself, the constant scramble for sponsorship money. Like any entrepreneur, he had to hustle, and – distasteful narcissism – the product he had to hustle was himself. Yet, his anti-romantic protestations aside, all the time he was sailing, a kind of love affair grew in spite of himself.

Once, at the start of our interview, Laurent let slip a suggestion of that ardour. He wasn't sure why he had kept sailing when he was a boy and hadn't tried to get back into the judo class he had signed up for. It must have been an early intimation of why he had continued to sail and had moved through the sailing ranks to become a professional, almost by default. That was just the way things had sorted themselves out, he said. But then, too, there had always been this feeling: 'From the beginning, I was fascinated and attracted by the sea and I wanted to be on the sea all the time. That's all.'

By the time the foremost boats entered the belt of the trade winds, the fleet had bunched up again – just the vagaries of the wind. Auguin's fear that he would be left too far behind to make up the distance turned out to be groundless. Roufs, in seventh place, was now only 130 miles behind Parlier, still steadily in the lead. For the first time since the start, the leading boats were moving at top speed day and night, sailing Kipling's 'sweetest way . . . in the heel of the North-East Trade,' the sailor's nirvana. The racers luxuriated in the wind's perfect, constant strength.

At the same time, Tony Bullimore, his autopilots now working, had left Les Sables-d'Olonne for the second time, had cleared the Bay of Biscay and was sailing close down the coast of Portugal. It hadn't been a good choice, however, and he was moving at an irritatingly slow pace. Dubois had fixed his damaged hull and was just about to sail again. When he left, he would be more than twelve hundred miles behind the leaders and, like Bullimore, sailing only for the experience and the glory.

The trade winds are a necessary meteorological corollary of the zones, or cells, of high pressure roughly thirty degrees north and south of the equator in the areas of the north and south horse latitudes – the North Atlantic or Azores High in the northern hemisphere and the South Atlantic or St Helena High in the southern. While not permanent phenomena, these high-pressure centres nevertheless remain persistently in place. Around the centres, large areas of light and uncertain wind stretch in all directions. Sailing vessels always try to bend their courses around the perimeter of these regions. They must still cross the horse latitudes, but they try to do so at the peripheries of the Highs – nearer the European or North American coasts in the northern hemisphere, closer to African or South American shores in the southern – where there's usually more wind.

Wind flows from high pressure to low pressure. The trade winds are really the flow of air (downhill, as it were) from the North and South Atlantic Highs towards the permanent low-pressure trough around the equator, the doldrums. As with the movement of all air and ocean water on earth, however, the planet's rotation affects the direction in which the trade winds actually blow. The moving air is directed towards the west. The trade winds in the north, therefore, blow from the north-east, and since winds are labelled by the direction they blow from, they become the north-east trades. Currents, on the other hand, are described by the direction they're flowing to. It's not really inconsistent when one realises that the reference point is the sailing vessel itself. The important things for the sailor are where the wind is coming from, so that sails can be trimmed accordingly, and where the current is taking the boat to, so that allowance for its effects can be made in finding the boat's position. The boat is the referential centre of the sailor's world of relativity and uncertainty.

The low-pressure trough towards which the trade winds blow – the doldrums – is a relatively narrow belt, wider at its eastern end in both the Atlantic and the Pacific. And its position and width varies with the seasons. It's centred just north of the equator in February and March and may be only a few miles wide. By July and August, its centre has moved to around seven to nine degrees north latitude, and it may be several hundred miles wide if the sailor is really unlucky. In November, when the Vendée Globe skippers were preparing to cross them, the doldrums were roughly in between these two extremes – a few degrees north of the equator and wide enough to slow or to stop a boat for several days.

The French call the doldrums the *pot au noir* literally, the 'pitch pot' – a dreadful muddle of weather, a black hole. The English word *doldrums* is of unknown origin, but the *Oxford English Dictionary* speculates that it may be a colloquial variation on 'dull'. The French version is certainly more dramatic and expressive. It captures the sheer chaos of weather in the region, its uncertainty and, most frustrating for sailing vessels, the extent of its calms. The old square-riggers, their bottoms weed- and barnacle-fouled, were sometimes delayed for weeks. Often, their small boats were launched and the crews put to the oars for exhausting days at a time, slowly towing the mother ships out of the airless calms.

The Vendée Globe racers, with their minimal wetted surface and huge sail areas, could ghost along on a whisper. Yet they too feared the doldrums and the fickleness of their wind. Getting through them involved luck and an element of the sailor's art as well. The skippers, like the old sailing-ship captains, used the look of the sky and the water, refracted through long experience, to judge their best route through the calms. In fact, close observation of the appearance of the actual world surrounding the vessel was the sailor's only option until very recently. Moitessier or Hiscock, crossing the doldrums twenty years ago, listened to, and watched for, the same intuitive whispers and hints as sailors two hundred years earlier, which mostly meant sitting, waiting, hoping for the best. Now, the fine, orbiting web of electronic sensors and feelers, gathering and transmitting data to chart-table instruments, has almost completely replaced the old techniques.

One by one, as the leading boats picked up the north-east trade winds and began their rush towards the equator, the skippers considered their choices. The boats coalesced into two groups with Autissier, Auguin, de Broc and Roufs keeping closer to the South American coast, and Parlier, Laurent and Dumont choosing a route farther east. The differences weren't that great; the flotillas were less than one hundred miles apart.

As it turned out, their careful positioning didn't make much difference. The intricate, enigmatic processes that unexpectedly, and often inexplicably, change big climate phenomena like the doldrums, as well as little weather events like an afternoon squall, had been at work. This time around, the doldrums proved toothless for the three leading boats. Where there should have been light breezes and calms, there was a cracking twenty-knot wind that drove Parlier, Autissier and Auguin straight through the pitch pot without a falter. The following four boats weren't quite so lucky. De Broc spent twelve motionless hours under a huge cloud. As he sat there, Laurent, not far away, ghosted past on his own private breeze into fifth place. Roufs, Thiercelin and Dumont lost time as well. But it could have been much worse. Roufs's new boat began to show its stuff in the lighter wind, and he dramatically improved his position. Now in fourth place, he led the second group of five boats trailing the three leaders by between 250 and 400 miles. But it was still a close enough race.

Getting through the doldrums relatively easily meant that the leading boats had a chance to beat Lamazou's record time of 109 days. He had slipped across the doldrums without hindrance as well, and a fast passage both ways across the equator was probably essential to set, or beat, the record.

At the equator, the skippers celebrated the traditional crossing-the-line ceremony. This pagan homage to Neptune – dressing up as the god, casting libations or food into the sea for his favour – is an ancient custom. It gives thanks for both being at sea and still being alive; it acknowledges human frailty and the ocean's undiminished power. What sailor headed for the Southern Ocean would fail to keep the custom? Snug in their unmoving and unmenaced buildings ashore, people can afford to ignore superstitions. At sea, even the most rational of humans would hesitate to do so. The sailor's prospects are always undetermined, threatening, unpredictable, and it just makes sense not to stretch your luck with smug, smart-assed deference to sensible, logical thought. This is the sea! 'The dragon-green, the luminous, the dark, the serpent-haunted sea.' 'The scrotumtightening sea,' as Joyce called it, for different reasons. With his trident, Neptune could call forth storms, shatter rocks, shake the shores. According to the *Ocean Almanac*, 'He lived in a golden palace beneath the sea. His sea horses had brass hooves and golden manes, and when they drew his chariots over the sea, the waters became as smooth as a mirror before him, all sea monsters tame in his path.'

The Vendée Globe skippers toed the line of irrational observance in different ways, but in each case, just as one would somehow have expected them to. Parlier, the ascetic athlete, shared a sugar biscuit with Neptune. The cosmopolitan Autissier offered the god a bouquet of flowers and a little champagne. Auguin, well-provisioned, every-thing prepared for, by now settled into his steady, almost serene race rhythm, had a splendid Gallic meal of foie gras, a cassoulet, and a *grand cru*, and watched a video.

Parlier would have been happier if he had a little fresh water to share with the sea god. The unusually fair wind had hustled him quickly through the doldrums, and there was almost no rain. He reduced his ration to a litre a day and tried not to eat any food requiring much liquid to digest. If not yet dehydrated he was certainly thirsty, and he would be in a difficult situation if the southern hemisphere westerlies didn't have some rain in them early on. Ironically, as Roufs was making his slower way through the doldrums in the more characteristic weather that followed the passage of the first three boats, he spent hours in a downpour, 'Enough to irrigate the Sahara,' he said.

The official race doctor, Jean-Yves Chauve, estimated that the sailors needed about three or four litres of water a day, more in the tropics. This was based on a formula of one millilitre of water for each calorie consumed, and the assumption that the sailors, moderately active in their small spaces, would take in three thousand to four thousand calories per day. The cruising sailor's rule of thumb (in the days before affordable desalinating water-makers, when boats had to carry in tanks or jerrycans all the water they needed) was half an imperial gallon per person, per day for all purposes: drinking, cooking, brushing teeth and so on. It was assumed that the crew would use salt water for washing themselves and, whenever possible, for other purposes. This ration also assumed, however, that the crew would drink soft drinks, juice, beer and other canned or cartonned drinks to supplement their water intake. The Vendée Globe skippers, however, had to rely almost entirely on water for liquid. If they were cutting toothbrushes in half to save weight, they certainly weren't about to lug around cases of Coke or beer in the bilge. A little wine, perhaps – these were mostly French boats, after all – but not much else.

'*Water, water, everywhere/Nor any drop to drink,*' the Ancient Mariner famously lamented. It was the most ironic dilemma for sailors: they could die of thirst in the midst of the seventy per cent of the planet covered by water. And sometimes they did die – if the water they carried, precariously, in oak casks went bad (and it often did), and if they didn't get rain in time. After scurvy and shipwreck, lack of drinking water was the square-rigger sailor's nemesis. The horse latitudes got their name because ships caught in their calms, running low on water, drove their cargoes of horses overboard to drown. It was either them or the crew.

In windless tropical heat, parched sailors developed cases of calenture (from the Latin *caleo*, to be hot), a tropical fever under whose influence they had the sudden impulse to jump into the sea. In their inexplicable delirium, they imagined it to be a moist, consoling green field. The sea's saltiness made its water as undrinkable as sand. Saint-Exupéry describes how, in the desert, the stranded flyer would first drink his urine, perhaps a little blood, then gasoline or diesel fuel and, finally, battery acid. Any liquid to stave off the body's desiccation. For the sailor, in his moist air, with rain in the offing, the danger of death was comparatively remote. But the principle was the same: crossing the ocean or the desert, humans had to carry what they would need there, or find it along the way – in unpredictable rain or at scattered and obscure oases. Nature in both places possessed what Yeats said of the sea: a 'murderous innocence'.

Parlier's problem was an anachronism, caused by bad luck and a ferocious emphasis on saving weight. With their steel water tanks and desalinators, modern sailing vessels could provide for all the water needed for drinking – and even for the most wasteful of western indulgences, the daily fresh-water shower. The French press got into a frenzy about Parlier's condition. His wife was pestered by callers, including some doctors, who told her she should persuade her husband to quit. But Parlier wasn't particularly worried. He was thirsty on a quarter of the liquid his body needed each day, but felt all right otherwise. It would rain eventually, and he was prepared to wait.

On 20 November, however, something far more serious occurred. A steel pin holding part of Parlier's genoa jib roller-furling gear broke. This was the equipment that allowed him to reef or furl his huge jib from the safety of the cockpit by simply hauling on the furling line as he slackened off on the sheet. Without it, Parlier would have to risk the foredeck and take on the exhausting work of changing to smaller headsails, rather than simply rolling up his genoa, whenever he needed to reduce sail.

There was nothing mysterious about the cause of the breakage. It was yet another result of insufficient preparation time. As the novel rotating mast on Parlier's boat turned in response to varying wind direction, it stressed and eventually broke the pin, which was undersized as well. If he and his team had had more time to test the boat before the race, they certainly would have seen the inadequacy. It would have been obvious – it took only seventeen days of moderate stress to do the damage.

When the pin broke at ten in the evening, Parlier's genoa tumbled down and into the water. He struggled for several hours to get the big, sodden sail back on board. He had to go into the water three times, in pitch dark, diving to free the tangles around the sail and the boat's keel.

'The race is lost,' he said.

Later, after he had slept for a while and then reinforced the mast with an additional makeshift forestay, he was less pessimistic. He was managing to sail at eleven knots under his mainsail.

'The mast is still up. The race goes on. I'm less certain of winning than I was yesterday; but one never knows what will happen.'

Within a day, the balance within the race shifted. Autissier took the lead; Auguin moved into second place, fifteen miles behind. Parlier, recovering his equilibrium, managed to get a jib hoisted, as well as his mainsail, and kept moving fast enough to hold on to third. Roufs, finding stronger wind than the other boats in the second group, and his new boat's greater speed beginning to tell, was now only 250 miles behind Autissier. The other members of the group – Laurent, de Broc, Thiercelin and Dumont – were three hundred to four hundred or so miles behind the leader. Strung out behind them, finally clear of the doldrums, Dinelli, de Radiguès, Goss and Chabaud were about seven hundred miles back, the last three, against all the odds, within sight of each other. Dubois and Bullimore, their races born again, were sailing fast but well behind. The fourteen-boat fleet was stretched out in a line 1,750 miles long up and down the North and South Atlantic oceans. Two and a half weeks after the start, the race had already assumed the pattern that would characterise it until its conclusion: a line of widely scattered boats in several rough groupings; most of the pre-race favourites in front; most of the skippers, with little apparent chance of making up ground already lost to the leading boats, doggedly keeping on.

In their ragged order, the boats swung out in a wide arc, much closer to the coast of South America than that of Africa, staying to the west of the South Atlantic high pressure zone, with its calms and light winds. As they approached thirty degrees south latitude, they began a long curving turn to the south-east, threading their way along the southern fringes of the High, cutting across the South Atlantic towards the Southern Ocean.

Autissier and Auguin, followed by Parlier, duelled for the lead as they raced ahead of thirty-knot winds generated by a depression that allowed them to shorten their route a little around the high-pressure zone. Roufs had to heave-to for an hour in *Groupe LG2* to go over the side and cut away a fishing net that had wrapped itself around his rudders. He was close enough to the leaders to get some of the same wind that was driving them fast to the south-east, but couldn't avoid losing a little more ground on them. In the ideal conditions, unusual for this sea area, Autissier and her close escorts continued to widen their lead on the fleet as the length of the line of boats stretched out day by day.

On 27 November, Auguin moved ahead of Autissier. As Autissier's sponsors pointed out in a communiqué, however, the change in position wasn't really all that significant. Auguin had decided to head more to the east, while Autissier, overtaken again by the front before which the three lead boats had been running for days, had decided to head farther south in search of even more wind. The two boats had moved two degrees of latitude apart – more than one hundred miles. Parlier was diving to the south as well. Still hampered by the lack of roller-furling gear, he had, surprisingly, succeeded in staying within fifty miles of the other two boats. But he was expending more energy to keep up, reefing the mainsail more often, getting wet and cold on the foredeck as he manhandled foresails up and down their stays. South was where the strong, steady winds were. They would make things easier for him. There would be fewer sail changes – he wouldn't have to worry about his big genoa, so difficult to handle without roller-furling – and he could use his smaller foresails almost all the time.

Under cold, grey skies, and in waves growing and lengthening into typical high-latitude rollers, the three leading skippers began to see their first albatrosses. On 29 November, Parlier crossed forty degrees south latitude into the roaring forties. Auguin and Autissier were close ahead, a little to the north. The sailors were drawing in on themselves, making last-minute checks of the boats and their gear, bracing for the assault – the three boats running hard to the west before near gale-force winds.

'Now we have to look after our boats, to be very careful,' said the prudent Auguin. 'The important thing is to get to Cape Horn in good condition. Things will get better again only after that.'

A few days later, at thirty-seven degrees south, Roufs found himself surfing down long, high swells at close to twenty-five knots in sustained winds of more than fifty-five knots, force 11 on the Beaufort Wind scale – a violent storm. The Vendée Globe racers had begun their long journey through the Southern Ocean.

6

The Soul of a New Machine

That splendour of fine bows which yet could stand
The shock of rollers never checked by land.

– John Masefield

. . . the machine does not isolate man
from the great problems of nature but
plunges him more deeply into them.

– Antoine de Saint-Exupéry, *Wind, Sand and Stars*

WHEN I first saw one of the Vendée Globe boats, I had three
reactions almost at once. First, I thought, This is a gorgeous
machine. With its fluid curves, low and shining profile, tapered,
almost delicate-looking mast, its deft pattern of standing and running
rigging, the boat seemed more like a product of natural evolution
than a human artefact. It was like a perfectly evolved animal, adapted
to dominate a narrow ecological niche. It crouched like a cheetah
waiting to run.

My second impression was of the boat's potential for speed, but
also of its apparent fragility. These are very light boats. My thirty-six-
foot cruising boat had weighed two to four tons more than these
sixty-footers. I recalled the structural problems some boats suffered
in previous races when they'd had to do even a relatively moderate

amount of pounding into head seas. I knew that the boats were
stronger now, especially with the newer building materials, with their
higher strength-to-weight ratios. But the boat in front of me looked
so delicate. It had better be fast, I thought. It looked as if it would
need to skim, weave and dodge its way around the world, and
particularly around the formidable seas of the Southern Ocean.

In hindsight, my third thought turned out to be a dead-accurate
premonition of disaster. I think that any small-boat sailor like me,
who prefers more traditional hull forms, would have had the same
reaction. When I looked at this boat end on, with its wide dance-floor
deck, the tall mast that could set a sail area to move a clipper ship and
the slender keel with its proportionately tiny bulb of ballast at the
end, I thought: Even though it's a monohull, if this boat turns over,
will it ever right itself?

The great advantage of monohulls over multihulls has always been
that monohulls pick themselves up when they're knocked down by a
wave. The weight of the heavy keel acts like a pendulum and quickly
pops the boat upright again, even if it was completely upside down.
This sort of knockdown or capsize happens surprisingly often to
small boats in bad storms. They usually survive, although their crews'
nervous systems are never the same afterwards. It has never happened
to me. If it ever does, I'll take the old sailor's traditional retirement:
walk inland carrying an oar until someone says, 'What's that?'; buy
a chicken farm on that very spot and never move.

Multihulls are faster than monohulls because they reduce those
speed-limit factors, hull friction and bow wave, that kept our little
thirty-one-footer restricted to less than six knots. They can make fast
and exhilarating passages. I was once a crew member on a catamaran
delivery from Lake Ontario to Chesapeake Bay. It was a moment of
pure joy sailing at fifteen knots on a flat sea off the New Jersey coast
as the cat vibrated and hummed with the glee of a perfectly running
machine.

But multihulls do have one significant problem: they're most stable
upside down. They have a great deal of initial stability – they resist
heeling – but no ultimate stability. Once they go over, they stay that
way. Multihull sailors often fit escape hatches into the bottoms of
their hulls so that they can look out of the overturned boat for rescue.
The Vendée Globe racing machine I was admiring looked to me as if
it might just behave more like a multihull than a monohull when it
met the wave with its name on it and was capsized.

Later, I read the corroborating, and alarming, view of these boats held by the yacht designer Bruce Kirby: 'While the newer Vendée boats are very stable at low heel angles,' he wrote, 'a boat that has a lot of initial stability might be sadly lacking in ultimate stability. Ultimate stability is a boat's ability to come back upright from a catastrophic knockdown or inversion by a giant wave. Some of the Vendée boats were dangerously weak in this area.'

When I first looked at the Vendée Globe boats, I had to admit they were elegant – but as machines, like certain cars or aeroplanes or weapons. I thought they were ugly boats. I liked overhangs, sheer-lines, tumblehomes, a little deck camber, and a sweet turn to the bilge – all the old design techniques that made a traditional sailboat beautiful, and seaworthy as well. But that changed. Maybe it was just a matter of getting used to the ideas and criteria their designers had used. I had to accustom myself to the look of these radical designs, so unlike the orthodox yacht, before I could appreciate their own peculiar beauty. A little like coming to see the appeal of cubism if you are a realism kind of guy. Part of the accumulating appeal of these boats for me was certainly the idea of being able to sail so fast. I'd come to hunger a little for the sensations of sailing at twenty-five knots, my appetite whetted by a few rides in multihulls. Even more compelling for a cautious sailor like me was the clear link between speed and safety. The less time you're out there, the less chance of getting dumped on, the more chance of being able to dodge bad weather. Safety at sea is its own aesthetic. Whatever the reasons, I came to like these racing machines as boats. I liked the delicate, gull-like dimple they made on the water's surface with their minimal underbody, so unlike the traditional boat's heavy, intrusive pene-tration *into* the water. I liked the more restrained and subtle curves – you can't ever get away from curves in a boat's hull – around the edges of the straight-up-and-down bow and the chopped transom. I especially liked the way they looked as if they were allowing themselves to be temporarily and grudgingly held back by shore lines and the proximity of harbour breakwalls, before taking exuberant, speedy flight.

Some of the boats in this Vendée Globe were brand new, designed and built just for this race. The majority were refitted veterans of one or more previous long-distance races. Nearly all of them were like very big racing dinghies with deep, narrow keels. On five of the boats, the keels were designed to be canted – swung from side to side up to thirty-five degrees for greater leverage. The most recently designed hulls, which reflected the latest ideas about how to build very fast sixty-footers, had flat, shallow bottoms for minimum hull friction. Their great width made them initially stiff, or resistant to heeling – no sailboat sails well lying on its side. While the ballast bulb at the bottom of each keel wasn't enough to completely balance the weight of the boat, and of the tall masts and rigging in particular, against the full force of strong wind and waves, it was supplemented, on most of the boats, by internal water-ballast tanks. The sailors could pump several tons of water from one side of the boat to the other to help keep it upright. The details of hull and deck construction were complex and arcane – layers of exotic, man-made materials like amalgams of immensely strong carbon fibre and kevlar, or the older technology of fibreglass, or, occasionally, aluminium, or epoxy-saturated wood. They were ocean-going surfboards, designed for maximum speed off the wind – the purest racing sailboats of their size ever built.

At the same time, and as a necessary element of that purity, the layout and rigging of the boats was surprisingly simple. The cabin in most of them took up no more than ten to fifteen feet of the overall length. Sometimes, there wasn't even enough headroom for a six-footer. They were spartan: simple bunks on each side against the hull – narrow sea berths, so that the skippers could wedge themselves in and brace their bodies against the motion, a single-burner propane stove, and a little stowage space for dry clothes. On many of the boats, the interior surface was unfinished, with bolt heads showing and wiring tacked up with staples. The bare carbon fibre or fibreglass made the cabins look seedy and primitive. The primacy of the race, and the imperative of getting somewhere, was reflected in the big chart tables. They dominated the cabins. Above them, the electronics were bolted in and down. The whole arrangement was really a sophisticated navigation console surrounded by cabin sides and a top that, grudgingly, included a few rudimentary amenities for the single-minded sailors. Usually, the toilet and the sink were buckets, which, *in extremis*, the sailor could also use to bail water out of the boat.

The theme of simplicity was carried forward, although with con-siderably more elegance, in the rigging. The boats needed steel forestays – usually solid stainless-steel rod, but sometimes steel wire, running from the bow to the masthead – to accommodate the headsail roller-furling gear or staysail hanks. Otherwise, the standing rigging supporting the mast, often steel rod or wire as well, was sometimes made of kevlar rope, many times stronger than steel in any event, but much lighter. Where weight could be saved, it was – that was the reason for buckets instead of nice, comfy little marine toilets with contoured seats. The scheme of standing rigging was relatively simple for boats this size. Complexity was the enemy of the single-handed sailor: more stuff to go wrong; more to do when handling the boat; more weight; more to worry about.

When the Nova Scotia boatbuilder Vernon Langille decided to build a fast schooner, a scaled-down version of the Lunenberg fishing boats, that would be able to work the Grand Banks as well as sail for pleasure, he whittled a model of what he had in mind out of a chunk of wood. The proportions in the model were scaled up into a full-sized version, which took shape in the boatbuilder's yard without a drawing in sight. The frames were set up and eyeballed into place – a foot here, a little shaved off there – until, when you stood back and looked at the whole skeletal assembly and imagined its covering hull planks in place, it just looked right. It was a sweet-looking shape that everyone agreed should take the sea well and sail fast too. The boat was called *The White 'Un* by its builder and *Cimba* by Richard Maury, who sailed it from Canada to the South Pacific. He wrote a classic literary book about the voyage, *The Saga of Cimba*.

The fast and sweet-sailing little schooner was built in the traditional way of East Coast working sailboats. The legendary racing schooner *Bluenose* was constructed in 1921 according to plans meticulously drawn by its architect, W. J. Roue. But the yard that built the boat didn't like it. They had built 120 vessels before the Bluenose, without a plan in sight – the way Langille built *Cimba*. They didn't see why they had to fiddle around with all that paper to build the 121st. The new boat worked out well anyway, of course. It worked the Grand Banks catching cod for half the year, and it cleaned up in races with fancy-brassed and varnished rich men's schooners the other half. It became a Canadian icon. And, like *Cimba*, it sailed like a dream.

Today, complex computer software figures out structural stresses, rotates three-dimensional objects on the screen, analyses a design's theoretical performance in various wind and sea conditions with different hull, keel, ballast and rig shapes and configurations. Not a chunk of wood in sight. Not even any of the finely constructed, pre-computer scale models that were used until recently in water-tank tests or wind tunnels – to gather information about the aero- and hydrodynamic characteristics of the various laboriously hand-drafted views of the hull lines and sail plan. There's no doubt that the design process is now much more technically informed. Less of a hit-and-miss affair. And most noticeably, yacht designers, like all computer users, can try out ideas, backtrack, tweak a variable here and there, and make changes easily. There's a flexibility in the whole routine that allows for instant feedback on the consequences for speed, stability or looks, of any alteration in any part of the boat's complicated structure. There is a lot of *data*. The result? A boat – a Vendée Globe rocket, say – as a product of the scientific method, a Cartesian construct by way of the microprocessor chip.

Well, not quite. The machine still has a soul. For several reasons, the technique of designing a sailboat remains an uncertain and indeterminate affair. This is sometimes the case because a boat may have to be a number of contradictory things at the same time: a dormitory for ten people, yet small enough that it's cheap to make and buy; a fast sailer, yet with sails a small, ham-handed crew can deal with; low and handsome in profile, but with headroom for a basketball player. The designer of pleasure yachts must try to dole out solutions to the conflicting clamours of the market like Solomon dispensing justice.

The purpose of the Vendée Globe or BOC designs, of course, is clean and uncomplicated by comparison. The architect just has to put something together that will bring one person home the fastest, in one piece, through the Southern Ocean. But even that is an equivocal process. First, the boat is a machine that must operate within a dynamic system of infinite variability defined by the open ocean. The boat will bounce around on waves whose form, duration and frequency are constantly changing. There's no way to accurately predict the stresses that the endlessly and sometimes chaotically forming and re-forming seas will inflict on the hull and rig. Wave energy is protean. What combination of forces will strike, twist or deform any specific part of the boat at any given moment, producing whatever measurable loads on its structure, is anyone's guess.

Second, the naval architect's job is difficult because even the single-purpose Globe boats must be a compromise. They have to go as fast as possible on different points of sail – upwind, downwind, the reaching angles in between – which call for quite different hull characteristics. A hull shape that is relatively secure and stable surfing monster waves at twenty-five knots in a Southern Ocean gale will be uncomfortable and inefficient beating to windward in the shorter, steeper seas of the North Atlantic. With its wide beam and flat, shallow profile, the boat will tend to pound, flopping from one crest to the next. It won't be able to pierce the waves as efficiently as a narrower, deeper boat. Roufs's friend Philippe Ouhlen said that sailing close-hauled in a Vendée Globe sixty-footer is like driving a truck with square wheels. 'It's really, really horrible.'

And impossible to sleep in. Each time the boat hits a wave, the sailor is trampolined a foot into the air. Because the wave-piercing hull form that goes to windward best will not help a skipper sleep soundly in a Southern Ocean dust-up, the designer must make choices, and create the hull shape and rig configuration that approximates everyone's best guess about the conditions in which the boat will likely be sailing for various amounts of time. In all of this, the designer relies not only on what the computer says will work this time, but also on experience, on what has worked well in the past.

All the Vendée Globe boats would sail the same route towards the same goal. There was a set of basic requirements each design had to meet. The boat had to be seaworthy and strong enough to withstand the extreme destructive and disintegrative wave forces it would encounter during the race, and especially in the Southern Ocean. It had to track well – that is, sail a straight course under self-steering; the boat would seldom have a human at the helm. It had to be stiff, so that it could stand up to the heeling forces imposed on it by the proportionately huge sail area. It had to also have good ultimate stability, and it should be easy to handle, because everything on board would be done by one tired human being for months at a time.

This last consideration was key: the boats would be sailed single-handed. That meant that things would happen to them that would never occur on, for example, a fully crewed Whitbread race boat, with its shifts of fresh and strong helmsmen. Because they were often unattended, and their autopilots were unintelligent, the Vendée Globe boats would sometimes broach – slew around broadside to an unexpected wave whose impact only a watching human could have avoided. The likely consequence was a knockdown or a capsize, both producing sudden, immense strains on hull, mast and rigging. The boats might go backwards if the skipper missed a tack, putting huge strains on the rudders as the whole weight of the boat pinned them against the resisting force of the water astern. Tacking was a lot of work all at once – adjusting running backstays, trimming sails, pumping water ballast from one side of the boat to the other – so it was hardly surprising that problems sometimes occurred. Most important, though, the boat would have to negotiate big waves unattended. It would surf into waves ahead with the danger of burying its bow. It would fall off waves into troughs, like dropping it ten feet or more on to concrete. All of these stresses and strains would occur frequently – that, at least, was a certainty – while the skipper was below sleeping, eating, contemplating fresh carnage on the weatherfax, chatting to family or support team members by satellite phone.

With these criteria in mind, there's a lot of room for variations on the themes. Different designers make different choices about which kinds of sailing performance to emphasise, when to shave the tolerances in one area to increase speed, or augment a design charac- teristic elsewhere. Among the boats in this race, for example, the English naval architect Adrian Thompson's plans for Goss's *Aqua Quorum* were much different from those by Jean-Marie Finot and Pascal Conq, whose several designs dominated the race.

The most obvious difference was that Thompson had to try to put together a fifty-footer, all that Goss could afford, that could compete with boats twenty per cent longer on the waterline. All things being equal, the bigger boats would go faster simply because they were longer. But the overall length was just a matter of scale. If he had used the same design and performance criteria as the Finot team, Thompson could have wound up with a smaller version of the French boats. But he didn't, and *Aqua Quorum* was a different animal from Autissier's *PRB*, Parlier's *Aquitaine Innovations* or Roufs's *Groupe LG2*, all recent Groupe Finot productions.

Of the dozen or so Vendée Globe boats that I spent time aboard or looked at from a dock, *Aqua Quorum*, nestled against a mundane marina pontoon in Southampton, was the one I liked the most. Part of that affection was a spillover from Goss himself – the modest, humorous, open-hearted hero. But mainly, his boat appealed to me because it wasn't really an extreme design. It was a boat I recognised: its proportions, curves and lines suggested an older more pleasing lineage. I was still in the process of adjusting my idea of boat beauty.

No sudden road-to-Damascus conversion, it was a matter of the slow absorption of a different aesthetic. *Aqua Quorum* was a transitional object, somewhere between the traditional ideas and the extreme design developments reflected in Finot's boats.

The most obvious and startling characteristic of the French designs was their very wide beam, carried back almost to the stern – the 'aircraft carrier' look. They're as wide as nineteen feet, several feet more than a modern conventional sixty-footer, themselves considerably wider than boats of previous generations. The impression of width is reinforced by low freeboard (the height of the hull sides from deck to waterline), and by the boats' flat, dishlike profile in their middle sections. Thompson had eschewed these extreme features, and that gave *Aqua Quorum* a relatively conservative appearance. If symmetry is pleasing to the human eye, Thompson's design effortlessly satisfied that innate preference.

Thompson didn't make his design choices for beauty's sake, although he too liked *Aqua Quorum*'s lines. It was a matter of safety. He thought once again about what happens to single-handed boats in the Southern Ocean. They broach, and that usually results in a knockdown; their masts go into the water; sometimes they turn turtle. And all of this may happen when the boat has a good amount of sail set. The boat has to have a good chance of righting itself under these conditions. The narrower the beam, the better the chance the boat can recover from extreme angles of heel and pop upright again. The wider the beam, the more likely the boat is to keep going all the way over in a severe knockdown, and to remain stable upside down. The hull characteristics that create a lot of initial stability or stiffness – wide beam especially – also tend to keep the boat stubbornly inverted once it's turned over. Its righting ability is limited. 'I couldn't reconcile going that extreme for the Southern Ocean,' Thompson said.

There are two considerations that push Vendée Globe architects to make the boats beamy and thereby create lots of initial stability. One way to think of initial stability is that it's a boat's ability to come back to an even position – in other words, right itself – from angles of heel up to about forty degrees, normal while under sail. Wind pressure on the sails tends to push the boat over on to its side, at the same time as it drives it forward. This heeling motion is energy lost to the boat's forward motion. The stiffness provided by a wide beam, therefore, diverts more energy to forward motion, so the boat heels less and drives ahead more efficiently.

The Open 60 rules, which govern the design of these boats, also encourage great beaminess. The so-called ten-degree rule requires that when all movable water ballast is pumped into the tanks on one side, and the canting keel, if any, is fully deployed to the same side, the boat shouldn't heel more than ten degrees in that direction. The wider the beam and the greater the initial stability, the easier it is for the boat to pass the ten-degree test.

At the same time, the rule establishes a standard for the boat's self-righting ability. This is its ultimate stability: how easily, and from what angle of extreme heel, it will come back upright again. The formula under the rule works out to roughly 110 degrees. That is, a Vendée Globe boat knocked down by a wave to 110 degrees, so that its mast points downwards at an angle of twenty degrees below the horizontal, will still come back upright. Beyond that angle of heel, it will keep going, and the skipper's floor becomes his ceiling. This may seem like a reasonably safe angle. But older cruising-boat designs can often right themselves from angles fifty degrees or more below the horizontal. Even the Whitbread race boats, designed under their rule to sail the same waters as the Vendée Globe boats, must be able to come back upright from thirty-five degrees below the horizontal. Most of them exceed that requirement by a good margin.

In a way, Thompson observed, everything was backwards. If the various rules were logical, you'd have the single-handers sailing the relatively conservative Whitbread-type boats. They're still fast and exciting boats to sail, and they recover so much better from a knockdown than the Open 60s. The inherently unstable Vendée Globe boats would be better off sailed hell for leather by full crews, always under the control of good helmsmen.

According to the naval architect Bruce Kirby, the 'greatest hydro-dynamic mystery' of this Vendée Globe was the stubborn refusal of Dubois's *Pour Amnesty International* to come back upright again after it was rolled over during the powerful low-pressure weather 'bomb' that capsized Bullimore as well. Any one of the big seas would have thrown a traditional design right side up again in a matter of seconds, a minute or two at most. What was even more surprising was that Dubois's boat had an intact keel and no mast. With the righting force of the ballast bulb at the keel tip, and without the tremendous stabilising effects of the eighty-foot mast and its rigging plunging deep into the sea, *Pour Amnesty*'s righting angle as it lay upside down should have increased from the relatively meagre Open

60 standard of 110 degrees up to a much healthier 140 degrees. (It made sense that Bullimore's boat wouldn't come upright – it had lost its keel completely, and its mast and rigging were still more or less attached to the boat.) But it didn't seem to matter. Once it capsized, this was a monohull in name only. Its stability characteristics upside down were those of a multihull.

Dubois's boat was similar to the Finot designs, although, at seventeen feet, its beam was two feet narrower. It had been drawn up by the French naval architect team of Joubert and Nivelt. Bernard Nivelt was as surprised as anyone when the inverted *Pour Amnesty International* continued to ride fifty-foot Southern Ocean waves like a duck, while its skipper clung precariously to a rudder, death a second-by-second likelihood. Nivelt could only say that the boat's extreme beam, and its flat deck must be the explanation for its unexpected behaviour.

Thompson agreed. He and his team had been also astonished when they saw photographs of Dubois's boat. They had a good idea of its lines and ran a computer-modelled analysis of *Pour Amnesty*'s plight. The model confirmed that the capsized boat had a stability range of at least ninety degrees, not far off its right-side-up stability figure. 'So it was quite happy sitting there.'

For Thompson, the insouciant upside downness of Dubois's boat proved his point about the dangers of design extremism. Jean-Marie Finot was, understandably, more sanguine. He knew as well as Thompson, or anyone else, what sorts of conditions the racers would have to deal with in the Great South. The safety of the skipper was his first priority too. But his solution to the dangers of the Southern Ocean was different: speed and a lot of it. The beamier boats went faster, especially downwind, where they were more stable than narrower boats in any event. The asymmetrical appearance of Finot's designs above the waterline belied their efficient dynamic behaviour below the waterline when they were on the move. Then they were the most efficient machines around, he thought, dealing as elegantly as possible with the problems of hull skin-water friction, bow-wave resistance, quarter-wave disturbance – all the hull-shape factors limiting the speed at which a boat could travel, and the relative ease with which it was able to move over and through the water. Theoretically, Finot said, a fast racer could adjust its speed to stay between waves for long periods of time. It would have to deal with far fewer of them. 'That's the objective. With these boats, you dominate the sea, and you try to dominate it for as long as possible. That's the principle.'

The idea that, in heavy weather, a fast-moving boat is a safer boat is now widely accepted. Everyone agrees, said Thompson, that boats are most vulnerable to capsize when they're moving slowly. The faster the boat, the better the chance of legging it away from threatening storms and the less impact one hundred tons of wave water will have on the boat when it hits. Goss was doing just the right thing when he surfed down waves at thirty knots. Travelling fast, the boat was dynamic. The more water that flowed past the rudder, and the faster it flowed by, the more powerful the rudder became. The boat was more easily steered, its reactions faster and surer, even under the purely reactive autopilot. Thompson speculated that Bullimore's capsize happened because he wasn't going fast enough. He had taken all sail off to run under bare poles. Although Bullimore's two wing masts provided a lot of windage with their large sections and all their standing rigging, his speed was still relatively slow. He wasn't confident enough in his autopilot's ability to handle the massive forces that would act on his rudder if the boat was going faster. The result was a series of broaches, each one subjecting *Exide Challanger*'s keel to immense stress. Eventually it was too much. The keel snapped off, and Bullimore's life hung by that long, fragile Southern Ocean thread.

Speed is a function not only of hull form, but also of weight. In this Vendée Globe, there was already a wide divergence in displacement between the older and the newer boats. Parlier's *Aquitaine Innovations*, the lightest sixty-footer in the race at a shade over seven tons, weighed fifty-eight per cent of Laurent's or de Broc's twelve-ton old-stagers. Finot thought that the innovative lightness of Parlier's boat was just the beginning. New and lighter (but even stronger) varieties of carbon fibre, new building methods involving thinner hulls and stronger framing material, and lighter carbon masts would result in an even lighter boat. This would require less ballast, which would, in turn, save even more weight. He foresaw boats that could eventually go thirty per cent faster than the fastest boats in this race.

Finot's vision of future sixty-footers zooming through the Southern Ocean at thirty-five knots, continually adjusting their positions in relation to weather systems, parking themselves in between six-storey waves for minutes at a time, is really the completion of a evolutionary change in the theory of how small boats should be handled in survival conditions. The revolution began, appropriately enough, with Moitessier.

If he was a poetic interpreter of the natural world, Moitessier also had to get *Joshua* across the sea's most dangerous regions. He was a hard-headed technician of heavy-weather sailing. In 1965, during the first of his two great Southern Ocean passages, he pioneered a novel method of dealing with survival storms. Until Moitessier's innovation, the accepted technique was to run square before the waves towing large-diameter lines called warps, their friction in the water designed to keep the boat's speed down. The reasoning was that the overtaking waves would lift and then pass under the boat, more or less. Keeping the stern square-on would, with careful steering, prevent a broach and a likely capsize. Maintaining a steady speed of four to six knots would allow steering control but prevent wild surfing, and the possibility of pitchpoling (capsizing end over end, a fate usually even more destructive than rolling over) if the boat surfed down the face of a wave and tripped over its bow as it buried in the back of the next wave.

On his voyage from Tahiti, around the Horn, to Alicante, Spain, Moitessier, this time sailing with his wife Françoise, was overtaken by a monstrous storm. He described the length of the seas as between 500 and 560 feet, breaking without interruption across 650 to 1,000 feet. They were absolutely unbelievable, with masses of white water behind each breaking crest. Waves like that would have been travelling towards the boat at a speed of thirty to thirty-five knots.

At first, Moitessier used the accepted approach and ran off to the east towing warps. But *Joshua* staggered as the building seas swept the deck. The boat almost pitchpoled in one wave. Moitessier thought that the boat wouldn't be able to withstand the storm's mature waves when they developed. Then, by chance, *Joshua* caught the next wave at an angle and seemed to handle it much better. This jogged Moitessier's memory: he recalled reading a brief description by the Argentine Cape Horner, Vito Dumas, of how he had survived a great gale by running off his heavy wooden ketch before the waves at speed, without warps, and taking the seas at a slight angle off the stern.

Moitessier thought that they had nothing to lose. He cut away *Joshua*'s warps and took the waves fifteen to twenty degrees on the quarter, allowing the boat to slide at that angle down the face of each wave at a moderate speed. This technique seemed to prevent the boat from doing any straight-ahead surfing (its traditional, full-keeled hull form wasn't suited for that), or from being caught beam-on and broaching. For six days and nights, without a respite, they hand-steered the boat through the fearsome seas. Steering from an inside position (being out of the wet and cold was crucial, Moitessier thought), facing astern, watching each sea with unwavering concentration, Moitessier and Françoise brought their boat through.

In the long, mature seas of the Southern Ocean, and especially when sailing the Vendée Globe surfboards, the method Moitessier pioneered is used universally. In part, of course, the skippers favour it because it keeps them moving fast where they want to go. Surfing down waves at twenty-five knots is what these machines were designed to do – they're in their functional glory. But it seems to be the safest practice for them as well.

As I listened to Finot's confident assertions of technological evolution, I wondered about the human factor in all this. It was true that sailing a Vendée Globe racing machine at speeds that were the sea-going equivalent of those reached by Formula One cars on a straightaway was the essence of the whole enterprise. This was truly the adrenalin-saturated edge that thrilled those temperamentally equipped to sail it, drawing them back over and over again. Doing it in the isolated reaches of the Southern Ocean just couldn't be topped – fear and exhilaration blended into one great surge of energy.

In dinghy sailing, at a certain point when the wind is just right, the boat begins to plane. This means that it suddenly leaps up on to the top of its own bow wave and stays there. Its speed more than doubles in a second or two. As it simultaneously creates and surfs on its bow wave, the boat seems to come alive. Everything vibrates and hums, almost ecstatically, the rigging taut and vibrating like guitar strings, the centreboard and rudder humming loudly in different keys. It's as if the boat is about to break the sound barrier. When I heard the Vendée Globe sailors talk about what it was like at twenty knots or more in their sixty-footers, it sounded something like hanging on to a planing dinghy as it strained to go airborne. No one seemed jaded by it.

'It's incredible,' said Autissier. The whole forward part of the boat, almost back to the mast, rises out of the water, the rest of the hull sits poised on the wave top, and water flies everywhere. And the noise! 'You cannot imagine,' she said. 'A roar, a rrrrrrrrrrrrrrrr,' – she bellowed out a long rolling r, laughing at the same time – 'it's really an experience!'

'It's lovely,' Goss assured me. 'The most exciting thing.' And with these boats, when you put an extra ten per cent of effort in, you don't just get an extra knot or two the way you do with most boats. You get another six or seven knots, just like that.

Even the cool, detached Laurent acknowledged that, if nothing broke, it was quite an experience. 'It feels good,' he admitted.

But along with the exhilaration comes fear. It comes when the boat goes too fast, for example, and the autopilots lose control, or when one of those irresistibly destructive waves overtakes it. There is, after all, an optimum speed for each boat, depending on its design and the conditions. It is possible to go too fast, and then the margin for error decreases alarmingly. The boat 'pushes the envelope'. A term usually used to describe aeroplane or spaceship performance, pushing the envelope applies equally well to boats. It occurs on a Vendée Globe racer when it's in a situation in which it may, at any moment, be driven to exceed its design tolerances. The envelope, created by the designer's computer and practical experience, defines the things the boat can safely do. Outside the envelope, catastrophe. In a Southern Ocean storm, the envelope contracts so that the zones of danger outside move much closer. It doesn't take much for the boat to be thrust into them, and into the maelstrom of a broach and perhaps a knockdown or a capsize.

The other problem with fast sailing is fatigue. Everything about surfing big waves at twenty-five knots strains the human nervous system: the motion, the very loud noise. Carbon fibre is an efficient transmitter of sound waves. Even water flowing past the hull is noisy. The sound of waves hitting the boat, or breaking over it, is momentarily deafening. And there is the wind as well. Although it screams at the best of times, there is a truly intimidating, keening screech as it rushes around the mast and rigging. All this goes on at high pitch for days at a time. Even when the weather isn't too bad by Southern Ocean standards, the tumultuous rush continues.

Parlier, as tough a sailor as there is, often wore a helmet and ear plugs to try to block out the racket. But he couldn't isolate himself from the noise for too long. It was important to hear what was going on – how the sound of the wind changed as it blew harder or lighter, the roar of threatening waves coming up astern, the myriad sounds of all the strained parts of the boat as they worked close to their limits. Alone with their boats for so long, the sailors relied on the sound of things to monitor the health of the whole complex operation.

'Every time you hear a little noise on your boat,' Chabaud said, 'you ask it, "What's happening? Tell me what the problem is." You speak to the boat – the sails, the helm, every little thing. And it speaks back to you, and you have to listen.'

Eventually, single-handers have to block out the racket to get some sleep. It seems inconceivable. You're doing the right thing: smoking down waves at twenty or twenty-five knots; stuffing the bow into the wave ahead; running with the low that's creating the big seas, keeping your speed up close to that of the waves. It's dark, no moon in the usual low cloud cover, only the phosphorescent curl of the breaking waves, maybe rain or snow, perhaps a few bergs or growlers about, spray driving back right past the stern, solid water regularly sweeping the deck, the boat at a forty-five-degree angle down some of the bigger five- or six-storey waves, the high-decibel noise. And in the middle of all that, the sailor crawls into one of the berths, wedges into it behind a canvas lee-cloth to avoid getting pitched across the cabin, and goes to sleep.

At that moment, the single-hander has given up control of the boat, which is now in the hands of the autopilot and subject to luck and ineluctable chaos. That's the moment Thompson and Finot thought about so often as they pulled and prodded at the idea of a new machine. All the computer analyses and twirling of three-dimensional forms, the experience of what has or hasn't worked in the past, even the underlying idea of what the boat should do when it's in danger – the object of all the necessary design compromises – have led to this moment of the single-hander's profound trust and faith in the machine and its creator.

7

———

The Tiger Heart

*Ocean racing is made up of many bad
afternoons, ugly mornings, and hard
nights.*

– William Snaith, *On the Wind's Way*

*The art of the sailor is to leave nothing to
chance.*

– Annie Van de Wiele

DURING THE first week of December 1996, almost as soon as
the Vendée Globe boats entered the Southern Ocean, things
changed dramatically for the race leaders. At the beginning of the
week, it was still a tight race among the first four boats. Auguin
gradually increased his margin over Autissier, who was almost a
hundred miles behind him, and over Parlier, 190 miles back – not
significant distances now that all three boats could count on more
than enough wind for six weeks to come. Even Roufs, now sailing in
his own solitary bubble and trailing Auguin by 540 miles, was very
much in contention. The second group – Laurent, Thiercelin,
Dumont and de Broc – was still north of thirty-five degrees latitude,
and sailing in frustratingly light winds between 950 and 1,250 miles
behind Auguin, straining to reach the constant wind farther south.

They seemed to be out of the running for a spot on the Vendée Globe podium. And even though they had sailed their older, heavier boats with eminent skill, it was the skippers with the new, radical designs who were out in front and apparently running away with the race. The third group – de Radiguès, Goss, Chabaud and the pirate Dinelli – against all odds, were still bunched tightly together, the first three within forty miles of each other, and trailed the leader by almost seventeen hundred miles.

But at sea, the only surprise for the sailor is to experience no surprises. In an ironic Möbius-like curve, that principle of un-certainty itself becomes a certainty in the Southern Ocean. It's no place for people who can't accept sudden and catastrophic change.

'When you go around alone,' Autissier remarked, 'really each minute, anything can happen. You have to remember that all the time, up to the end, right through the final miles. And in the Southern Ocean, who knows what you will see?'

By the end of the first week of December, the axiomatic truth of Autissier's remark was demonstrated. She herself had limped back to Cape Town for repairs, disqualifying herself after one of her rudders had broken off right at the hull in a collision with flotsam. Dubois, twenty-five hundred miles back after his restart a week after the fleet, had again hit flotsam and damaged a rudder. Finally discouraged, he was talking about heading all the way back to Les Sables-d'Olonne, even though he was less than thirteen hundred miles from Cape Town. And at the end of the week, one of Parlier's rudders snapped off when he smashed into a growler.

This rash of incidents pointed to the vulnerable location of the dual rudders on Vendée Globe racers – one on each side of the stern. They were far more efficient than a conventional single rudder located on a boat's centreline because they became deeply immersed when the boat heeled and retained their turning power. Out on the edge of the hull, however, they were prey to any floating object, while a single rudder was protected against flotsam by the keel forward of it.

Parlier decided to keep heading east, but towards Fremantle, Australia. He couldn't risk the long haul to the Horn without repairs. When he stepped ashore two weeks later, he too would disqualify himself. By 7 December, Auguin, trouble-free, was even more securely in the lead. Roufs vaulted to second. And the four sailors in the second group suddenly had a chance of placing. Of the original sixteen starters, ten were still officially in the race.

Autissier had been anticipating this December week with appre-
hension. It was a bitter anniversary for her. While no rational person
could believe in a jinx, no sailor, habituated to the uncontrollable
happenstance of the sea, could feel comfortable ignoring the possibility. Her rudder broke on the first day of December. Two years less
a day before that, she had been dismasted while leading the 1994–95
BOC. Three out of three. Two dismastings (she had also lost her rig
in the 1990–91 BOC) and now a smashed rudder. Autissier's luck, all
bad, had held in this Vendée Globe as well. In Les Sables-d'Olonne,
before the start, she had described her boat as one of the best
prepared. Her team had had the time to fine-tune the little details on
board *PRB*. But this preparedness didn't extend to replacing rudders
at sea. The boat had to be hauled out for the job. At least she was
lucky with the weather after her rudder broke. She sailed the 460
miles to Cape Town in two days. As she approached the Cape
Peninsula under full sail in a light wind, she was able to marvel once
again at how beautiful its scenery was. But mostly she thought about
how hard it was to lose when you lost so much. The sailors of the
South African marine-rescue service, who towed her the last few
miles to harbour, handed a tired Autissier a bouquet of red roses. She
hung them on *PRB*'s stern.

'It's a dreadful, brutal disappointment, but it won't do any good to
cry over it,' she said briskly. She would rejoin the race after her boat
had been repaired, 'not to win, but as a way of being faithful to my
commitments. The Vendée Globe is a hard race. No one can say
they're sure of finishing. But for me, in my mind, the race will go on
until I get back to Les Sables-d'Olonne.'

In May 1932, Amelia Earhart flew solo across the Atlantic Ocean, the
first person to do so since Charles Lindbergh five years earlier, and
needless to say, the first woman to make the flight alone. (She had
been a passenger on a plane that made the crossing in 1928.) She took
off from Harbour Grace, Newfoundland, in her red single-engine
Lockheed Vega and flew into bad weather almost right away. For
most of the fourteen-hour-long flight, she was socked-in, flying blind.
A few hours after take-off, her altimeter failed. When ice built up on
her wings, and she had to descend to try to get rid of it, she had no
idea how close she was flying to the waves. An engine exhaust

manifold vibrated deafeningly throughout the flight. At one point, it caught on fire. She had been trying for Paris, like Lindbergh, but all these problems forced her down in Northern Ireland instead. A little later, she flew on to London, to a heroine's welcome.

Earhart made the flight for the same reason she had become a flyer in the first place: it was her heart's desire. Being a woman was irrelevant. It was axiomatic for her 'that women can do most things that men can do'. In an interview, she said, 'I see no reason why a woman, properly qualified, should not fly the ocean as well as a man, given a suitable plane and favourable weather conditions.'

The story of Earhart's determined incursion into the male world of aeroplanes and flying – a small brotherhood of adventurers and daredevils – echoed Isabelle Autissier's entry into the elite of single-handed ocean racers. It shouldn't have. Sixty years later, it would be reasonable to expect that no one would think twice about a woman entering a BOC Challenge or a Vendée Globe. But Autissier had been the subject of a great deal of public and media interest from the time she first entered the MiniTransat and the Figaro single-handed races. The attention became more intense when she entered the 1990–91 BOC. To a certain extent, the media interest in Autissier's sailing career is a result of its own need for material, for a different angle on events. Yet she, like Earhart two generations before her, couldn't avoid becoming a genuine symbol of women's rightful expansion into all categories of experience, including the last all-male pockets of danger.

Like the pioneer flyer, Autissier, the pioneer sailor, was only living her life as she saw it necessarily unfold before her. When she arrived at Newport, on the United States east coast, for the start of the 1990–91 BOC, her first racing circumnavigation, she was surprised by the constant questions from the media. How would she deal with the physical demands of the race? Could she handle the gear? Reef and furl the huge sails? What was it like being the only woman? Autissier was surprised by the questions, because for her, by then, all that was nothing. 'I just did it because I wanted to do it, and that's all. Of course, I knew I was the only woman, but I didn't care about that. Everyone else cared much more than me.'

At the same time, she acknowledged that there was 'a little bit of resistance' to her presence on the part of the fraternity of male skippers. But that didn't last long. In most cases, no longer than the first leg to Cape Town. Certainly, by the end of the race, she was in. Within a few years, experienced skippers, like the Australian David

Adams or Gerry Roufs, considered themselves privileged to sail as Autissier's crew on her round-the-Horn speed-record attempt, or in the Tour de l'Europe.

But it was impossible to escape from the complicated perceptions and politics of gender. Both Autissier and her male colleagues are its prisoners. 'First of all, you are not taken seriously because you are a woman. People thought, "She's a woman. She's not as good as the men, so she'll be at the back of the fleet." But then, when you prove you can do it, that you can win, it's the opposite, you're put higher up than the men.'

Up on the pedestal, a different form of condescension. 'I dislike that very much. The race is difficult for everyone, for me and for the guys. We all have to deal with the same difficulties.'

Autissier acknowledged that she might not be able to change or reef a sail as fast as a man, because of differences in upper-body strength. But in a BOC or a Vendée Globe, it didn't matter if something like that took fifteen minutes, or even an hour, longer. These races were won at the chart table, by analysing weather and wind patterns or the strength and track of lows as they ranged across the Southern Ocean. The skipper who cuts the best trail wins. Autissier proved that conclusively with her wide-margin victory in the first leg of the 1994–95 BOC. I wasn't sure that the physical differences were too critical anyway. I wondered if the small 135-pound Roufs, wiry though he was, would have had any advantage over the tall and solidly built Autissier. Her physical strength was apparent.

Similarly, Catherine Chabaud was tall and robust, though she said that sometimes she regretted she wasn't stronger. It had been difficult for her to do certain things on *Whirlpool Europe 2*. 'I thought, now, a guy would have done that a lot faster than me. But then I realised I got it done anyway. I found a solution. As a woman, you have to imagine the solution differently.' In any event, like Autissier, Chabaud emphasised that tactical skills win these races. She never saw herself as a woman sailing, but only as somebody – a person – who wanted to sail, and who, therefore, went sailing.

I found Autissier and Chabaud to be honest, direct, humorous, modest – like the men. But unlike the men, they seem to be living on a different kind of edge from the one they flirted with in the Southern Ocean. Autissier and Chabaud inhabit the border area between what men are conventionally able and allowed to do, and the corresponding territory for women. They do it without pretension or self-consciousness. They look like they belong there. And if they do, what woman doesn't?

While Autissier put into Cape Town, the Southern Ocean snarled at all the other Vendée Globe sailors. Even Auguin's seemingly impregnable *Géodis* showed its fallibility. Slip-sliding along in fifty-knot wind, which rose briefly to near-hurricane strength in the frequent squalls, in cross-seas that were increasingly difficult to negotiate, Auguin was knocked down by a big wave. With great anxiety, he watched as his boat righted itself very slowly and reluctantly. He headed farther north, trying to dodge the worst of the depression. Thiercelin reported almost the same conditions in a different system a thousand miles back. He too was knocked down, his mast almost in the water, his mainsail damaged. There seemed to be no end to the procession of low-pressure systems. One followed the other with only hours, or a day or so, respite in between. On the same day that Autissier's rudder broke, Parlier gybed unintentionally in fifty-knot winds in the same depression from which Auguin was running north. The wind caught the boom on the wrong side and swung it instantly across the boat. Parlier was lucky that the shock of the boom and sail smashing into the standing rigging didn't damage it, or the mast. As it was, he broke five mainsail battens, the thin slats that slide into slots along the outer edge of the sail to maintain its shape and prevent the edge from flogging in the wind. He had to sail under jib alone until he had a chance to replace them.

Of the three leading skippers, Roufs seemed to handle the storm the best. He spent more than two days riding its wind. Blowing at a sustained fifty-five to sixty knots (Beaufort scale force 11, a violent storm), the gale drove him along at speeds as high as twenty-six knots as he surfed the long Southern Ocean waves. By 6 December, when Parlier collided with ice, Roufs had closed the gap between them to less than one hundred miles.

There is a fine skill involved in riding these depressions. It isn't just a matter of the boats lining up and surfing along before the wind like identical fast cars on a highway. If that were the case, the boats would simply remain in the order they were in when they entered the roaring forties. In fact, the skippers could do a lot to improve, or jeopardise, their positions.

The successive depressions are complex systems that share a common structure and sequence of events. At the same time, each one has its individual entrails, which the skippers must interpret from their weather data, or from using the sailor's traditional methods of observing wind and wave direction and strength, and sometimes, clouds. A skilled watcher can derive almost as accurate an analysis of a frontal system's progress and location as a weatherfax wonk. Within each low, the spiralling winds blow from different directions depending on their relation to the system's centre. At the same time, the whole massive turning wheel of wind is moving forward at anywhere from fifteen to twenty-five knots or so, occasionally much faster. The sailors must try to position themselves so as to avoid the system's strongest wind, and also to take advantage of the wind direction within the system that most consistently favours their eastward course. They also have to keep up the careful, minute-by-minute shepherding of the boat through dangerous waves.

Low-pressure systems are the day-to-day marauders of weather at sea. They're not nearly as powerful and destructive as tropical cyclonic storms – hurricanes, typhoons, cyclones and the like. But they make up for that by appearing very frequently. The winds of a high-pressure system may be dangerously high only on its periphery, but a sailor in the path of a low must assume that it will be dangerous over the entire sea area it covers – including the centre, where somewhat lighter winds allow chaotic and hazardous sea conditions to develop.

As he watched the low approach him on 2 and 3 December, Roufs searched for the fine line between maintaining his easterly course and dealing with the actual sea conditions created by the system. As the front passed over, its north-west winds, blowing across his boat's port quarter (the left side of the stern), would switch quickly to the south-west and blow even harder across the other quarter. The new wind would build up seas running across the existing strong north-west wave pattern, increasing the likelihood of dangerous breaking seas or even of unusually high rogue or freak waves forming from two or more seas. Roufs would have to edge southward so that he could take the dangerous north-west waves more directly on his stern. To reduce the danger of the system's conflicting wave trains, he would have to go farther south into the stronger and more southerly wind he was trying to avoid. It was a hard trail to cut.

Catherine Chabaud would find out how difficult it was to compromise her way through a dangerous storm. A little later in the race, as she was sailing in the southern Indian Ocean south-west of the Kerguelen Islands, she was overtaken by an intense low-pressure system. While she was working on deck at the base of the mast trying to secure her mainsail, *Whirlpool Europe 2* was knocked down. She hung on to the mast and boom and watched as the top of the mast, forced below the horizontal, disappeared into the sea. The boat itself was almost invisible for several seconds under the enormous onrushing wave. She had two thoughts. First, she marvelled at how beautiful the water was – like mountains with snow-white foam, but a deep blue and turquoise as well. She also thought: Maybe this is the end. 'It's bad to finish your life at thirty-four years old.' Then she added, 'I was not afraid, you understand.'

'No, I don't understand,' I replied.

But when her boat righted itself and she crawled back to the cockpit, she said, 'I was like that – aaaah!' – she mimed a slumping, shaking survivor of near-catastrophe.

The knockdown had been her fault, she said. She hadn't taken Moitessier's advice. His account, in *The Long Way*, of his tactics in dealing with Southern Ocean lows reads like a precise, magisterial analysis of the systems and how sailors should react to them. It's like reading a technical manual. And in a way, nothing could be more deceptive, partly because the reader is lulled into forgetting the conditions under which all of Moitessier's (or Chabaud's, or Roufs's) calculations and manoeuvres had to be made: shrieking, screaming wind; ear-popping explosions of waves on hulls like soundboards; whipsaw, muscle-straining pitching and rolling; the sheer intimidating size of the waves. On square-riggers, canvas shields were often rigged behind the helmsmen – it took two or three men to control the wheel in heavy weather – so that they couldn't look back and see the size of the waves roaring down on them.

The sailor knows that every storm spawned waves or combinations of waves that, meeting a boat in one chance configuration or another, could destroy it. Whether or not that meeting took place was a matter of luck, the obscure operation of the laws of chaos. However it was determined, it was certainly out of the sailor's hands. In boats of the latest design, built out of the latest materials, equipped with the most sophisticated safety and communications equipment available, the Vendée Globe sailors, like all sailors before them, still couldn't avoid disaster if it happened along.

'I heard the groan of a big wave,' Autissier had said. *'But of course, I could do nothing.'*

Moitessier was careful to include a caveat with his advice on how to meet storms: the more he learned, the less he knew. The sailor never knows what will happen. A small change in a wave's size or shape and everything changes. A chance cross-sea at the wrong moment and the game's lost. Moitessier wrote, dogmatically but truly, 'Above all, there is the great and most beautiful unknown, the sea itself.'

Near the end of the first week of December, as Roufs closed in on him, Parlier's troubles were continuing. Riding the winds of the same storm as Auguin and the Canadian, he had had no chance to repair his mainsail battens. He was running fast under foresail alone, but his speed was necessarily lower without his mainsail, or the reefed portion of it he would have used in these fifty-knot winds. To most sailors, it would seem bizarre that a boat sailing in a force 9 or 10 storm ('Very high waves with overhanging crests,' advised Admiral Beaufort about the latter. 'Sea takes white appearance as foam is blown in very dense streaks') would think of having any sail up at all, let alone a mainsail. Or that a skipper would consider it a dis-advantage sailing under only a small storm headsail. In the past, a boat would have been running under bare poles, or at the most, a scrap of a storm jib to provide some directional stability among the waves. Its skipper would have tried to keep boat speed down, trying not to surf down the waves and bury the bow in the back of the wave ahead. But as Jean-Marie Finot had emphasised, these Vendée Globe and BOC boats had changed everyone's idea of the best way of dealing with extreme storm conditions, at least in vessels with their radical design characteristics. Speed meant everything: maximum helm control, reduction of the waves' concussive power. Going fast with a following wind reduced the apparent wind – you could subtract the boat's speed from the wind velocity, and carry more sail in the lighter wind actually blowing across the deck of the fast-moving boat. And of course, there was the race. Speed won. In the Southern Ocean, the only strategy was to go flat out.

Parlier's difficulties suddenly got much worse when he collided with the growler on 6 December. At less than forty-three degrees south, he was well north of the official iceberg drift line. But the growler was there nevertheless. Smaller pieces of ice, and sometimes larger bergs, often drifted well to the north. It could have gutted *Aquitaine Innovations* and sunk him in a few minutes. Or it might have ripped off the keel and the boat would have capsized instantly. Instead, the ice bumped, alarmingly but harmlessly, down his hull and took out a good part of one of his rudders. The good news was that it was possible to hit ice without suffering ruinous damage. Just a matter of luck.

Parlier considered following Autissier's example and turning back to Cape Town. After talking things over with his technical team, however, he thought he could make it to Fremantle on the west coast of Australia. It was in the direction he was going and he would lose less time. He could also fix his genoa self-furling gear and take on fresh water. The most isolated part of the Southern Ocean, from south of New Zealand to Cape Horn, still lay ahead. Fremantle would be a welcome chance for Parlier to get his boat back in shape.

He had some difficult moments after his collision as he tried to secure *Aquitaine Innovations* for the two weeks it would take to reach port. The part of the rudder still attached to the boat – a substantial piece of carbon fibre and kevlar – flailed around with the boat's motion and repeatedly bashed the hull. It could do serious damage. Parlier tried to secure it with an elastic shock cord, but it kept breaking free and continued its mayhem. Finally, he lowered the shaft and the remains of the rudder down and dropped it out of the bottom of the hull. Water poured in and flooded the entire aft watertight compartment. He had to heave-to so that the boat lay to one side to reduce the water inflow. He couldn't reach the hole from the outside. His electric bilge pumps malfunctioned, and the compartment filled with water again. He climbed into it through the hatch in the watertight bulkhead. But because of the water flooding the compartment, he had to seal off the opening to the rest of the boat. Then he had to work fast.

'I plugged the hole, but some water kept coming in. Unless I could patch the hole and stop the flow, I wouldn't be able to get back into the boat again because the bulkhead cover was underwater. I glued a piece of plastic over the hole, and I sat on it up to my chest in the freezing water. All the time, I was saying to myself. "I hope this sticks." It was one of the difficult moments during the race when I was afraid.' The patch stuck, and he was able to pump out the compartment with a hand pump, open the hatch and get back into the boat's cabin.

Then Parlier continued his water-short run towards Fremantle. He now had about thirteen litres of drinkable water left and was hoping for rain, but he was also packing four bottles of good-quality Bordeaux. If they didn't reduce his dehydration, they'd at least keep him happier.

'But the Vendée Globe was over for me when I hit the ice,' he said. Under the race rules, his status as an official racer would end when he accepted a tow into Fremantle harbour or, if he made it to a dock under his own sails, at the moment his foot touched land.

A little more than a month into the race, there had already been five collisions with ships or flotsam – and now, ice: Autissier, Dubois (twice), the Hungarian sailor Fa, run down by a freighter in the Bay of Biscay, and Parlier. All of the mishaps had led to abandonments or disqualification's as the boats put into port for repairs.

In their passages through the North and South Atlantic Oceans, the racers crossed dozens of major shipping lanes: between Europe and the United States east coast; between Europe and the Panama Canal; for the shipping that poured in and out of the Mediterranean; the lanes originating in the Far East or the Middle East, running around the Cape of Good Hope to Europe or the Americas. The skippers had to watch their radar and the horizon especially carefully as they crossed each of these notional lines in the sea. They also had to worry about wide-ranging, long-distance fishing boats, or tramp steamers off the usual shipping routes (until they reached the Southern Ocean, of course, one of whose defining characteristics is that there's no one there). The ships' radar could detect the Vendée Globe boats with their tall rigs reasonably easily – in good weather. It was more difficult to find them in rough seas, amid the jumble of waves. However, many ships keep no consistent radar, or visual, watch, and incredibly, the radar sets on some vessels are often turned off.

I once read about a US freighter that arrived in Yokohama after crossing the northern Pacific from San Francisco. When it docked, the crew discovered parts of a sailboat's mast and rigging lodged in the ship's anchors, which were secured at the bow. No one had been aware of a collision, but somewhere in that vast ocean, someone's luck had run out. I never found out whether a sailboat had actually been lost, or had survived a dismasting and had made it to port under jury-rig.

As the boats sailed south into high latitudes in the Southern Ocean, they left behind any danger of collision with large ships, and reduced a great deal the chances of hitting flotsam such as logs or shipping containers. Ice became their biggest worry.

In heavy weather or at night, the skippers relied exclusively on chance, and the dubious protection of watertight, or collision, bulkheads, to avoid or survive catastrophic collisions. Because these deep-keel surfboards were so fast, collision had serious consequences. Hitting a berg or a growler at a cruising boat's five or six knots might be survivable; it was a different matter smashing into one at twenty or twenty-five knots.

The Vendée Globe race rules require the boats to carry radar. It's certainly useful for the skippers when they're in or near shipping lanes. And it picks out the larger icebergs. But there are problems with the device. In many ways, it is a technological sop to dangers at sea that really cannot be guarded against. Radar, like all the other electronic wonders on board, can break down. Laurent's never worked properly all through his Southern Ocean transit, and he mostly ignored it. Other skippers had periodic problems. More crucially, though, radar can't pick up anything floating low in the water – flotsam or smaller bergs and growlers. In rough weather, with five- or six-storey-high waves, quite big icebergs could easily get lost in the sea clutter. There was no rule which said that a boat would not encounter ice in rough weather. In the end, the chance of hitting ice was another one of those chaotic uncertainties – like the random freak wave – that Southern Ocean racers had to accept.

Ice was worse than a storm, in a way. The sailor in heavy weather could at least do something to affect the outcome: reduce sail; change course in response to the passage of the system and its changing wind; steer among the waves avoiding the dangerous breaking crests. Eventually, the storm passed over, the danger lessened. But south of forty degrees, the risk of ice was always there. The sailor was free of it only after the Horn, when the Falkland Islands were nearly abeam. And during that whole time, not much could be done, apart from looking around while on deck and plotting the big bergs that did show up on the screen. If you bothered with the radar at all.

'I never turn mine on,' Goss said. 'It's just there for the rules and it's a waste of power. In truth, the waves are so big, the bloody things just get confused. My view's a bit fatalistic really. If it's got your name on it, you'll hit it; if it hasn't, you'll be fine.'

As for the watertight bulkheads, reinforced bows and so on – well, a boat won't necessarily hit ice head-on. A growler can rip a hull down the side, exposing several walled-off compartments at a time. After all, the *Titanic* had watertight bulkheads.

'Let the Russian roulette begin,' Thiercelin commented sardonically in one of his faxes, as he began his descent south of the ice line in the southern Indian Ocean.

Things settled down for the Vendée Globe sailors at the end of the eventful first week of December. Autissier left Cape Town with a new rudder just before dark on the eighth. Her support team members had been helped by some of the mechanics on board one of Jacques Cousteau's ships, *L'Alcyon*, which had been lying nearby. Following her custom, Autissier clipped a bouquet of fresh flowers to each end of *PRB* as she put out to sea again. With luck, she would be able to rejoin the race, as an unofficial competitor, somewhere between the second group of four – Laurent, Thiercelin, Dumont and de Broc – and the third group, also of four – Goss, Chabaud, de Radiguès and Dinelli.

The previous day, a revived Dubois reversed his dispirited decision to trek all the way back to Les Sables-d'Olonne. He announced that he too would sail for Cape Town, make repairs and set off from port for the third time in the race. Dubois's fateful decision would take him into the Southern Ocean after all. His expanding experience with misfortune was far from over.

Eric Dumont, in seventh place and almost two thousand miles behind Auguin in the increasingly attenuated string of boats, hit a growler, or maybe just a particularly hard wave, and began taking on water through a split on the port side of his hull near the bow. It was the same spot he had repaired with resin and sealing compound while he was sailing off the Canaries soon after the start. At first, he thought that he too would have to put into Cape Town, reducing to nine the number of competitors still in the race. His boat needed serious repair work with material he didn't have on board, and he turned towards South Africa – a ten- to fourteen-day sail in the prevailing conditions. By the next day, however, he had changed his mind. He could keep going after all. In a rush of inspired, and optimistic, improvisation, he plugged the leaking hole, stuffing the outside with an old T-shirt and plastering it over with resin. On the inside, he wedged a piece of wood cannibalised from the interior furniture across the damaged area and epoxied it into place. He would go on, and think about putting into another port later in the race. His boat had a demonstrated weak point, a gap in its defences, which he'd have a lot of time to worry about.

While Dumont was finding a use for old clothes, Dinelli got bad news. The French Federation of Sailing had rejected his appeal of the decision by the race jury in October to exclude him from official status in the race. He had taken the chance of sailing as a 'free competitor' hoping that the federation would make him official. But it agreed with the jury that Dinelli hadn't completed the required qualification sail, and more critically, that his real experience on sixty-footers was 'non-existent'. An ironic conclusion, since at that moment, he was sailing one of those sixty-footers at forty-four degrees south latitude in a fifty-knot gale, and managing to stay afloat. In a few weeks, however, the federation's opinion of Dinelli's competence would arguably appear more accurate. Sixteen hundred miles behind the leader, he would have to sail on as the race pirate.

With the removal of Autissier and Parlier from official contention, the fight for places in the race had boiled down to a simple proposition. Unless Auguin was capsized, dismasted or collided with something, he was going to be very hard to catch. In fact, over the course of the second week of December, he steadily widened his lead over the now second-place Roufs. Auguin seemed to have settled into a groove. Carefully administering his energy in the wet, cold, stormy sailing, meticulously checking and maintaining his boat's gear, he drew away from the Canadian day by day. He was lucky too. During the thirteenth and fourteenth, he found himself on the leading edge of an approaching low. In just the right spot in relation to the system's spiralling winds, he surfed ahead of the worst of it for two days in waves that hadn't yet had a chance to become dangerous. In fact, over a twenty-four-hour period during those two days, Auguin broke his own speed record, set in one of the legs of the previous BOC. He sailed 374 nautical miles at an average speed of 15.6 knots. The stability of the wind's strength and direction as he kept station at the front edge of the low were the essential conditions for his achievement, Auguin said. This was the sort of thing Finot had in mind when he talked about future Vendée Globe designs: boats that were nimble enough to be able to adjust their positions in relation to the weather. Auguin had been able to do it this time because of the relatively small area, quick development, and slow speed of the system, and because he had been lucky enough to find himself in just the right spot in relation to its centre. Maybe his achievement would turn out to be prophetic, as the boats became even lighter and faster. At the rate he was going, Auguin had a good chance of beating the Vendée Globe race record of 109 days. On 15 December, he passed south of Cape Leeuwin, one of the three stormy capes. Two down, one to go. Now there was just Cape Horn.

Roufs had fallen back more than eight hundred miles by the week's end. He was sailing well himself, and during one day, he averaged more than fourteen knots over twenty-four hours. But he had not managed to find Auguin's same charmed path through the wind. And now, perhaps, the Frenchman's experience through the Southern Ocean in two BOCs was beginning to tell. Roufs was ambivalent about the charms of the 'Great South'. The long, high swell, unlike wave patterns anywhere else on earth, was magical and fascinating, he said. But when the winds of the next low whipped those swells into toppling, roaring monsters, it was different. 'There's no joy here. It's nature's version of Beirut,' he wrote in an e-mail.

One night, in winds blowing up to sixty-five knots (just over the line into force 12, hurricane strength), a combination of cross-seas almost capsized *Groupe LG2*, rolling it around 'like a chef at a pizzeria spinning his dough'. In the violent conditions, he got no sleep at all for two days. He passed a group of icebergs about two miles to windward, after spotting them on his radar. In the driving spray and snow squalls, it was impossible to see beyond the bow of his boat. At one point, a growler bumped, scarily, along his hull. He had a dilemma: as a racer, he wanted to go faster; but the sailor in him said, 'Slow down,' and he did. 'The race was second priority, and too bad about the miles I was losing.'

Near the beginning of the week, Roufs had a problem with his mainsail halyard. In a lumpy sea, he climbed his mast to check on it, using a mountaineer-like climbing system. While he was up nearly eighty feet, the wind and sea increased, and he had a difficult time just hanging on with that murderously exaggerated masthead motion. He nearly fell several times. 'I was frightened,' he said. 'I could have easily fallen. And at twenty-five metres, there's not much room for dancing.'

The halyard was all right, but then, on the way down, his climbing lines got tangled. One of them wrapped itself around his neck, and he just about hanged himself. After several frantic minutes, he managed to untangle the lines and get back to the deck. It had been his worst moment since the beginning of the race.

Behind Roufs, the rest of the battered but still spirited Vendée Globe fleet stretched back almost four thousand miles across the desolate reaches of the Southern Ocean. Laurent and Thiercelin duelled for third place, only eight miles apart. Autissier was just a few hundred miles behind them, and was gaining fast on the veteran boats in her swift new one. Goss and Chabaud were a hundred miles from each other. She had already passed the seventh-place Dumont and would catch de Broc in a day or so. Paolier, beginning his swing north-east towards Fremantle and disqualification, had dropped back out of contention. Twenty-five hundred miles behind the leader, de Radiguès was suffering from the faulty electrical system that would plague him for the rest of his race and lead to his disqualificaton when he too was forced into port in Fremantle. Goss was convinced now that his smaller boat, with its lower hydro-dynamic speed limit, had no chance of keeping pace with the new sixty-footers. Dinelli was a few hundred miles behind Goss, a proximity that would very soon have the greatest significance for both men. Bringing up the rear was Tony Bullimore, although he would soon be joined by Dubois, after his Cape Town repairs were completed.

The weather patterns at those latitudes were so constant that the racers were experiencing much the same range of conditions across the whole length of ocean. Auguin and Bullimore could have been ten miles apart as they swung along to the harsh rhythms of the gales of the roaring forties and furious fifties. Everyone faced the same challenges: knockdowns, scary surfs down the white-water faces of waves like waterfalls, the bitterly cold water and air, ice lurking and always the noise.

It was seven years since Philippe Jeantot had sailed in the Great South, but he could never forget what it had been like there. In the Southern Ocean, he told me, he had always felt that you weren't just living, you were trying to survive as well. And the real problem was that that lasted for forty or fifty days.

'And during all that time, you are cold, you feel so lonely, you are frightened.' The tough veteran looked at me and smiled. 'You have to admit that, you know.'

In the summer months, the usually execrable conditions in the Southern Ocean sometimes improved, but even then, by any reasonable standards of sea-going, they were very nasty. Laurent mentioned to me with no irony that he had been able to fix something on his boat one day between Australia and Cape Horn because the weather was quite good. When I asked what that meant, he said that the wind had dropped to thirty to thirty-five knots sustained and the seas were below twenty-five feet. To me, and to most sailors, those are severe and potentially dangerous conditions. And even if conditions are 'good', or even good in the normal sense of the word – occasionally in the southern summer, the wind does fall away – the sailor knows that they won't last long. Waiting to get hammered can be almost as bad as the event itself. The single-hander waits alone for the onslaught.

'You know it's going to happen,' Robin Knox-Johnston said of his five-month-long single-handed Golden Globe race marathon in the Southern Ocean (he was at sea continuously for 313 days). 'Even on calm days, you know that in a few days, it's going to come at you again. It's a constant threat – a miserable, mean, vicious place.'

The Vendée Globe sailors themselves acknowledge that, in some ways, things are getting easier in the Southern Ocean. The communications and emergency devices the boats carry make it so much safer than it was for Moitessier or Knox-Johnston, or the square-rigger sailors. It's a very different kind of experience when you can spend hours each day chatting to your wife or shore team by satellite phone, exchanging faxes or e-mail with anyone, talking around the world by single-sideband, long-range radio. The sociable Auguin admitted that he often spent two or three hours a day on his Inmarsat M satellite phone – at a cost to his sponsor of $3.50 a minute. The EPIRBs sit in their storage brackets, always comforting, proven life-savers.

Apart from the EPIRBs, however, the skippers were ambivalent about this easy accessibility. Autissier thought that the communications gear was good in many ways. It was fun to stay in touch with family and friends; it was satisfying to share the amazing experience of the Southern Ocean with the public. But sometimes, it was all a nuisance, a huge distraction. All the ways of being in touch jeopardised the connection that meant everything in that dangerous place: the sailor's bond with herself and with her boat. With all the distractions, sometimes you lost concentration. The domestic detail intruded on the elemental struggle.

'I mean, we are alone, and we have to stay alone in a way. We need to focus on what we are doing. I don't like to have a phone ringing when I'm alone and doing something on the boat.'

Chabaud was glad when her fax broke down in the Indian Ocean, and even happier when her radio gave up after Cape Horn. Early in the race, she had faxed back and forth with her friends on shore, sometimes five or six times a day. She was so excited to be living the great adventure of her life that she needed to discuss it. But more and more, as the sea embraced her in its beautiful and precarious routine, Chabaud wanted to be alone. When her fax broke, she tried to fix it, but soon gave up. It was a relief. Even more so when her radio went down. After that, she said, her race was quite different from that of Auguin or Autissier. Her experience of the sea was much more like Moitessier's: the sailor and her boat in uninterrupted symbiotic communion.

Goss felt the same way. The whole communications system on board was useful, often pleasant, to have. But it had to be carefully managed. You had a responsibility to share what you were going through with the public from which your sponsor hoped to recoup its outlay. That was a necessary part of the business of sailing professionally. Still, when he lost his radio, Goss was as happy as Chabaud had been. There was always the 'off' button on each piece of equipment. But a breakdown relieved you of your obligations to the world – it was a permanent 'off' that no one could blame you for.

In a way, these feelings were a less extreme version of Moitessier's revulsion, as he rounded the Horn in 1969, at the idea of what would happen to him if he finished the Golden Globe race – all the hoopla and fuss. He felt this way partly because of his own personality, estranged from the world and in permanent exile. But this tendency had been sharpened by the months he had spent alone at sea on *Joshua*. In his mind's eye, the real world had become his boat and the great ocean they were travelling together, it seemed forever. The world of finish lines, spectator boats and prize money had come to seem false and inconsequential. It wasn't just a matter of not wanting to go back. There was no real 'there' to go back to. So Moitessier went AWOL from the world; he just wasn't in their army any more.

When I read Moitessier's description in *The Long Way* of his defection, I thought that he had done it just because he was Moitessier. It seemed a purely idiosyncratic decision. But then I remembered reading about Francis Chichester's reaction to a small press plane that flew overhead as *Gypsy Moth IV* rounded the Horn in 1967 on his record-setting, one-stop circumnavigation. He hated the plane and its intrusion beyond measure. If he could, he would have shot down the noisy little bugger. He hardly acknowledged it, and went below into his cabin until, finally, it buzzed away. Chichester went through the same angry reaction at the end of his voyage, when he was met by hordes of small boats and planes, their occupants celebrating his accomplishment.

Then Knox-Johnston, the steely, steady, no-nonsense lifelong mariner, surprised me when I talked to him about the Golden Globe. He understood completely Moitessier's decision to abandon the race, he said. He knew exactly what the Frenchman was going through, what he was thinking. After he rounded the Horn, Knox-Johnston, too, felt a strong impulse to keep going, in part because he had the same sort of reaction as Moitessier to the thought of having to deal with the world again. He also felt, in a rush of foolish hubris, that he had beaten the Southern Ocean, and that maybe he'd go around again just to rub it in, 'cock a snook' at it. Fortunately, he said, these feelings didn't last long, and, unlike Moitessier, he turned to the north for home. It was still a very tough arrival, though. He had profoundly mixed feelings. He wanted to see his family and friends again, but it was all such an unwelcome interruption. He and his boat had been in their own little world for so long; he wasn't sure he wanted to break it up. He titled the book he later wrote about his voyage *A World of My Own*.

In spite of the technology that was available to the Vendée Globe sailors, the experience of actually getting through the race remained a dauntingly difficult and challenging task. Being able to talk about it with other people didn't reduce the rigours of handling the boat, reefing, steering, keeping your nerve in appalling weather. The Vendée Globe was still a pact between the sailor and the boat, said Parlier. According to Autissier, it makes no difference how many boats sail the route to the Horn: 'That doesn't change anything. When you are there, you are there. Even if you sail the Southern Ocean ten times, it will be difficult each time.'

8

A Spectacle for the Gods

I dare to all that may become a man;
Who dares do more is none.

– William Shakespeare, *Macbeth*

Our interest is on the dangerous edge of
things.

– Robert Browning, 'Bishop Blougram's Apology'

THE DIFFICULTIES in this race weren't long in coming. So far, there had been withdrawals, collisions, knockdowns – the normal quota of trouble in any Vendée Globe or BOC. Only ten boats remained officially in the running. But at Christmas, seven and a half weeks after the race began, its rough yet familiar tenor suddenly shifted. The catastrophic events of the ensuing two weeks changed the race so completely that it seemed to become a mutated version of itself, a new species, recognisable in form but exhibiting novel and frightening behaviour. The Vendée Globe fleet staggered as the EPIRBs began to go off, one after the other.

Remember 25 December – Dinelli's boat capsizing in the force 11 winds and big rollers of the unexpected, close-isobar depression. His mast smashing a hole in the boat's deck, and *Algimouss* filling with water, the boat rolling sluggishly upright again, Dinelli lashing himself to his awash deck, beginning his wait, his life a toss-up.

Now the fragile line of succour between sailors in the Southern Ocean would stretch to the limit. Would it hold?

Dinelli's EPIRB signals were picked up quickly by satellite, his personal signal identified and relayed to race headquarters. Philippe Jeantot moved fast to try to cobble together a rescue. Patrick de Radiguès, only sixty miles away from Dinelli's position, was the closest sailor and, most important, he was upwind. Even in these extreme conditions, he stood a good chance of being able to guide *Afibel*, his fast-running boat, downwind towards Dinelli. But de Radiguès was incommunicado. The electrical problems that had plagued him throughout the race meant that neither his radio nor his fax was working. Jeantot tried to raise him for two or three hours, without success.

The only other possibility was Pete Goss.

Goss was close enough to Dinelli – about 160 miles downwind of him – to have experienced the rapid onset and development of the same storm. Christmas Day had started out genuinely blessed – bright and sunny, with a pleasant twenty-knot northerly wind. But Goss knew it wouldn't last. It was unusual enough to have sunshine and light winds in the first place. And he too had heard Chabaud's warning about the moderate low-pressure system she was sailing through, and that would overtake him and Dinelli before the day was out. Goss had a feeling about this one, however, a sense that it was going to be worse than Chabaud had suggested; it was an intuition of impending disaster, he said later.

And no wonder. The barometric pressure dropped forty-six millibars in twenty-four hours, most of that in the last twelve hours of the day. That was a very steep drop, and no sailor could have doubted that something big and menacing was in the works. Weatherfaxes and high-seas weather forecasts were all very well, with their neat, coloured satellite pictures and detailed predictions, but they were unreliable in the Southern Ocean. Weatherfax information was a matter of supply and demand. No one went there; why waste resources on forecasting its weather? Both the pictures and the forecasts covered vast sea areas. The sailor could never be sure what would actually happen at any given moment in any particular square mile of sea. The barometer, that old harbinger of weather change could sometimes tell you more than modern instruments about what was ready to drop on your head.

At sea with low and falling glass, / Soundly sleeps the careless ass.

A diving mercury wouldn't, by itself, identify the centre of the low or tell you what else was on the way. But it was certainly a predictor of generalised misery, and its likely intensity. You knew that shit was about to happen, and right on top of you. A fast-falling glass was like the slow scream of a shell coming in on the soldier's position. Pain was inevitable.

Goss's premonitions were right. Because of *Aqua Quorum*'s location in relation to the dense low's centre, the wind went round to the south-west almost right away. And it rose like an elevator – forty, fifty, up to about sixty knots in three hours, as the tightly packed mass of the low swept over him. Conditions got so bad so quickly that he spent almost all that time continuously reducing the boat's sail area, just keeping on top of it. And then the boat was screaming and surfing at twenty-eight knots, under bare poles – no sail up, driven by wind pressure on the mast and rigging alone.

As the storm grew, things quickly became dangerous for Goss. The race receded into the background as he found himself in survival conditions, trying to cope with the increasingly dangerous seas. It was a classic development of Southern Ocean low-pressure-system waves. The northerly wave set, created by the storm as it first approached, was crossed by the south-westerly seas that ensued after the quick wind change, resulting in truly vicious breakers. He was knocked down three times and started to sustain damage. 'It was bloody hairy really. I nearly pitchpoled a couple of times, and a lot of water got in everywhere.'

In the middle of this mayhem, his computer beeped, and he noticed that a mayday had been registered somewhere, but he was too busy to check the position. He didn't recognise it as Dinelli's emergency beacon. Because the Frenchman had been a late entry, Goss didn't register the name of Dinelli's boat – he was used to dealing with the other skippers using only their first names. The distress signal could have come from anywhere off the Australian coast. It just didn't occur to him that it could be one of his fellow-racers. When he had a few seconds' breather, he began to look for a chart in the scrambled mess of his cabin so that he could see where the mayday was originating. Just then, his computer beeped again. It was Jeantot telling him that the mayday was Dinelli.

'I asked Pete, what was his condition,' said Jeantot. 'Because I knew he was sailing under bare poles and that conditions were very,

very bad. And I asked him, do you think it's possible for you to head back and help Dinelli.'

Goss faxed back immediately to tell Jeantot that he had problems, that he'd been knocked down, that things were a bit dicey. He wanted more information. What about de Radiguès? he asked Jeantot. Goss knew the Belgian's position, and that he was only three hours upwind of Dinelli. And he knew that trying to go upwind 160 miles in the storm would be very dangerous. He might not survive.

But right after he had sent the fax, he thought, Well, I've got to go back anyway. No matter what information Jeantot responded with.

'People have often asked about the decision to go back,' he said. 'But it was easy. It's just what you do when someone's in trouble. I suppose it was a decision made by tradition of the sea. Having made it, and thinking about it, I had to come to terms with the consequences of it. You know, you sit down for thirty seconds and think about your family and everything. But at the end of the day, for me, it's a simple process: you either stand by your morals and principles, or you don't.'

Goss was responding to the unwritten law of the sea, the sailor's prime directive: that aid must be rendered to anyone at sea who asks for help. Even if it cost a lot of money – supertankers or big freighters, for example, steaming days out of their way and incurring hundreds of thousands of dollars in extra operating costs, or delivery-delay penalties, to search for a single sailor in trouble on a small yacht. Even if it put the helper's own life in some jeopardy.

According to Jeantot, Goss then simply told him, 'I have no choice. I'll do it.'

Goss crawled out into *Aqua Quorum*'s cockpit and, in hurricane-force winds of seventy knots or so, in the enormous and confused seas, he hoisted a tiny storm jib. He needed some sail up in order to have any chance of beating back upwind. It took him a long time to get the sail up. It was only possible at all because, with his boat's speed, the apparent wind strength was only about fifty knots (Beaufort force 10, a full storm). Goss couldn't distinguish sea from air because of airborne spray and spume. The boat's motion was extremely dangerous – violent, quick, unpredictable. And the fear, which only an insane person would not feel, permeated everything. Sailing his boat to windward in this storm could subject it to stress that no designer would ever build into a hull, let alone into the more vulnerable mast and its supporting standing rigging. It was a real possibility – in fact, it might be more accurate to say that it was probable – that *Aqua Quorum* would not survive the punishment Goss was about to inflict on it.

The time had come. If any man has a moment in his life in which everything is in the balance, where death is as likely, or more likely, an outcome as life, Goss was entering such a moment now. It would be a prolonged moment, two days or more to get back to Dinelli's position if he got back at all. Goss's self-jeopardy would last a long time.

He put the helm over and turned his boat into the wind and waves. The apparent wind immediately increased the twenty-five-knot speed the boat had been travelling downwind, and Goss felt the full force of the hurricane he was turning into. It knocked *Aqua Quorum* down right away and pinned it there, flat on the water, the mast top across the waves, the guardrails under the surface. Goss thought, Shit, can we do anything in this at all?

For a minute or so, willing though he was to risk his life, it looked as if the wind just wouldn't let him. He might not be able to move the boat towards Dinelli.

Then, in a slight lull, the mast came up very slowly and grudgingly out of the water, and the boat began to move to windward. Goss found that he could sail at five or six knots about eighty degrees off the wind. Remember what this is like: the five- or six-storey buildings, some even higher; the toppling crests, two storeys or so high, with their tons of avalanching water moving at thirty miles an hour; the wind lulling in the troughs of the waves as the sea to windward blocks it, the boat losing speed and steerage way; the long, steep-angled climb to the wave top, the wind increasing in force as the boat climbs, until, on the crest, the full force of wind accelerates the boat down the fifty-foot slope of the wave into the next trough.

Goss couldn't open his eyes to windward and it was difficult to breathe. The noise was unrelenting and deafening, at a decibel level approaching that of a nearby jet engine. In gusts, the wind blew well into the range of hurricane force, and *Aqua Quorum* and her skipper felt the full strength of every knot of it.

As his boat made its slow, concussive progress, climbing one mountainous wave after another, Goss kept wondering if it would hold together. No boat, and no specialised Vendée Globe design in particular, could be counted on to withstand the shocking loads this violent motion was inflicting on its components. Other boats had begun to come apart in much less severe conditions than this.

In fact, not even *Aqua Quorum*'s designer was sure the boat would remain intact. When Adrian Thompson and his associates heard what Goss was up to, they were very apprehensive. 'To be honest,' said Thompson, 'we were sitting in the design office in a state of extreme nervousness and stress.'

None of the hull load calculations had been the result of exact science. As their boat confronted the Southern Ocean in its stormy spate, they could only hope they had been on the right side of the line when they drew up their specifications. This was the most extreme test imaginable, but, they hoped, not a test to destruction.

With his ingrained soldier's approach to danger, Goss broke his rescue mission into a series of distinct phases. Phase one was to survive the storm. Rescue phases would follow. It was a very grim night. He was knocked down every half-hour; there was lots of damage, gear everywhere. At one point, he was hurled across the cabin and landed hard on the elbow that had become infected early in the race. It had been bothering him ever since, in spite of his self-treatment with antibiotics. The punishment it took that night began a chain of complications that would test Goss in a different way later. In the meantime, he was being thrown around so much that he had to climb into his bunk and tie himself down.

Luckily, the next day, the worst of the low passed over. It was a shorter than usual shellacking because, for once, the boat was heading against the storm's track rather than running with it, and the system passed over quickly in the opposite direction. The wind dropped to forty-five knots. It seemed like a calm day to Goss; it was amazing what you could get used to, he thought. He began to repair damage to his mainsail and other gear. His aft watertight compartment was full of water, and he bailed it out.

Goss had no idea whether the French sailor was still alive. But he was sure that Dinelli's 'clock was ticking', and that it was just time that would save his life. Goss received hourly satellite weather information from Météo France via Jeantot, who spent a sleepless day and night himself. Another low-pressure system was on the way.

By nightfall, Goss finally heard from the Australian air force. It had been notified of Dinelli's distress signal, standard procedure, and one of its planes, operating at the very limit of its useful range, had homed in on Dinelli's EPIRB signals and found him. He was alive, the

Australians told Goss, and had managed to get into one of the two life-rafts they'd dropped to him just before his boat sank.

He hadn't felt afraid, Dinelli said, as he had stood on frozen feet in great pain, tethered to the deck of his sinking boat, ice-cold waves breaking over him.

'I think that this is in no way heroic. I think that when man faces an extreme situation, if he becomes afraid, he loses all his capacities. I stayed this way for thirty-six hours without eating or drinking. At the end, my eyes were burnt by the sun, the salt, the wind. My feet were freezing; I could not feel them any more.'

He hoped that the Australians or de Radiguès, or perhaps Goss, would get to him before he sank. But he knew it would be close. The Australian plane located him an hour before dark. Ten minutes after he tumbled into the life-raft, his boat sank.

'I knew I only had one hour left before dark, and if the aeroplane had not shown up, it was finished. I would be dead. Death was one hour away. I knew the limits.'

Dinelli was too cold. He knew he couldn't survive until a ship got to him. Everyone involved in the rescue knew that too. No ship was dispatched. Goss was Dinelli's only hope – his ferry away from death.

It took Goss the rest of that day and until midnight the next night to get to the general area of Dinelli's mayday. He was, after all, still beating to windward into the teeth of a strong gale (force 9 on the Beaufort scale), with big seas left over from the storm system. He searched for Dinelli's life-raft for the rest of the night, but the mayday position fix kept jumping, a quarter-mile or so every two hours. True to its wild form, the Southern Ocean flung the predicted front across the area, and in the deteriorating conditions, a quarter-mile might as well have been a hundred miles. Visibility was bad, with heavy rain. Goss would cover an area as best he could, then a different position would come through. So he'd search that area, and then another. With growing desperation, Goss hunted through the valleys and crests of the big seas for the tiny, low-lying, eight-foot diameter raft.

Goss would not have found Dinelli's raft on his own. At one point, he probably passed within a few hundred yards of it without seeing anything. He could look around him briefly when his boat was on the crest of a wave but the rest of the time, he could see only the walls of water hemming him in. He was exhausted; he hadn't slept for more than two days, he was battered and bruised and he was drained of nervous energy by the beat through the storm. He also hadn't eaten anything, or had much to drink. In the thirty hours it took him to get back close to Dinelli, he lost an estimated seven or eight pounds in weight.

The next morning, the Australian air force plane came back out. From its vantage point, it found Dinelli's tiny raft and dropped smoke flares to mark his location. Goss couldn't see even those in the driving spray and big waves. Finally, the plane flew over Dinelli and, as it did so, turned on its landing lights. Goss saw them and got a compass bearing. He was about three miles away from the raft. He thought there was a good chance that Dinelli was badly injured, or had died during the night from exposure and hypothermia. He worried it would be Dinelli's corpse that he would have to drag out of the raft. He wondered what he would tell the French sailor's family. Then the Australian plane radioed him with news: Dinelli had waved to them. He was still alive.

When Dinelli first saw Goss's boat, he thought it must be de Radiguès; he thought it very unlikely that Goss could make it back to be his rescuer. The pick-up went like clockwork; it was clinical, Goss said. He beat to windward of the raft, then turned downwind, and ran towards it. Two boat-lengths away, he rounded up into the wind again. He backed his little storm jib and drifted down beside the raft, the boat rolling violently, but creating a slightly calmer lee for the raft, smoothing the transfer. Stricken though he was, Dinelli came aboard *Aqua Quorum* with professional panache. He handed up his emergency beacons to Goss – so they wouldn't keep transmitting maydays. Then, to Goss's astonishment, and in a quintessential Gallic gesture, Dinelli handed him a bottle of champagne. He'd managed to hang on to it through everything, in a pocket of his survival suit. Goss hauled him aboard.

Dinelli's coolness masked his desperate condition.

'I got him on to the boat,' Goss said, 'and we were rolling violently and I thought, All right, I'll leave him there, he's fine, and put the storm jib about, and get the boat going downwind, and I can come back to him.'

But when Goss let go of Dinelli, the French sailor fell flat on his face, almost breaking his nose. He was as stiff as a board and could barely move by himself. Then Goss realised how far gone Dinelli was. He rolled him over on to his back. 'And all you could see was his eyes,' Goss said. 'And it was just . . . the emotion in the pair of eyes was just amazing really. He was trying to say, "Thank you, thank you"; he couldn't really talk. He was very cold.'

And the two men hugged each other.

As he was telling me this, Goss paused for a few seconds, staring out of *Aqua Quorum*'s hatch at the tarred and barnacled Southampton dock nearby. Six months afterwards, the emotion of the moment of rescue – when he returned Dinelli's life to him – was still strong.

Goss dragged Dinelli to the shelter of his cockpit spray hood and propped him on a little seat. He got the jib trimmed and turned the boat downwind under autopilot. Dinelli was so stiff that Goss had trouble bending his arms and legs to angle him in through the small companionway hatch and into the cabin. He stripped off Dinelli's sodden survival suit and got him into his own thermal suit and then into his sleeping bag. He radioed the Australian plane and asked them to tell Dinelli's family that he would survive, and that he could handle the situation – not that there was a lot they could do anyway.

'Raphaël is on board,' Goss told them. 'He is very cold and happy. He has no injuries. I have just given him a cup of tea. I have all his ARGOS on board. Cheers.'

In an exchange of national stereotypes, Goss replied to Dinelli's gift of champagne with his now-famous English cup of tea. It was a cyclist's bottle, to be precise – warm, very sugary tea that Dinelli could suck up through the nipple on the bottle. It was important to get his core body temperature up again.

'And then, I was absolutely knackered,' said Goss. 'Oh, completely shagged, and I thought, Great, I need an hour's sleep, and I'll get back to it.' But Dinelli was high on the adrenalin rush of his own, un-expected survival. He wouldn't shut up.

'He was bloody rabbiting away,' said Goss.

'Poor Pete,' Dinelli said. 'He had to look after me during the day, and then I kept him up all night talking.'

Goss couldn't speak French. But Dinelli had a sort of pidgin English and, because he was very bright, his language improved quickly. The two men drew pictures and went through charades. By the end of their ten-day sail to Hobart, Tasmania, where Goss would drop Dinelli off, they were having deep conversations.

Dinelli couldn't feel his hands or feet, and long strips of skin began to peel off the frostbitten limbs. For five days, he was a helpless invalid. Goss had to lift him on to the toilet bucket and hold him there, and feed him every four hours; he gave him muscle relaxants and pain medication. By the time they arrived in Hobart, Dinelli was, shakily, back on his feet. He would make a complete recovery

For Goss and Dinelli, it was the beginning of a profound friendship. It was ironic, Goss said. You start off to do a sail around the world by yourself, and you come back with a particularly good friend. It was a lucky situation all around.

'I mean, he could have been an arsehole, couldn't he? But he's a wonderful guy. We would have become good friends after the race. But something like that is quite an intense experience, a bit of a catalyst. We're like brothers now. We'll be friends for the rest of our lives.'

In August 1997, Goss was best man at Dinelli's wedding. In October of that year, they sailed together in a transatlantic race for two-person crews.

Philippe Jeantot had been around the sailing block himself more than a few times. Dinelli's rescue was a miracle, he said.

Of Goss's decision, he added: 'I can tell you that he had very, very, very bad weather, and it was very courageous for him to go against the wind and to go back. He was going downwind under bare poles, and I asked him to beat back with some sails on. He is a very, very brave man.' Not everyone in the race could have done what Goss had done, Jeantot implied. Jeantot knew the Southern Ocean. He'd been there and had no difficulty imagining what it must have been like for Goss.

Jeantot emphasised his admiration when he asked the French government to award Goss the *Légion d'honneur*. President Jacques Chirac pinned it on Goss's chest a few months after the race ended. The English sailor joined Eric Tabarly as a recipient of France's highest civilian honour.

The professional sailors of the Vendée Globe try to control the risks of Southern Ocean storms and other hazards of the race through preparation and experience. Most of them are the sort of people who, they discover over time, have the capacity to withstand the stresses these risks produce. Their performance leads them to reasonably expect that they can master the perils the race will inevitably present. But this confidence has its limits. Familiarity with the sea increases sailors' expectations that they can handle bad weather, or other dangers, and survive. But experience also teaches that catastrophe is a constant, unforeseeable and unpreventable possibility. The chance explosion of disaster or death could hit anytime – the wave with your name on it, the growler likewise tattooed, the roving sea-junk, the last slip and fall of your life.

Even very experienced single-handed sailors on superbly designed, built and prepared boats can't deny the ocean its due, if chance and brute force combine to take it. I thought that my wife and I had got to the Virgin Islands on our thirty-one-footer only by the benign grace of the sea – a considerable overestimation of the danger in that part of the ocean at that time of year. But in the Southern Ocean, it's always an appropriate evaluation to say, 'We got by it that time.' Often, as with Autissier, Bullimore, Dubois, Dinelli, Roufs, and a score of other sailors in previous races, the single-hander doesn't get by it. Knox-Johnston commented on the silly talk or writing he sometimes came across about sailors 'conquering the sea'. 'No one ever does that,' he said. 'It's always left on the battlefield; you're not. You might escape unscathed, but you never conquer it.'

Apart from this quota of irreducible luck, the Vendée Globe sailors rely on skills that are almost beyond the comprehension of the average sailor. Roufs's friend Philippe Ouhlen tried to make me understand the level these people sail at. 'These are guys who can go downwind in thirty knots of wind, surfing on twenty-foot seas, carrying a spinnaker and full mainsail. And in those conditions, they'll gybe the boat, with the spinnaker – at night, in the dark, alone!'

The spinnaker is the big, lightweight, pot-bellied sail that's generally used for downwind sailing. In coffee table-book photographs of yachts, the spinnakers are the huge, multicoloured, parachute-like sails billowing out ahead of the boats as they run before the wind or broad reach with the wind blowing across the quarter. A spinnaker can also be used in light conditions for beam reaching (wind blowing across the boat's beam), and a determined racer may use it, as Ouhlen described, to run downwind in relatively heavy conditions – even though it's traditionally a light-weather sail.

The spinnaker is the most unwieldy, unruly and difficult sail to manage. It's often flown attached to a spinnaker pole, a spar (the general term for mast, boom and poles) in its own right, which can seriously injure or kill a clumsy or unwary sailor if it's not properly handled. Instead of one line controlling a poled-out spinnaker – a sheet – it has four: a sheet, a guy, an uphaul and a downhaul. Spinnakers are usually flown and handled by three or four members of a racing crew. On many of the Vendée Globe or BOC racers, the lone skippers use a simpler arrangement. One corner of the triangular sail is attached directly to the boat's bow eliminating the heavy pole and its control lines.

The gybe is one of the most technically difficult, and dangerous, manoeuvres on a sailboat. Controlling a gybe is particularly tricky in heavy wind and seas, especially if a poled-out spinnaker is involved. The pole must be disconnected from one corner of the wind-distended sail and reconnected to the other corner, as the sail is brought from one side of the bow to the other; the mainsail and the heavy boom to which it's attached must be brought simultaneously from one side of the boat to the other in a tightly controlled movement. The sailor must make a careful course adjustment, so that the wind will carry the sails across. An unintentional, or uncontrolled, gybe in strong wind can damage rigging or even tear the mast out if the boom is allowed to slam from one side of the boat to the other. The boom can seriously injure or kill a sailor if it hits him. This is a frequent accident on racing boats. The spinnaker can get tangled and torn to shreds in a moment. The single-hander must meticulously plan the whole operation – which lines get connected and disconnected in which order; when the sailor must dash back forty or fifty feet to the cockpit to adjust the course and handle the mainsail sheet. There are a score or so separate actions. A gybe is easier if the spinnaker is flown without a pole. The skipper can then use a 'sock' or 'snuffer', a bag attached to the head of the sail. As the bag is hauled down, it gathers up the sail which ends up neatly stuffed into it. Gybing with a sock involves snuffing the spinnaker and then rehoisting it after the boat has been put into its new tack. With or without a pole, however, one mistake, or a step out of sequence, can be disastrous.

Doing all this in the dark obviously adds a little heat to the whole routine. The procedure is analagous to a pilot landing a warplane on the deck of an aircraft carrier at night in rough weather, or a driver driving a Formula One racing course in the rain, or a mountain climber negotiating a technically difficult section at very high altitude (the Hillary Step, just below the summit of Mount Everest, for example). Gybing a spinnaker in the conditions Ouhlen describes really is the sailing equivalent of rocket science.

I've always regarded spinnakers with the cruising sailor's distaste – they're nasty, brutish sails that make you sweat, worry and pay constant attention. But I have grudgingly participated in wrestling with them on racing boats I've crewed on – often enough to be certain that the Vendée Globe sailors are in a completely different spinnaker bracket from me. And it's one I don't want to enter; in fact, never could. It's an example of the sometimes profound difference between the amateur and the expert professional in any sport.

The Vendée Globe sailors could also control risk and reduce danger with new and elegant technology. The various electronic and satellite-linked communications devices carried by each boat tethered the distant sailors to the web of faxes, e-mail, radio and telephones. Although physically remote, the sailors in the Southern Ocean remained intangibly intimate with home. The Vendée Globe racers were like spaceships compared with the Golden Globe boats. The sixty-footers varied a little in the kind of high-tech instruments they carried, but most had a large complement of gadgets. These typically included a single-sideband, long-range radio and two VHF short-range radios for voice communication (one hand-held so that it would work if the VHF antenna was destroyed). Some skippers had a more sophisticated satellite phone – on *Géodis*, for example, Auguin used a land-mobile Inmarsat M terminal, which provided clear and reliable voice communication throughout the race. Weatherfaxes were the main source of weather and wave-height information. In the areas of the Southern Ocean where weatherfax information was unreliable or non-existent, real-time satellite pictures of weather systems could be had from a Dartcom weather satellite receiver. Once these pictures were routed through computer software, the skipper could construct a reasonably accurate forecast. Text communication – e-mail and faxes – was carried by an Inmarsat C satellite system, which also transmitted Météo France one- to five-day weather forecasts.

Navigation was completely electronic – although each boat had to carry a sextant as a back-up – and centered on a global positioning system (GPS) position fixer. The GPS receives an almost constant stream of simultaneous signals from several of almost a hundred geostationary satellites, and adjusts its readings to the boat's motion second by second. It is accurate to within less than one hundred yards. (In comparison, a position derived from sextant sights from the bouncing deck of a small boat is a real achievement if it's accurate to less than five miles.) The device also gives constant data about the boat's actual course and speed, thus providing inferential information about the effects of leeway or currents on its progress.

All Vendée Globe and BOC boats are required to have radar, with its largely theoretical protection against collision with ice. The boats also carry a set of free-standing instruments that show boat speed, course, wind speed and angle, and water depth. The hub of this whole busy web is a bolted-down laptop computer which handles the information from Inmarsat C, the GPS and the various individual instruments. It may also be loaded with electronic charts (the boats carry the traditional paper ones as well), which display a picture of the boat's location and movement derived from the stream of data it's receiving.

Some of the skippers had weather-routeing software. Auguin, for example, used a sophisticated program called MaxSea, which he ran on his Mac laptop. MaxSea linked up to the GPS so that positions could be updated on the system's electronic charts. The program also recorded boat speed in relation to apparent wind velocity and direction. With all this and data on forecasted wind from Météo France wind-vector charts, MaxSea could derive an optimum course for the boat to steer. The race rules forbade routeing advice from shore-based experts but the skippers were allowed to use this powerful software, so long as they alone were its confidants and interpreters.

In parts of the Southern Ocean, boats experience big magnetic variations that play havoc with conventional compasses. These aren't essential for navigation any more, but they are needed to run the autopilots. Some boats carried a gyrocompass, which is immune to magnetic influence. Skippers who couldn't afford this very expensive device had to sacrifice sleep to hand-steer or keep a constant eye on their autopilots whenever they were sailing through areas of magnetic anomaly.

All of this communications and navigational equipment is a lot to keep track of and fiddle around with each day. No wonder the Vendée Globe skippers spent the single largest chunk of daily time at their chart tables – often more time than they spent sleeping in a typical twenty-four-hour period.

Each boat had to carry three of the older ARGOS EPIRBs which, when activated in alarm mode, sent out signals to the ARGOS system's three polar-orbiting satellites. One, attached to the stern rail, acted as a continuous position indicator. The two other ARGOS on board were stored below, and the skipper could also activate them in alarm mode if necessary. One of the three ARGOS had to be equipped with a GPS unit as well. The skippers were supposed to activate this unit when they rounded the obligatory race marks: Cape Horn or the two waypoint latitude-longitude positions in the southern Pacific, for example. The GPS attachment, which used the whole panoply of the global positioning satellite network, provided a much more accurate fix than a simple ARGOS using that system's three satellites.

Each boat in the race also had to have one of the newer SARSAT 406 EPIRBs, the number referring to the megahertz frequency on which the digitally coded identification signal was broadcast. It can take up to an hour before the satellites are able to transmit the signal to a search-and-rescue centre, although it's usually much quicker than that. (Signals from the later-generation Inmarsat E transmitters, which first came on the market in early 1997, are received by the centres within two minutes. More recently, GPIRBs incorporating GPS technology improve accuracy to within two or three metres.)

The Vendée Globe skippers were obliged by the rules to carry four EPIRBs, and some of them had five. Redundancy was especially beautiful in the case of these little devices: the more the merrier.

Some part of these complex systems failed at one time or another on most of the boats – Laurent's radar, Goss's and Chabaud's radios, de Radiguès's whole electrical system. The equipment could be fragile, depending on sensitive chips and circuits withstanding damp, cold and physical shocks, and on the continuing health of the older technology in generators, wiring, and batteries. By and large, how-ever, enough communications gear kept working so that, most of the time, the skippers could keep talking, e-mailing and getting weatherfaxes. And of course, at the back of each skipper's mind was the knowledge that if the worst happened, and they had the chance to activate an EPIRB, the world would at least know where they were. Depending on who or what was nearby, they would have a fighting chance of getting out of it alive.

But if all this sophisticated gear was a shield against danger, it could also be a sword against each sailor's throat. Because they could stay in contact with the world and call on its search-and-rescue resources when they needed them, the sailors did things they might not have done otherwise. The reckless swings deep into the higher latitudes of the fifties, sailing fast through the drift-ice, cutting the mileage to the Horn – these were all recent Southern Ocean tactics, adopted in the various BOC and Vendée Globe races. It takes only one sailor's decision to go south to stimulate the others' competitive ardour. If one goes, many follow. Indeed, the very existence of the extreme, non-stop, no-help Vendée Globe, revived twenty years after the Golden Globe race, probably owed a great deal to the existence of EPIRBs and the other shiny new stay-in-touch gizmos. At the very least, the nature of the race – its flat-out, round-the-buoys intensity – was partly a result of the safety net, fragile though it was in the Southern Ocean, provided by the new communications and emergency equipment.

Knox-Johnston speculated that you could probably solve the whole problem of the Vendée Globe sailors' assuming excessive risks by taking away their EPIRBs. I don't think that the skippers would be more cautious; the races are too competitive. They'll push their surfboards to the limit in the Southern Ocean storms and waves, no matter what. They are prepared to court death to win. Besides, there are those long stretches of the Southern Ocean where you are always a boat too far, too distant from the more traditional technology – ships and planes – to be reached.

EPIRBs trigger another kind of paradox as well. Their state-of-the-art communication relies on one of the most sophisticated kinds of technology – satellite reception and transmission of radio signals – the unseen pulses of energy relayed by a type of spaceship rocketed into orbit. But once distress signals have been passed along to potential rescuers, the technology suddenly becomes much more primitive. The real live human crews of planes and vessels of one kind or another launch out into the far reaches of the earth's last great wilderness, almost to the end of their endurance or range, to try the hard, crude job of dragging live or dead bodies out of the sea.

Things are so different now from the time of Knox-Johnston's heroic endurance in the Golden Globe, just thirty years ago. He navigated with equipment hardly different from that of Captain Cook two hundred years earlier: a chronometer that kept Greenwich Mean Time for longitude calculations, and a sextant that operated on the Ptolemaic principle that the earth was the centre of the heavens. The sextant measured the altitude of celestial objects, usually the sun or selected stars, and their angular distances from the sailor's position on the earth's surface. Together with the essential numerical information contained in the Nautical Almanac and the sight reduction tables (which reduced complex calculations to simple arithmetic), these were all that Knox-Johnston or Moitessier had to work with. Although Knox-Johnston had an unreliable, long-range radio transmitter, Moitessier did not, and neither man had any kind of emergency beacon. EPIRBs were still in the future. When they entered the Southern Ocean, they knew that they were profoundly alone. If they couldn't reckon their course, make repairs or survive on their own, they were done for.

The ethos of complete self-reliance which was adopted by these sailors owed a lot to necessity as well. If you went to sea, especially to a remote, godforsaken sea, you had to be completely self-sufficient. This unavoidable condition of ocean sailing was stated most uncompromisingly by the ex-cockleshell commando Blondie Hasler, whose half-crown bet with Chichester began single-handed ocean racing. Solo sailors who got into trouble had no right asking for help, no matter where they were. Having voluntarily assumed the risk, they were morally bound to accept the consequences. They should, said Hasler, 'drown like gentlemen.'

Knox-Johnston had a creed that was not much different: the Lord helps those who help themselves. *You* had to hand, reef and steer as best you possibly could. That was it. You could never count on help, and in the Southern Ocean, you could count only on not getting help. This was unavoidably true for Moitessier as well. He embraced the most conservative tactics possible in the Southern Ocean. He was obliged to go south into the forties to clear Tasmania and New Zealand, and couldn't avoid the swing south to almost sixty degrees to round the Horn, but for the rest of his high-latitude passage, he hugged the fortieth parallel to try to avoid ice and bad weather. Moitessier's prudence extended to the most mundane aspects of his voyage. He described how, twice each day, he would rub cream into his hands, examine them closely and tend to them immediately if they were strained or cut – sea-water cuts quickly develop nasty infections. During his long months alone south of the three capes, Moitessier knew that his hands were his essential tools for survival. No one could help him if they failed him. He pampered them as if they were a pianist's supple, indispensable conduit of music.

Four days into the new year, the string of Vendée Globe boats stretched out to more than five thousand miles. Day by day, Auguin increased his lead over Roufs and was now sixteen hundred miles ahead of the Canadian and just nine hundred miles from the Horn, his 'gate to the exit from hell'. He'd had it with the cold, the wind, the stress. Then something strange happened to the weather. Auguin and the next four boats – Roufs, Thiercelin, Laurent and de Broc – found themselves in an unusual weather system, two thousand miles across, with light wind, frequent squalls and snow. In the changeable conditions, the sailors had to constantly reef the sails, then shake out the reefs, trim the sheets and adjust the course. Auguin had an hour's sleep in twenty-four. Laurent complained that Météo France had predicted a day of light winds, but the calmer conditions had unaccountably stretched out to three days. It was a break from gales and big waves, but it wasn't getting them out of the Southern Ocean, and more of the usual lows were on the way – boats farther back were getting them. As Knox-Johnston had said, waiting for it was almost as bad as getting it. For once, the Southern Ocean weather wasn't more or less uniform for the whole fleet. Dumont, for example, three thousand miles back, was going through an average forty-knot gale with heavier squalls. Nothing special. Chabaud, four thousand miles behind Auguin, was in the middle of sixty-knot wind.

At the back of the fleet, Bullimore and Dubois, sailing within forty miles of each other, had a strong north-west gale on their hands. More ominously, however, the weather forecast for their area seemed to be picking up the early signs of what meteorologists call a 'bomb' – a very fast-developing and intense low – which would soon overtake them. They could expect a high-latitude depression, typical in its structure, but with more explosive winds than usual and a very abrupt wind shift from west to south-west as the centre tracked by. This wasn't just another depression. This was trouble.

And indeed, the rescue of Dinelli quickly became merely the opening act in the Vendée Globe Christmas drama. Goss was still sailing the lucky survivor to Hobart when the beacons went off again.

Bullimore's boat flipped when its keel suddenly broke off. Not even a preliminary broach. *Exide Challenger* just rolled over as it surfed down a wave, Bullimore rolling with it. No mug of tea left, but finishing his cigarette, thinking out what to do next. Then the window smashed by the boom, the boat instantly flooding, the cabin contents sucked out into the sea. Bullimore diving down and through the companionway hatch to try to cut away his life-raft. The hatch slamming shut, chopping off his finger. Floating one of his ARGOS beacons out of the broken window through the swirling wreckage of rigging and spars, up to what he hoped was the surface. Climbing up on to his little shelf, half in, half out of the freezing water. Waiting for whatever might happen: most likely death.

Almost simultaneously, the dismasted Dubois rolling over again and staying that way. After two hours, climbing out through the transom hatch, unable to reach his 406 EPIRB, and setting off two of his ARGOS beacons, lashing them to his body the way mountain-climbers do, scrambling up the steep, slick slope of the hull to cling to one of the twin rudders. Getting washed off into the sea. Somehow managing to clamber back on to the hull again, exposed to the full force of bitterly cold waves and sub-zero wind-chill. Waiting, like Bullimore.

Jeantot and the regional search-and-rescue operational centre in Brittany – CROSS in the French acronym – passed along to the Australians the job of responding to the distress calls. These may-days, like Dinelli's, were their bailiwick. This time, no other racers were within striking distance of either Bullimore or Dubois. Running at the rear of the Vendée Globe fleet because of their forced port calls, they were particularly isolated. The closest sailor was Chabaud, more than twelve hundred miles downwind to the east. It was impossible for her to get back. Only the Australians had any chance of rescuing the two men, assuming they were still alive. The Australian maritime rescue-coordination centre in Canberra asked the air force and navy to help. An air force P-3 Orion long-distance search-and-rescue plane was dispatched right away, followed the next day by a frigate, the *Adelaide*.

Even this fast warship would take four days to reach the wounded boats – assuming that the weather would allow it to negotiate its Southern Ocean passage at top cruising speed. Assuming, too, that it didn't run into trouble itself in the strong winds and big waves. Like most modern warships, it was a lightly built aluminium vessel, and its three-eighths-inch-thick hull had finite wave-impact resistance. Large amounts of ice had been reported around fifty-two degrees south, not far from the yachts' positions. The *Adelaide* was as vulnerable to ice damage as the Vendée Globe boats were. It wasn't designed to surf on Southern Ocean combers either – no one had complete confidence in its handling abilities in heavy southern weather. It would need to be refuelled as well, to have any chance of getting to the ARGOS positions at top speed, manoeuvre there and get back again. A naval tanker was authorised to sail from Fremantle and rendezvous with the *Adelaide* on its way back to port. Bullimore and Dubois had been sailing at fifty-one degrees latitude. They were considerably closer to Antarctica than Australia. No one had conducted a rescue this far from land before, and this was as dicey an operation as you could get – a quick thrust through stormy seas towards Antarctica in a race against the next big low already showing up on the weather charts.

As for the planes, the Orions could fly out that far and back if they stayed no more than three hours at the scene, if the fuel calculations were correct and if there were no unforeseen head winds or mechanical problems. The usual operational requirement that the planes land with at least enough fuel for forty-five minutes' flying was waived. They would be allowed to reduce their grace period to just fifteen minutes. This is a very fine margin. The operation would risk the planes and the ship, and would put their men in jeopardy too.

Following standard procedure, the rescue centre put out a call for commercial ships in the area. A tanker responded, the only vessel in that remote sea. The *Sanko Phoenix* was more than seven hundred miles from the mayday positions – half the distance to Fremantle, where the *Adelaide* was coming from. But the heavily loaded ship could do only eleven knots and, if the weather didn't deteriorate further, would take at least two and a half days to reach the search area. The ninety-thousand-ton ship's diversion towards the two ten-ton yachts and back to its course again afterwards would cost its owners close to $100,000. But the unwritten law of the sea is compelling. The tanker's master responded to the Australian request right away, and turned towards the ARGOS positions.

The first Orion to fly out on the morning of 5 January was lucky. Flying three hundred feet above the five-storey waves in a raging seventy-knot wind, it found Dubois's boat in spite of the stale position information from the old polar-orbiting ARGOS satellites. The plane's crew could make out Dubois, still perched on the bottom of his boat, its keel intact, with one arm around a rudder, frantically waving. As it turned out, apprehensions about the righting ability of the Vendée Globe designs hadn't been misplaced. In spite of its keel's weight, Dubois's boat had remained upside down for half a day and seemed comfortably stable.

The Orion managed to drop two life-rafts into the water close to Dubois. Under the circumstances – with storm-force wind and seas, allowing for the plane's airspeed and the boat's drift – this was a difficult job. Judging the long, flying parabolic curve of the rafts from the plane's belly to the water's surface was purely a matter of innate hominid hand-eye expertise – like the long forward pass or the looping three-pointer into the basket. Low on fuel, the Orion immediately had to climb away from the Frenchman and head back. As the plane disappeared, Dubois, frozen and desperate, launched himself from his boat into the sea to swim the hundred yards to the rafts, like an untethered astronaut stepping away from his ship into the void of space. It was the swim of his life. As he tried to climb into one of the rafts, a wave flipped it over. He was too far from his boat to be able to swim back to it. Once again, he thought he was about to die. He felt the peculiar sadness and regret of a man dying too soon. But he didn't panic. Eventually, he managed to drag himself into the damaged and slowly deflating life-raft, where he lay in a pool of water enduring the bitter cold.

An hour later, a second Orion arrived, homing in on the signal from a buoy dropped by the first plane. This Orion dropped another raft almost on top of Dubois. He was finally able to crawl into a functioning life-raft with some emergency food and water stowed inside, sheltered from the -30°C wind-chill, mostly out of the freezing water – though temporarily, as it happened. Within an hour, the raft was capsized by a wave and Dubois was thrown back into the sea. With the gale still blowing between force 9 and 10, up to fifty-five knots, he somehow got it turned right side up again and climbed back in.

The Orion turned to search for Bullimore's boat. It was close to nightfall and no more planes would come out until the next day. Visibility was a half-mile or so, the ceiling less than three hundred feet, the wind still blowing at fifty to sixty knots. With position information from the ARGOS satellites coming in slowly, the crew reverted to a standard visual-search pattern. Against all odds – everyone's luck was flowing freely on this rescue operation – the plane found Exide Challenger, upside down, low in the water, without its keel, surrounded by bits and pieces of its rigging and masts, no signs of life on board. It was impossible to tell whether Bullimore was dead or alive inside the white, fragile-looking, over-turned hull, or if he'd drifted away in his life-raft. At the end of its on-site fuel limit, the Orion could do nothing else. In the Southern Ocean dusk, the storm still howling, it turned back towards land.

Bullimore was still alive. He was cold, nine-fingered, with no idea if his ARGOS beacons had worked or if a rescue was under way. The world would know he was in some sort of a jam because his ARGOS transponder would have stopped beeping his position when he capsized. But if his emergency signals hadn't been received, Jeantot might not start a search for some time. He might ascribe the loss of signal to electrical problems, or to a malfunction that Bullimore was unaware of. If his emergency beacons hadn't worked, if there was no recent position, what rescuers would ever find him in this wilderness? Add his name to the list of disappearances without explanation. But in the faint daytime glow of light through the swirling waves – not enough to see much of anything by, but encouraging nevertheless – and in the absolute blackness of the Southern Ocean night, he was going to hang on.

'Tough as old bootlaces,' he said. 'A bit unusual; things don't rattle me.' Still going through the pluses and minuses of his various survival plans. At fifty-seven years old, far from finished.

The waves poured in and out of the cabin; 'It was like a washing machine from hell.' In places, when he stood up, the water reached his neck. Occasionally it washed right over his head. The cold made his eyeballs hurt. Waves continued to break up the inside the cabin – the chart table, his food, the instruments, the sextant, pieces of his berth, all sucked out through the hole of the big broken cabin window. The water swirling in and out set up a kind of siphon effect, which pumped air in and out of the boat with each roll or pitch. 'The wind was like a bloody blizzard in the boat'.

On top of everything else, Bullimore had to deal with the effects of wind-chill inside his shattered cabin.

He found and ate a salty-tasting chocolate bar. Only a few ounces of fresh water survived the roll-over, but he salvaged his hand-desalinating pump. One thousand strokes made one cup of drinkable water. He pumped away for hours with the end of the hose in his mouth, sucking out the precious water drop by drop.

His life-raft was still intact, but was tied down on the floor of the inverted cockpit. He dived down into the frigid water a dozen times to try to free it. For hours after each dive, his head ached with the cold. He wanted to drag the raft into the cabin and prepare it for launching from there. He thought he could push it out through the cabin window on a line, then follow the line himself, up to the surface, where he could inflate the raft. Because there was no guarantee that *Exide Challenger* would stay afloat, getting the raft ready in case it didn't was one of his survival plans. But it wouldn't budge: the raft was too buoyant for him to manhandle down and through the companionway hatch.

Finally, in the austral summer morning of 9 January, four and a half days after his capsize, the *Adelaide* reached Bullimore's boat. He was lying on his shelf, by now frostbitten, hypothermic, almost in shock, but alive. He heard a chugging noise, and then a loud banging on the hull. It was the warship's inflatable. One of the crewmen was hitting the resonant carbon fibre with the blunt side of an axe. They thought they would have to chop a hole in the hull to get at Bullimore, alive or dead. If he was there at all; if he hadn't drifted away in his life-raft.

'By then, I'm down in the water, aren't I. I'm down like a rocket. I've got my ear against the side of the hull.'

Bullimore wanted to be sure there was someone there before he tried to dive down through his hatch and up to the surface. If he was hallucinating and there wasn't anyone there, he wouldn't be able to get back into the boat again. He would be swimming alone in the Southern Ocean with nowhere to go. Then he was sure he heard people talking in English. He shouted that he was there, took a deep breath and dived – down through the hatch into the cockpit, mustering all his strength against the bulk and buoyancy of his survival suit and the drag of his seaboots to dive down even farther below the coamings, through the lifelines, then finally, up through the rat's nest of lines and pieces of mast and boat, his lungs barely holding, arms and legs tangling and then untangling in the web of wreckage.

Then: pop! He was on the surface. Sitting right in front of him was the *Adelaide*. He had never, as the saying goes, seen anything so beautiful in his life. He felt a surge of relief; the tension drained away immediately. Then he felt euphoria, elation, joy. He realised how surprised he was that he would live.

The inflatable was on the other side of his boat from where he surfaced, its crew deliberating about how to chop a hole in the tough hull material. At first they didn't see Bullimore desperately treading water. Then, over the top of the overturned hull, they did see him. A navy diver got to him first, wrapping his arms around him, lips against his ear: 'I've got you; you'll be OK.'

In the inflatable, the crewmen wrapped him in a foil heat blanket and hugged him. His head was cradled in a lap. He waved the stub of his severed finger at them, worried that someone might try to grab his hand.

'You'll be all right, mate. You'll be all right!'

Bullimore heard the Australian accents, so much like his own, on the far side of the earth from England. An inheritance of the British empire of the sea. They lifted the whole inflatable out of the sea and on to the ship's deck with tackles, rather than trying to get Bullimore up a ladder. On deck, to Bullimore's astonishment, Dubois stepped forward, grabbed his hand and shook it. Bullimore, of course, knew nothing about the Frenchman's ordeal. The *Adelaide*'s Seahawk helicopter had finally been able to fly when the wind dropped to below forty knots. It had picked Dubois out of his life-raft a few hours earlier.

The weather forecast predicted another imminent depression: a large system lying to the south-west, the whole mess moving fast towards them at forty knots. They were lucky to have found the sailors so quickly: the *Adelaide* did not have enough fuel to ride out a storm, and then conduct a sea search and rescue. Within hours, the north-west wind had risen to storm force once again, the seas, still big, began to build higher. By evening, when the front passed by, the wind, following its custom, would back to the west and then the south-west, and blow even harder. As the warship turned north for port, the abandoned Vendée Globe boats drifted away on the wild Southern Ocean rollers.

A brave man struggling with adversity is a spectacle for the gods. Seneca, the philosopher of stoicism, was talking about how people react to the unavoidable, unsought misfortune and suffering that life brings. Every man a Job. The gods supposedly watch our passive endurance with their usual lofty and detached curiosity. But what about the adversity that humans bring upon themselves? When we put our own necks in the wringer? Every man or woman a hero, looking for adventure, seeking out risk and mastering it. Surely that interests the gods as well, provokes in them admiration for our boldness and ingenuity. If we succeed, doesn't that mean that we are blessed?

If there are no gods, or if they don't care what we do, then we can make a secular conclusion. The four men who had been part of the Vendée Globe Christmas miracles – Dinelli, Goss, Dubois, Bullimore – had responded well to the challenge of their lives. The profound risks involved in sailing the Southern Ocean could not have been more vividly demonstrated. But they had come through all right; they'd kept their nerve, and survived.

9

A Zone Unknown

The 'call to adventure' . . . signifies that destiny has summoned the hero and transferred his spiritual center of gravity from within the pale of his society to a zone unknown. This fateful region of both treasure and danger may be variously represented . . . but it is always a place of strangely fluid and polymorphous beings, unimaginable torments, super-human deeds, and impossible delight.

– Joseph Campbell, *The Hero with a Thousand Faces*

I was a warrior in danger.

– Antoine de Saint-Exupéry, *Wind, Sand and Stars*

I T IS interesting to contemplate what combination of compulsions and desires drives these sailors to the Southern Ocean. The 1994–95 BOC is an excellent test case. In that single-handed, round-the-world race in four stages, Nigel Rowe, an urbane Englishman, tired of organising the race for his employer, British Oxygen, joined in the fun for once. He discovered soon enough that the professional racers, the sailors who made a living from it and who dominated the race standings, were playing in a different game with different rules.

Rowe was near the back of the fleet in his forty-eight-foot boat, trying to deal with a sixty-knot Southern Ocean storm. As he looked out of his companionway at the huge waves, amid the terrible, deafening, 'banshee scream of wind' in the boat's rigging, he was gripped by profound fear. In the fierce cold, he was sweating. He couldn't breathe.

'Some great fist was squeezing my stomach with an iron grip . . . Dear God, save us all from this hell. What had begun as a dream, to sail alone around the world, had become a living nightmare.'

Ahead of him, the race leaders were going through the same sorts of conditions – sixty-knot wind with snow squalls – but handling them differently, with an almost psychotic disdain for safety. Most of these boats had damaged sails and broken gear, but not because of carelessness or lack of skill, Rowe noted. It was their 'relentless quest around the clock for that extra fraction of a knot of boat speed, shaving margins for error to the finest limit they knew, that put them in a league of their own'. He was in awe of them.

The American Steve Pettengill, who was sailing one of the big, state-of-the-art sixty-footers in the same race, sometimes wore a T-shirt with the words 'If you're not on the edge, you're taking up too much space.' The professional sailors in the BOC, like the Vendée Globe racers, often take the sorts of chances more appropriate to sailboat races on lakes or shoreside bays, a few miles from shelter or rescue. They drive themselves and their boats as close as possible to the breaking-point of human and machine components – into that narrow space between control and barely averted disaster. At one point in the storm that terrified Nigel Rowe, Pettengill, the most successful American single-handed racer, was knocked down, the boat's cabin so deeply submerged that his ears popped.

The wryly laconic Australian David Adams, with his fifty-footer, *True Blue*, was sailing right up with the big racers, manoeuvring his boat like a huge dinghy.

'I'm absolutely stuffed,' he reported to race headquarters. 'Been twenty-four hours at the wheel in 40 to 60 knots. Had four knockdowns, with the mast in the water. Once we went down a wave like that, on our ears. It's just survival out here, not racing.'

He later wrote: 'In a huge storm when you're running on sheer adrenalin, it's enough to get through the next half-hour alive and bugger the race.'

Adams was actually washed overboard at one point. He was wearing a harness and stayed attached to the boat, but he got back on board again only with considerable difficulty.

His arch-competitor (and good friend) in class two was the Italian Giovanni Soldini. They'd been racing neck and neck, often in sight of each other, since near the beginning of the race. But it seemed that there were degrees of insanity even on the edge. Soldini refused to match his rival in everything.

'Adams! What a shit!' he faxed. 'He got one hundred miles ahead yesterday . . . but he's mad. He never stops steering outside. It's a crazy risk. I won't do it. I don't want to kill myself.'

Adams hadn't necessarily stayed in the cockpit to get ahead – his motivation was even more basic.

'People often asked how I managed to hand-steer for hours and even days through these storms,' Adams wrote. 'Fear is a great motivator. I thought if I stopped steering I would die. Simple as that. So I kept steering.'

And sailing: Adams has competed in several long-distance ocean races since the BOC. The rescued Vendée Globe sailors too will keep sailing. Dinelli said he hadn't been afraid as he waited on his sinking boat. Maybe so. But he later paid the price, and he's still paying it. 'In my head, these images are terrible, very hard. At night I have nightmares.'

At one point, as he told me about his ordeal, Dinelli abruptly stopped talking, stood up and walked over to the door of the house. He opened it and looked out over the road and the nearby neat, hedge-rowed fields of the Vendée towards the sea in the hazy distance. After a minute or so, collected again, he came back to his chair and resumed the story.

Later, when he went out for a while to pick up some visiting English sailing friends, his future wife Virginie told me that Raphaël had been fortunate in having had the opportunity to deal with the trauma of his sinking. It was a matter of getting back on the horse right away. After the rescue, Goss set course for Tasmania, more than two thousand miles away. They were overtaken by the heavy weather of yet another frontal system almost right away; Dinelli, still in shock and severely hypothermic, was fearful and at times almost panicky in the too-familiar din and clamour of a sixty-footer in a storm. Had he escaped by the skin of his teeth only to delay his inevitable death at sea? Day by day, as the bad weather continued and Dinelli regained health, his fear diminished. By the time *Aqua Quorum* reached Hobart ten days later, he had completely recovered his emotional poise. But without that immediate experience of bad weather, Virginie believed, he would have found it very difficult to go sailing again. Dinelli will, though. When we spoke, he was beginning his campaign to find a sponsor for the next Vendée Globe in the year 2000. He will almost certainly find the money – he's a high-profile media star in France now.

The title of Dubois's book about his miraculous survival is *J'y retournerai* ('I Will Return'). Bullimore also regards the Vendée Globe as unfinished business. In spite of his wife's misgivings, the *merveilleux bouledogue* would like to do another one. When we spoke, he had a design proposal on his table for a new boat from Groupe Finot. Autissier and Thiercelin competed in the 1998–99 Around Alone. Goss has already lined up sponsorship for the £4 million he'll need to sail 'The Race' – a mad round-the-world speed dash for crewed boats of unrestricted design that starts on 31 December 2000. Adrian Thompson has designed a big multihull for him in this anything-goes extravaganza – a 115-foot-long, wave-piercing catamaran with twin rotating masts, one on each hull. It will sail at close to forty knots. Until the starts of these big races, all the sailors will compete in various lesser events across the Atlantic.

I tried to imagine my own reaction to conditions in the un-imaginable maelstrom of a Southern Ocean storm. I don't know what I would have done. At best, I suppose, hang on like Nigel Rowe and wait for deliverance. At worst . . . perhaps set off my EPIRB and scream for help. I admired Rowe tremendously for getting through his ordeal and actually making it to Australia – he withdrew from the race shortly after the start of the third leg from Sydney, following a recurrence of chronic rig and rudder problems. He seemed much more like me than Adams, Pettengill, Goss or Dinelli. His responses appeared to be those of a 'normal' person, and I understood the way in which he expressed and reacted to his fear. I couldn't grasp how the 'on the edge' crowd could keep going, or why they kept coming back for more, race after race.

A number of terms have been coined to describe people like the pro-fessional BOC and Vendée Globe sailors: edge-workers, sensation-seekers (the term was coined by the psychology professor Marvin

Zuckerman), practitioners of paradoxical behaviour. The sailors aren't unique. They fit into a class of people who pursue a variety of dangerous activities out of choice and as often as they can. These are almost always sports – most often characterised now as 'extreme sports' like mountain climbing, race-car driving, skydiving. Just about anything that life-insurance companies list specifically on their application forms as risk factors, and that they want a lot more information about before they'll even think of insuring you. The insurance companies know. They're in the business of risk assumption and assessment. Why should they agree to fork over money to the beneficiaries of some lunatic whose idea of a good time is to scan the face of death every weekend, or indeed for months at a time in an ocean race?

Besides sports, the other main source of stimulation for sensation-seekers is war. The soldier driven by the elemental experience of combat, driven to re-experience in spite of his terror the wild ecstasy of the moment of contact. The fighter pilot making a night landing on to the deck of an aircraft carrier in bad weather is the flying equivalent of gybing a spinnaker alone at night on board an onrushing Vendée Globe sixty-footer. This is 'right stuff' territory. The Apollo astronauts, graduating from their warplanes to little capsules that were catapulted with negligible safety margins into orbit or to the barren wilderness of the moon, are the only humans who have been farther from the planet earth than sailors on the planet ocean. I remember reading that as the landing module from Apollo Eleven was rising from the moon's surface to dock with the mother ship the pulse rate of the mission commander, Neil Armstrong, rose to only ninety beats a minute. Even allowing for the calming effects of experience and preparation, this was the reaction of a man whose emotional and physiological response to danger is quite different from mine.

In *Dispatches*, his book about the Vietnam War, Michael Herr describes what he often encountered among the soldiers who fought there. When they were in Vietnam, all they wanted to do was get out – they obsessively counted the days left to go in their year-long tour. But when they returned to the United States, all they wanted to do was go back to Vietnam, a place of death where they had sometimes felt so alive. When Philippe Jeantot told me how he felt about the Southern Ocean, he sounded just like a veteran hungering for the crystal-pure excitement aroused by danger.

'It's amazing, but when you are there, you want to be somewhere, anywhere, else. But when you round the Horn and head north, you forget the troubles you had there. All you want to do is go back.'

Why do you want to go back? I asked.

'For the South, for the South,' Jeantot replied. 'Not for the doldrums; not for the trade winds. Not for that. The South.'

Catherine Chabaud told herself during the race, and for several weeks afterwards, that she would never again go back to the South. When she first saw the photographs of Thierry Dubois clinging to his upturned boat adrift in huge waves, of Tony Bullimore in the water and of Raphaël Dinelli on the deck of his sinking boat, she began to cry. For a month, she couldn't bear to look at the pictures again. 'I hadn't realised before how hard it had been for me to live through it.'

In spite of that, her feelings gradually shifted. When I spoke to her three and a half months after her return to Les Sables-d'Olonne, she had changed her mind completely. 'Today, I want to go to the South again, alone. Why?' She laughed. 'Why?'

There's an element of compulsion here, a whiff of addiction. Drugs are involved: the seductive high of adrenalin, for example. It's a powerful substance. The athlete, the daredevil, the extreme-sport practitioner, sometimes the soldier, all return to the action in part to recapture the physical sensations produced by the body's own chemistry when it is in danger. There's also dopamine, the chemical produced in the brain when people have good experiences. It's what makes us feel pleasure, and we try to repeat the actions that trigger its secretion.

For some of us, however, getting enough dopamine may require more extreme activities. My brain may get more than enough of it when I spend four hours crossing Lake Ontario in a small boat on a blustery day. Tony Bullimore may need to sail a Vendée Globe to get his share. Neil Armstrong may need to fly to the moon. Moitessier's inspiration, Saint-Exupéry, also thrived on life-threatening mishaps. Indeed, says his biographer, Stacy Schiff, he made a cult of adversity. According to one of the mechanics who flew with him on the early, hazardous Saharan mail routes: 'In those moments when it would have been normal to give in to despair he seemed to experience extreme exaltation, intense happiness.'

Some recent studies suggest that there may be a genetic predisposition for some people to seek out new and challenging sensations, based on how their bodies respond to dopamine. One form of the gene that is responsible for dopamine receptors is larger than others. That gene form produces a receptor that doesn't respond as well to dopamine as the smaller form. People with that larger version of the gene won't experience the effects of dopamine secretion as readily as people with the smaller one. They may, therefore, be driven to activities that stimulate the production of larger amounts of dopamine. Depending on many other factors, both genetic and environmental, those activities may take the form of extreme sports or other dangerous adventures. Perhaps the Vendée Globe and Around Alone professional sailors tend to have large dopamine-receptor genes. Maybe it takes the Southern Ocean to squeeze enough of the chemical into their receptors to give them that nice natural high.

Not all extreme sports are the same, nor are the types of experiences their practitioners have. It's mainly a matter of where, and for how long, they go on. It's one thing to jump out of an aeroplane on a Saturday afternoon, or snowboard, or hang-glide, or to drive a Formula One car on the edge for two hours. It's another thing entirely to spend four months alone on a boat. That's not to say that the feelings of exaltation while confronting and mastering the dangers of those shorter-duration sports aren't intense. Although the race-car driver spends a relatively short time driving in a race, each moment is filled with the possibility of catastrophe that only great skill, steady nerves and fast reflexes can avoid.

Sailors, however, can be in these peak situations for long periods. David Adams, steering his boat from outside in the cockpit for twenty-four hours in a Southern Ocean gale, would understand the racing driver's sensations. So would Autissier when *PRB* leaped up like a planing dinghy on to a roaring wave, water flying in all directions. So, for that matter, would any of the Vendée Globe sailors, when their boats surf the long, five-storey rollers of the Southern Ocean at twenty-five knots.

It's another category of action to climb a mountain – with Everest as the most extreme example. Even then, the time of ultimate hazard lasts only a few days. In the Everest of sailboat races, the action goes on for a long, long time – a biblical forty days and forty nights in the Southern Ocean, more if you have bad luck. And it's no picnic on either side of that pivotal section of the race. Another two or three months of hard, solitary, sleep-deprived work. I can't think of any other sporting event that puts these sorts of demands on competitors.

When he was preparing his book *Beyond Endurance*, about survival in extreme circumstances, the psychiatrist Glin Bennet picked out long-distance sailing as a focus for his research. 'I have elected to study behaviour at sea . . . because I know of no other circumstances where it is possible to endure such physical and psychological hardship in isolation for such long periods yet with the possibility of keeping some sort of record,' he wrote. Certain adventures are analogous: crossing to the poles on foot, for example. Or certain kinds of wartime experience. Perhaps the political prisoner in solitary confinement.

To put it simply, to pass through the Southern Ocean, these single-handed sailors must have courage. They certainly need to possess superb technical sailing ability, but their skill won't get them far unless they also have nervous systems that can endure the strain of the constant and random possibility of traumatic accident or sudden death. Their own possible deaths are an inextricable part of the enterprise they're engaged in – part of the contract, as it were. They have all had good friends lost at sea, and still, they sign on. They must each find a way to govern the fear that every sane person feels in the face of premature and violent death. Yet at the same time, the Southern Ocean is an alembic, distilling the pure exaltation all the sailors feel when they survive and surmount its dangers.

There must be sublime moments for the solo sailors, when they become aware that an immediate danger is subsiding, that this time it looks as though they'll live. What an unworldly hiatus they must go through before that moment – when they're not sure whether or not they'll survive, when anything is possible, when the balance could be tipped either way. Like Bullimore, Dubois and Dinelli must have felt, or any of them in particularly bad weather or during a severe knockdown. The realisation of survival must feel like a glorious reprieve. The ardour and force of life at moments like that would be worth seeking out again. Maybe trying to recapture it is compulsively unavoidable.

The body's physiological response to fear and excitement is identical, different masks on the same face. The autonomic nervous system responds in exactly the same way, and the brain's arousal is identical in either situation as it prepares for action. In his book *The Dangerous Edge*, the psychologist Michael Apter describes such physiological arousal as an undifferentiated process, a gross bodily activation, that doesn't distinguish between the emotional labels that we attach to the experience. How humans define their bodies' reactions, says Apter, depends on the context. Our state of mind as we assimilate our bodies' arousal may be 'excitement-seeking', or 'anxiety-avoiding'.

Which of these mind-sets we adopt depends on the existence, and extent of, what Apter calls the 'protective frame'. This is a kind of psychological fortress, a way of seeing the world which implies we're safe from any danger. If I feel I'm still protected by the frame, then I will interpret my body's arousal as a pleasurable one – excitement. But if the protective frame isn't there, or if it is suddenly removed, then I feel my body's state of arousal as a very unpleasant one – fear and anxiety. I may also discover, without warning, that the protective frame I thought was firmly in place is, in fact, an illusion. My confidence in it was misplaced – it did not provide the protection I thought it would. Or I may have miscalculated my own ability to handle danger. My skill and nerve aren't what I thought they were. The frame collapses. The terror that I thought I could keep outside comes crashing down on top of me.

In the seminal 1968 Golden Globe race, one of the competitors experienced a complete collapse of his life-preserving frame. The enthusiastic but impractical Donald Crowhurst set off in a newly built trimaran which was as unprepared for the sea as he was. Sailing south through the Atlantic, he belatedly realised that he would never make it through the Southern Ocean. But he had staked his business livelihood and personal reputation on finishing, and he couldn't face what he saw as the opprobrium of withdrawal. Over the next several months, he jogged around the light-wind areas of the South Atlantic while creating the impression through false radio reports that he was in fact circumnavigating. In the absence of satellite beacons to track boats at sea, Crowhurst could easily lie low in that lightly travelled part of the ocean. But he soon realised that the phoney log documenting his imaginary race would not stand up to scrutiny. He hadn't been able to make the voyage, and now he couldn't go home. His inherent psychological fragility asserted itself, and he began to descend into delusions and disordered thought. Seven months after leaving England, he jumped off his boat into the sea. His trimaran was later discovered drifting along, its cabin table littered with the tapes and notes of a man sliding into despair and madness.

The Vendée Globe sailor's mainframe, so to speak, is the boat – the integrity of its hull and rig, the reliability of its communication and emergency gear. If all of this *feels* intact, then surfing in the Southern Ocean is exhilarating. When the frame is compromised – the hull is pierced by ice, the rig goes over the side, the whole cocoon of the boat turns turtle and stays that way – or if its integrity is seriously threatened by ferocious weather, the skipper's brain isn't likely to interpret his body's aroused state as pleasure. Underlying every moment of the race is the knowledge that the protection provided by the frame of the boat, its gear, the possibility of rescue after a catastrophic event, is far from guaranteed. Key parts of the sailor's protective frame can dissolve in seconds, as in the three Christmas capsizes. The alternation of fear and excitement, or the experience of both at almost the same time, reflects the fragility of the little redoubts that carry the Vendée Globe skippers across the ocean. In crossing the start line off Les Sables-d'Olonne, they sail beyond the pale into that zone unknown, where heroes flourish.

I can see the attraction or, in a sense, the usefulness of those forays beyond the pale of safety. We're all heading for the same place. In death, we leave the pale for ever and enter the universal unknown zone. The protective frame of life is always illusory. Everything dissolves into chaos sooner or later. If I had that knowledge firmly in my mind, if it were a constant part of my understanding of the nature of my life, perhaps I wouldn't view fierce ocean storms in the same way at all. I would look differently at the ways in which the Vendée Globe sailors place themselves closer to death. These risky adventures become a kind of reconnaissance. Isn't it human nature to want to take a closer look at where we're all going? There is possibly nothing better than these bold and exuberant sorties for cosying up to the inconceivable idea of it all. And the rest of life, its day-to-day progression, is transformed too, the significance and pleasure of its mundane activities affirmed.

Hervé Laurent told me that the race has changed him: 'Everything is simple. To cook, to eat, to pee, to go home at night – everything is easier. I appreciate life and people more. Since the race, I look for contact with people a lot more. I want to see people and talk to them. Before, I was more of a loner. Now, I'm always with my family, with friends. It's easy and simple to be with them.'

Perhaps Laurent was changed by his 116 days and twenty hours at sea. Without any question, going to sea very quickly reveals what sort of a person you really are – your emotional and psychological capacities. Indeed, it becomes very important to gauge those abilities dispassionately and accurately. The revelations are pressed upon you, whether you like it or not.

When I spoke to the Vendée Globe sailors, I was struck each time by how similar they were. Without exception, I found myself speaking to a direct, frank, humorous, unaffected person. They are unassuming about what they've done, tentative about claiming much credit for remarkable or heroic acts. Partly, I suppose, these traits are valuable in helping a sailor through single-handed ocean races. But their defining characteristic, I realised, is mature wisdom. It's an acquired maturity, the result of having to change in response to the pressures of events. Interestingly enough, no one changed for the worse. Only for the better, they all agreed.

'It shows you the sort of person you are when you are pushing your own limits,' Isabelle Autissier said. 'You can touch them. I know better who I am now. And I know it's genuine because I arrived at that self-knowledge directly, by way of my own experience and feelings. No one else told me anything. And because you're so intensely alone for so long, you feel closer to other people.'

You realise how connected we are, she added, how much we need one another. 'It's something really human, really very simple. Wonderful, in fact. It's from one person to another.'

Because you feel more confident with yourself, you feel more confident with other people too. 'For me, it's a big difference, and it's a good difference.'

'It sounds like a purifying experience,' I said.

'Yes, you purge yourself,' Autissier replied. Everybody should be obliged to do it, she added. That would take care of the problems of the world.

Goss, the soldier, already knew something about where his limits lay. The race hadn't changed that part of him. But there was certainly more, he said. 'It's hard to describe, but I've come back with a great sense of inner peace or stillness. Quite a special feeling.'

He didn't want to talk too much about it, afraid of pissing it away against the wall. He's not religious, and it's not really a religious feeling. Just the peace and confidence.

Catherine Chabaud felt very much older. She had thought that she would feel the way she did after the race when she was maybe sixty or seventy years old – the wisdom of age. When you're thirty, you realise you weren't very smart when you were twenty. After the race, you realise you weren't very smart before the race. 'I think I've won wisdom that, without this experience, would have come much later.'

Now she finds it easy to excuse the faults of others. She hardly ever feels the destructive anger that used to overwhelm her. Nothing is important enough to get so angry about. 'When I was waiting for wind, or for less wind, or for the sun, or for Cape Horn, or for the end, I told myself, 'Be quiet, you are learning patience'. Moitessier once wrote that 'sailing is a long lesson in patience'.

Bullimore, nearing the end of his sixth decade, learnt his sailor's patience long ago. But in this race, he had stared at death's face for four days. Indeed, he had believed that, on a balance of probabilities, he would die. But suddenly, he had heard Australian voices, had dived deep down through the frigid water one more time, to pop up in sight of the life-giving warship. You couldn't go through that and not be changed. 'You know, if you nearly buy it, but then you don't, life's bloody really got to be shiny and nice. It has to look a lot better. I'm still here. You know: God, it's good to be alive and start living your days, day by day.'

Jeantot, the founding father of the Vendée Globe and a veteran of five races through the Southern Ocean, must have been asked a hundred times what he had felt and how it had changed him. Although his days in the Great South have long been over, the passion of his answer was astonishing: 'Because you feel you are living something so strong. You have to push your limits. Every day, you are at your ultimate limits. The force of life is so strong there. Sometimes you feel it's too much for you, but after you've left it, you feel it was the most important time in your life. You live at a higher level, a higher speed. With the strongest sensations about everything.

'You think of yourself and your small boat, two thousand miles from the nearest coast, and the winds are blowing so fiercely. At that moment, you feel how small you are. When you are in the South, you have a humility lesson every day, every minute.

'When you come back from this kind of trip, you can't be the same as you were when you started. You never forget the lessons the South taught you. It changes you. You can't be the same after. Appearances seem so useless. Why make everything so complicated? You know you are as you are.'

Knox-Johnston had longer than anyone in the Southern Ocean, except Moitessier, to absorb the lessons of the sea. He was a very aggressive young man before he left, he said. But that, and much more, changed.

'You get humbled by the sheer size, the immensity of nature,' he told me. 'You realise how insignificant we are. You look at a big wave in the Southern Ocean, you're looking at something fifty or sixty feet high and it stretches from horizon to horizon. And you realise it could wipe you out and finish you off and not notice you.'

When he came home again, bailing his leaky wooden boat, living on ten-month-old tinned and dubious corned beef and a handful of rice each day, drinking rain water, like an ancient seaman on the *Flying Dutchman*, life was very different. 'You're wary of being too boastful. It's as if you don't want to tempt fate. You don't like to say, "Bloody fool shouldn't have done that." It's more like, "There but for the grace of God go I."'

Moitessier's burden was that he was really happy only when he was at sea, alone on his boat. Like his spiritual predecessor and guide, Saint-Exupéry, who quickly became desperate, irritated, depressed when he couldn't fly, Moitessier – Ishmael-like – could relieve the damp, drizzly November in his soul only by getting to sea as soon as he could. He learned his lessons there early. When he was a young man, sailing his wooden ketch, *Marie-Thérèse II*, from his Asian home to exile in Europe, he was swept overboard in a knockdown off Durban, as his boat lay hove-to in a gale blowing against the Agulhas current. He found himself swimming in the sea looking at his capsized boat, its main hatch cover ripped off. It couldn't stay afloat with a hole like that in the deck. But Moitessier felt no despair or bitterness. He said to himself, This time, old man, your number is up.

He remembered Saint Exupéry's page in *Wind, Sand and Stars* on the absolute necessity of following one's fate, whatever it was. 'I, too, was going to end up like Saint-Exupéry's gazelle, whose destiny it was to leap in the sunshine and die one day under a lion's claw.'

He had no regrets as he trod the warm water, but as chance and luck had it, *Marie-Thérèse* righted itself before shipping a fatal wave (the virtue of the traditional design yet again). Moitessier was able to climb aboard, bringing the hatch cover, which he had found floating nearby, with him. 'Then I pumped for five hours straight, glad to start living again.'

A few years earlier, Moitessier had fought in a colonial regiment of the French army against the Viet Minh in Vietnam. He learned what it was like to frantically plough the earth with his body in an ambush, trying to escape the sudden rain of bullets. He also learned about the attractions and the complexity of the body's arousal in danger.

'I learned to recognise the enormous rush that you get in the Great Game of War, a kind of total alertness throughout your whole being, a heightened state where the fear of never again seeing the sun or feeling your buddies' warmth is swept away by the burning fraternity of your comrades in arms, who can change into a single, almost divine man.'

The sea provided Moitessier with the opportunity to again feel the addictive intensity of war. Later, in *The Long Way*, when he was approaching the Southern Ocean, he observed that he was about to engage again in 'the great game of the high latitudes'.

Boats and the sea were also a path of escape from his beloved Vietnam, from which he, and all the colonial French, had become permanently alienated. In exile, he never found another home, except the tenuous one provided by the sea. Only there could he recapture the rapturous absorptions of his Asian childhood. Like all exiles, Moitessier felt nostalgia keenly and often. At sea, after two months in the wilderness of the Southern Ocean, he listened to 'the sounds of water on the hull, the sounds of wind gliding on the sails, the silences full of secret things between my boat and me, like the times I spent as a child listening to the forest talk'. He always remembered, with Proustian clarity, the idyll of his childhood. The sea was a substitute for the beautiful Vietnamese jungle where the wild boy hunted with his slingshot. 'It was not so much to kill birds as to listen to the murmurs, the reflections, the imperceptible crackings and the abrupt silences of the forest, full of clues and secret things.'

After happy childhoods, adulthood is a form of exile. Saint-Exupéry shared a great deal with Moitessier, including the same sense of acute loss of their childhood paradises. Monkishly alone at his airbase deep in the desert, Saint-Exupéry, like Moitessier alone on his boat in the Great South, remembered his home – the childhood house he had ruled over like a little prince – with painful, yet comforting, nostalgia: 'Somewhere there was a park dark with firs and linden trees and an old house that I loved. It mattered little that it was far away, that it could not warm me in my flesh, nor shelter me . . . It was enough that it existed to fill my night with its presence. I was no longer this body, flung up on a shore; I oriented myself; I was the child of this house.'

Saint-Exupéry's biographer, Stacy Schiff, observed that happy childhoods can take their hostages. For Moitessier and Saint-

Exupéry, sailing alone on the sea or flying alone over the desert eased the difficulty and pain of adulthood; their adventures were chances to avoid its complexities and responsibilities.

I was born in Belfast, Northern Ireland, and have returned for visits over the years to see relatives there, although their numbers have dwindled to a handful now, with death and emigration away from 'the troubles'. The city was a very tense place during the worst times of the 1970s. Visiting my grandmother soon after the imposition of internment without trial, I lay in my cold, damp bed and fell asleep each night to the crackle of gunfire round the borders of the nationalist 'no-go' areas, and even into the city centre, the whump of occasional explosions, the hee-haw of sirens. By day, the Saracen armoured cars, the police, the soldiers were everywhere. As a dark-haired, bearded young man, I 'looked' Catholic even though I wasn't. I was stopped, asked for identification, searched thoroughly or patted down perfunctorily a dozen times a day. One day, I was stopped and searched twenty-two times. There were random, tit-for-tat killings. Restaurants and downtown streets were bombed. From Saracens and armoured jeeps, soldiers scoped me with their rifles as they cruised by. Belfast was a place anyone would have been pleased to leave. I was. I could only imagine wanting to go somewhere peaceful and a little dull. I came home to Canada.

People living in Belfast during that time, or where daily life is anything but regulated and secure (which includes most of the world), won't go to sea in small boats or climb Mount Everest. Why look for risk when there's plenty of it in daily life? But where life is routinely safe and controlled, where the incidence of risk has been reduced through affluence and good government, it's a different matter. In the claustrophobic setting of the so-called nanny society – condoms, crash helmets, smoking regulations – some people need to look for danger, to seek more sensation than our society can legally provide. Extreme sports are one result. They're practised primarily in North America, Europe and European-settled countries like Australia and New Zealand, and consist of sports like skydiving, hang-gliding, auto racing, extreme snowboarding, skiing, surfing and so on. Ordinary risk-seekers have to fall back on these sorts of activities in part because the traditional safety-valves of war, and of frontiers and wilderness elsewhere in the world, have disappeared. There are a few exceptions: the polar regions, the great deserts, the high mountains and, above all, the Southern Ocean. These still offer what the more selective, skilled and affluent edge-worker needs.

The French have 'owned' long-distance, single-handed sailboat racing in recent decades. They are the most innovative sensation-seekers. Extreme sports more often than not have originated in France, and new forms and variations continue to arise there. It's an old tradition. When Saint-Exupéry first became fascinated with flying in 1911 (he flew for the first time a year later), it was the French who had embraced the new air machines before anyone else. In that year, there were more flying licences in France than in the United States, England and Germany together. The French held the world altitude, endurance and speed records. In a preview of long-distance sailing, French pilots dominated the early long-distance flying competitions as well.

The special significance in France of single-handed racing through the Southern Ocean has a kind of Saint-Exupéry–Moitessier lineage. In *Sahara Unveiled,* his book about crossing the Sahara, the American William Langewiesche writes about the French love affair with the barren and apparently limitless desert. They fought to control its emptiness for more than a century. He thinks it may have been, in part, the natural antidote to the particular regulated and 'de-natured' part of Europe in which they were confined.

The French had been shut out of wildernesses farther afield by the overbearing presence of the English maritime empire. The modern French fascination with the sea arose at about the same time as they were being thrown out of the desert. I thought it was an interesting transition. As the French lost one wilderness, another presented itself. Or more accurately, another was presented to them by Moitessier and Tabarly. The Southern Ocean replaced the Sahara as the liberating wilderness. Moitessier inherited from Saint-Exupéry the role of literary adventurer. The lone sailor replaced the lone desert flyer as the interpreter and medium for the French of this new, and even more remote, desert.

When the Apollo space programme was in full swing in the 1960s, many Americans objected to the huge cost of doing something that was almost entirely symbolic: putting a human on the moon. There was no scientific, technological or other rational reason for doing so. Instruments could give us the data we were looking for, as they have done more recently on Mars. When men did get to the moon's surface, they mostly bounced around, collected a few rocks, hit golf balls, planted flags and maundered inarticulately about the beauty and significance of it all.

But the defenders of the costs involved in the moon programme always argued that much more was involved than just collecting rocks or data. Landing on another world was a profoundly human quest – a continuation of the curiosity and daring exploration that was at the very heart of the human character, and that had made us lords of the earth. Someone referred to the great medieval cathedrals of Europe as symbols of human spirit and faith, as humanity then felt compelled to express them. The moon landing was the contemporary expression of the same enduring spirit, went the argument. The space flights were our cathedrals. Can the adventurers who climb Everest or who sail through the Southern Ocean make a similar claim? Do these expeditions keep validating humanity's coupon – its claim that, among many other terrible things, we're also brave, tough, ingenious? Maybe the race, like other dangerous and demanding activities, celebrates the good stuff that all humans have in them, as well as the right stuff that some have.

If it was worthwhile to spend money to get humans to the moon, then, for the same reasons, it's all right to spend big money outfitting people with boats and gear to sail these races, and to rescue them when they get into trouble doing it. The vicarious benefits to our societies are worth it. Jeantot defended the huge costs involved in rescuing Dinelli, and especially Bullimore and Dubois. How much money do we spend on repairing the consequences of crime or drug or alcohol abuse, for example, he asked. The answer is, many times more than the amounts it took to pluck these people out of the Southern Ocean. You could say that the example set by the sailors – their courage, self-reliance and endurance – paid this money back many times over. Perhaps we're all encouraged to live better lives, roused by the example of our heroes when they're summoned by destiny to answer the call to adventure.

For the inspiration to be real, however, the heroes must be authentic. To be authentic heroes, they must face real and incontrovertible dangers, including the possibility of death. Sailing the Southern Ocean seems enough to satisfy this condition. The three Christmas and new year disasters and subsequent close-run rescues in this Vendée Globe proved it. Early in January 1997, the demonstration of authenticity continued.

10

***

Remotest and Most Savage Seas

Below 40 degrees south there is no law; below 50 degrees south there is no God.

– Old sailor's saying

The sea was surreal, huge in its beauty, bursting with life, a sea you could never describe, with waves five hundred to seven hundred feet long that broke over hundreds of feet without tumbling down the swells that bore them. Six days and six nights of taking one wave after another, drunk with exhaustion and amazement . . . one after another . . . a million times, with water everywhere . . . water to infinity . . . water all the way up to the steering dome at times . . . water that roared and sang with the same voice for six days and six nights, binding us to Joshua forever.

– Bernard Moitessier, *Tamata and the* Alliance

E ven before the *Adelaide* picked up Bullimore and Dubois, before anyone knew whether Bullimore was dead or alive, whether he was, in fact, one of the miracles, the ARGOS satellite position beacon on Gerry Roufs's *Groupe LG2*, suddenly stopped transmitting.

It might be nothing. Roufs had not activated any of his EPIRBs. He had five on board, three ARGOS types and two SARSATS, the newest 406s. In the absence of an EPIRB mayday, maybe all that had happened was that his ARGOS had been damaged. One wave could do it, and he might not know anything about it. Roufs could be sailing blithely on, unaware of the malfunction and the concern at race headquarters. *Groupe LG2* might have suffered more general damage. Perhaps it had been dismasted. The ARGOS might have been destroyed, along with the boat's communication antennae, or even its entire electrical system. Roufs would be unable to com-municate, but he wouldn't activate an EPIRB if everything else was all right. For an elite professional sailor, an EPIRB was the very last resort. Dubois did not set off his even when he was rolled and dismasted. Neither did Autissier in the same circumstances in the BOC. Roufs, too, would try to deal by himself with anything less than outright catastrophe. He might have been preoccupied with setting up a jury-rigged mast. Perhaps he would soon be sailing along again, still in the race. He might be counting on people to not worry about his silence since he hadn't set off any of his emergency beacons. He might already be trying to figure out some way of communicating that he was OK.

On the other hand, the cessation of the ARGOS beacon might mean the worst. Everyone connected with the race was jumpy anyway, in view of what had happened during the last ten days and because of Bullimore's yet-unresolved condition. Dubois was still freezing in his life-raft, his rescue not a sure thing. On that tense 7 January, people erred on the side of pessimism when interpreting ambiguous signs. If the ARGOS had stopped sending because of some sudden and calamitous event, then things looked very bad. Roufs should have been able to find some way of activating at least one of his emergency beacons so that a signal would get out. Switching on one of his spare ARGOS units in alarm mode for a few minutes, then shutting it off again, would imply that he was there, wounded but able to handle his trouble. Dinelli, Bullimore and Dubois had all managed to activate EPIRBs even in their most extreme jeopardy. If Roufs couldn't do the same thing, there might not be much hope for him, even at this early stage. If he hadn't had the time or the opportunity to flick a switch, maybe it was because he'd tripped and fallen overboard, or was swept away by a big breaking wave. *Groupe LG2* might have sailed on for a while and then capsized, silencing the ARGOS. Or Roufs might have been in the cockpit when the boat capsized. He could have drowned quickly, unable to get on to the overturned hull as Dubois had, his EPIRBs out of reach. Or maybe it was ice, everyone's nightmare. Smashing directly into a berg at twenty knots, the boat could have disintegrated and sunk so quickly its skipper had no chance.

There were other worrying indications. Autissier was still sailing close to Roufs. On 6 January, she was probably no more than twenty miles away, close enough to talk by VHF radio. But on the seventh, Autissier reported that she hadn't been able to raise him for some time. That was ominous because Roufs had a hand-held VHF, which was not dependent on a masthead or other antenna that might have been damaged or destroyed in a knockdown or dismasting. Then, as usual, there was the weather: near-hurricane-force winds; five-, six-, seven-storey seas roaring down on them at thirty knots. 'It's war out here,' Autissier faxed her shore team early on 8 January.

With all these fears and uncertainties, Jeantot felt he had to do something. In cooperation with the CROSS, he ordered a search and began to look around for someone to carry it out.

There weren't many possibilities. Roufs was sailing smack in the middle of the most remote part of the Southern Ocean, in the uttermost part of the whole world. He and Autissier were about equidistant from New Zealand and Chile, about twenty-four hundred miles from each coast. They were much closer to Antarctica, but that meant nothing to a boat in distress. The Orion long-range search-and-rescue planes that could reach Bullimore and Dubois and spend almost three hours overhead, couldn't even get to Roufs's position and back to base again. Fast warships, dispatched from New Zealand or Chile, wouldn't arrive in the area for a week, assuming reasonably good weather en route. And they would need to be refuelled to get back again. The Chilean naval commandant in Valparaiso told the CROSS that Roufs's last-known position was too far from the closest airport, in Punta Arenas, on the Strait of Magellan, just north of Cape Horn. His planes couldn't begin to get there and back, especially in bad weather.

It was as if a sailor in that region of the sea had travelled back through time. Roufs was in the same situation as Knox-Johnston or Moitessier had been, or Cook or Magellan, for that matter. If he couldn't save himself, he was dead. Or nearly so. Roufs *did* have a chance his predecessors didn't: other racers within striking distance and a freighter less than 250 miles away.

Of the racers, Autissier was the closest. The CROSS asked her to turn back towards Roufs's last-known position, by then close to 150 miles away upwind. This was almost as dangerous and difficult for Autissier as it was for Goss to go back for Dinelli. But Autissier had several big problems that made her chances of success more unlikely. First, there was no EPIRB location to aim for. All she had was Roufs's last-known position – where he had been when his ARGOS stopped – adjusted for assumed drift patterns or slow jury-rigged progress in the interval. Second, there were no planes around to help her home in on Roufs. Goss would almost certainly not have found Dinelli without the help of the Australian Orion. Third, Autissier had her own problems. She had been badly knocked around by the severe storm for more than twenty-four hours. She was exhausted. Her boat had suffered damage in half a dozen knockdowns, and she had broken one of her fingers. After two of the knockdowns, only the off-centred weight of her canting keel had stopped her from capsizing. Most important, the damage to *PRB* included broken mainsail and staysail halyards. She couldn't hoist either sail. All she could muster was one-third of her storm jib's area; the sail itself couldn't be adjusted because of damage to its furling gear. Fourth, the search area was directly upwind. She had to tack – sail a zigzag course as close as possible to the wind direction – enormously difficult with such a small sail in the strong storm conditions. Fifth, she estimated that visibility was less than one mile, sometimes only a hundred yards or so. Finally, *PRB*, with the more extreme Finot design features which made it a particularly good downwind runner, was not as efficient a boat to windward as Goss's more conservative *Aqua Quorum*. In other words, Autissier didn't have as capable a tool for the job.

But she tried. After several hours, she had managed to get four miles closer to Roufs's last position, which remained, stubbornly, in the wind's eye.

'Several capsizes,' she reported (she meant knockdowns). 'I am in survival conditions, but am trying to sail back. It's a real mess inside. I am at my last physical limits.'

She napped at her chart table in her foul-weather gear in case she was knocked down again. Later, as the wind moderated, she was able to make six knots to the north. From Brittany, the CROSS sent her another position to head for. She replied that it was likely impossible for her to reach it without her mainsail. She kept trying. But after twenty-five hours of punishing windward sailing, Autissier was still well over one hundred miles from Roufs's position. The CROSS thought that she had done enough. 'We give you full freedom to manoeuvre. Thank you for your cooperation.'

In spite of this formal release from her search obligations, Autissier continued to try to beat to windward. But even in the moderating wind (now only twenty-five to thirty knots) and seas, she was unable to make headway dead to windward in her wounded boat and her own debilitated condition. The CROSS again: 'You may sail your former course to the east. Again, thanks for all.'

Autissier turned back downwind at last.

'I am sailing east now,' she told her team. 'I am thinking of Gerry constantly. I hope we will find him. I have to try to sleep now.'

Before she left she checked the weather. Two more strong depressions were bearing down on her. She set her course south-east, heading towards fifty-eight degrees latitude. She thought she might be able to squeeze between the worst of the systems, which would be on top of her within a day or so. Before they arrived, the exhausted Autissier would have to haul herself up her eighty-foot mast and replace the two halyards.

While Autissier tried to drive her boat into the wind, the only nearby ship, a Panamanian freighter, the *Mass Enterprise*, steamed towards Roufs's assumed position. The ship arrived late in the evening of 9 January, but couldn't do much searching before night fell. It began a methodical quartering search at dawn the next day, but by then the search area had grown to almost eight thousand square miles. That morning, the ship saw an iceberg a quarter-mile across and fifty yards high, with other smaller bergs and growlers nearby. They weren't directly on Roufs's assumed course, but they weren't an encouraging sign either.

Other assets were becoming available to the search organisers. Because Roufs had been sailing near the front of the fleet, the competitors coming up behind him could be pressed into service as well. Thiercelin would arrive in the search area late on 10 January.

The CROSS could also divert Laurent and de Broc, running farther south, to join in. Roufs's best friend in the race, Eric Dumont, was even farther back, more than thirteen hundred miles, and he had problems: a broken boom and heavy weather. He managed to repair his damage by lashing a spinnaker pole along the fractured boom like an aluminium splint. He notified the CROSS that he was heading for the search area. Anguished by Gerry's silence, he hurried, sailing fast among the growlers and small bergs with only two-hundred-yard visibility.

Hitting one of the smaller chunks of ice wasn't necessarily fatal. Parlier had lost his rudder but not his boat when he hit a growler. Other racers had heard small bergy bits rattle alarmingly but harmlessly along their hulls. Size mattered. A piece of ice like a bread bin probably wouldn't hole a boat in a collision; one the size of an automobile probably would. The outcome also depended on other factors: the boat's speed; where the ice hit. The bow was much stronger than the hull panels aft of it, and some of the boats' bows were fitted with collision bulkheads, recommended but not required by the race rules. Dumont couldn't know whether his danger was great or small. That old Southern Ocean Russian roulette again, he observed.

Thiercelin, also a good friend of Roufs's, joined the *Mass Enterprise* in the search area on 10 January. He had to heave-to for a while to get some sleep. Then he began a routine of alternating thirty minutes on deck and thirty minutes below, resting, getting warm – it was below zero Celsius with the wind-chill – and watching his radar. As he got close to Roufs's assumed drift point, he spent forty-five minutes on deck and fifteen below. Conditions weren't bad during the day of the eleventh: twenty-five-knot winds but with rough seas left over from the most recent system to pass through.

Then some more disappointing news arrived. Both Laurent and de Broc, only about 160 miles away from the search area on 11 January, decided to keep going. They cited the weather forecast for that night and the next day: low visibility in fog and heavy rain, winds up to sixty knots, very rough seas.

'It's a difficult choice,' de Broc said. 'My heart is broken.' He urged Jeantot to insist that the *Mass Enterprise* keep looking. It was much better able to do so than he and Laurent. In the weather that was due to arrive, they could hope only to cross the search zone as they ran downwind before it.

Laurent agreed. The weather would make a search impossible. 'It isn't an easy decision to make. Maybe I'm wrong. But it's still a long race, and I have to take care of my tired boat.'

The CROSS, reluctant to second-guess the opinions of experienced sailors on the spot, declined to order Laurent and de Broc to join the search. They had seen the forecast too, and decided they couldn't ask the two skippers to put themselves at more risk than they would already be in when the new system slammed into them.

Meanwhile, the sea area within which Roufs could be drifting grew by the hour. Jeantot, who was momentarily elated by the news of Bullimore's survival, became more and more pessimistic about Roufs's chances. He had a terrible feeling of powerlessness. His familiarity with the Southern Ocean only made it worse. He knew as well as anyone how a sailor could suffer there. He could imagine without effort what Roufs might be enduring if he was dismasted or capsized, unable to get a distress signal out. After more than two weeks of uncertainty and near-disasters, he was as exhausted as if he'd actually been duelling with the Southern Ocean himself. With more hope than sense, he speculated that perhaps all of Roufs's EPIRBs had broken down at once; maybe he was making for a Chilean or Polynesian port under jury-rig. But the signs were mostly bad and Jeantot knew it. With no actual position for the two searchers to aim for, Roufs was *une aiguille dans une botte de foin* – a needle in a haystack. All Jeantot could hope for was another miracle, that Gerry's ordeal would somehow end as well as had those of Raphaël, Thierry and Tony. Even though Laurent and de Broc kept going, Jeantot thought that Dumont, Roufs's close friend, would make a search no matter what the weather was like. Anyway, he would arrive after the worst of the imminent storm had passed over.

There was another reason for faint hope as well: more technology. The Canadian Space Agency operated RADARSAT, the most powerful non-military radar satellite in the world. A careful analysis of its photographs might disclose *Groupe LG2*'s mast, if the boat still had one. If it had been dismasted, however, or was floating upside down, there would be little possibility of picking the hull out from the wave clutter. Still, it was a chance. The satellite would pass over the search area on 12 January. If it did get a position fix of some sort, maybe Dumont could get there.

The *Mass Enterprise* had to end its efforts late on 11 January. After two days of determined searching, it was running low on fuel. Its captain believed that no damaged boat could survive the storm due to arrive on the scene late on the eleventh. But there was more than the usual amount of commercial traffic about, and an Indian freighter, the *Aditya Gaurav*, en route from Australia to Argentina, was approaching the area. It might have a chance of finding Roufs if the satellite could provide a fix.

As the new storm bore down, the CROSS decided that Thiercelin had done enough. It gave him 'complete freedom to manoeuvre' – his obligations were over. But 'Captain Marck' (his nickname, after the title of a sailing board-game he had invented and sold to raise some money for the race) kept searching through the day of the eleventh, as conditions continued to deteriorate. Late in the day, the weather was so bad that the CROSS sent Thiercelin a blunt order: 'Leave the area and continue your route.' The missing boat could be anywhere within a zone of twenty-seven thousand square miles. It would take him a month to cover it, said the CROSS. It congratulated him for his work and wished him luck. 'You don't have to thank me; I'm only doing my job,' the exhausted skipper testily replied.

Sadly, he turned to the east. A multi-talented expert cabinet-maker, ex-artistic director of a Brazilian advertising agency and magazine illustrator, Thiercelin was very depressed and anxious, unable to sleep in spite of his fatigue. All this reminded him of the MiniTransat he had sailed in 1991, in which two sailors had been lost. He had known them well and had a difficult time accepting their deaths. He desperately wanted to find Roufs, to do his humble sailor's duty and save a friend, as he said. But the weather had intervened. During the night of the eleventh, running off fast before the storm, he nearly pitchpoled. *Crédit Immobilier de France* surfed down a big sea and sliced into the wave ahead, burying its bow right back to the mast. The aft end of the hull and both rudders were fifteen feet out of the water. Thiercelin, helpless to do anything, numb and discouraged, watched his boat slowly resurface and resume its breakneck flight to the east. 'I am truly fed up,' he faxed. 'I hate this place.'

The satellite wasn't much use after all. It took four series of pictures during orbits on 12 January, and over the ensuing few days. At the time, the latest low was pounding the area. The high waves made it difficult to identify any floating objects. By late on the thirteenth, the Canadian Space Agency had picked out eighteen possible locations. For the next day and a half, the *Aditya Gaurav* methodically tracked them down, but found nothing. Out of time, and with no more to do, it too resumed its course towards the Horn. There were no other commercial ships within a thousand miles. Now Eric Dumont was the only remaining searcher. There were other racers still farther back, of course, but they were just too far away to help.

Chabaud, Goss and Parlier were far out of the picture. Chabaud was fifteen hundred miles astern of Dumont, still sailing her conservative race, staying well to the north – it was dangerous, absurd even, to go south near the ice, she said. Parlier, after his stop in Fremantle, had rejoined the race in his rejuvenated boat. But even sailing as fast as he was, he was still only a few hundred miles ahead of Chabaud and was well south of the search area. Goss had left Hobart the day after Roufs's ARGOS stopped, having dropped Dinelli off there. It would be too late by the time either Goss or Parlier got close to Roufs's last-known position. The search area would have swelled to an impossible size. They could keep an extra eye out as they sailed through towards the Horn, but that was all.

On 15 January, RADARSAT took more pictures of the search zone. Jeantot hoped that the Canadian analysts could provide some possible positions for Dumont to investigate. But they couldn't identify any likely looking blips or objects. Dumont arrived near Roufs's last position late on the fifteenth. He had a bad time just getting there. At one point, he came on deck to find his boat, *Café Legal le Goût* 'nose to nose' with a big berg. He hadn't slept for nearly three days, driving as fast as he could in forty-five-knot wind and big seas. Too fast – even in those relatively moderate conditions, he had suffered knockdowns. He thought he was now 'permanently awake'. From time to time, he confided, he broke down and cried. He was exhausted and frustrated, and afraid for Gerry.

By the afternoon of the sixteenth, however, Dumont had to abandon his search. The wind had increased to fifty knots sustained (Beaufort force 10). He had seen more ice even though visibility was less than half a mile. Sailing under his smallest storm jib, he was still moving at twelve knots. With no positions to aim for, in a search area that now occupied a significant chunk of the southern Pacific, Dumont's job was impossible. As dusk approached on the sixteenth, he turned and ran his boat off to the east once again.

And that was it. Jeantot had exhausted all possible sources of aid.

The CROSS asked ships passing through the area to keep a watch. The Chileans continued their air patrols in the vicinity of the Horn. The only hope now was that Roufs was in fact still sailing, perhaps under jury rig, towards a port of refuge, most likely in Chile. If this was all just a communications problem, and he was sailing normally, he would round the Horn any day now. If neither scenario was true, he was a dead man.

Michèle Cartier, Roufs's wife, was waiting out the race in Montreal, where she had enrolled their daughter Emma in school. She was certain that Gerry was still alive, she said. He would certainly have been able to activate at least one of his ARGOS or 406 EPIRBs if he was in trouble. He was such a good sailor; she had complete confidence in him. He hadn't entered this race to die. The sea was his life. For Michèle and Emma, that meant six months each year of anxiety. Still, this wait was the hardest thing she had ever had to endure. Emma came home from school and told her, 'Papa is dead.' Her schoolmates had heard from their parents about the news reports of her father's disappearance. During their last satellite telephone conversation, on 6 January Roufs had asked Cartier about some cheques he'd written before the race began. She had told him not to worry about cheques; just sail the race. Cartier publicly thanked Autissier for her rescue effort. She was terrific, brave. She had risked everything to go back to search. The same went for Thiercelin. She thanked Dumont – who would arrive on the scene shortly – in advance. She made no mention of de Broc or Laurent.

She and Emma had given Roufs his Christmas present before he left, Cartier said – a lighter for his one-burner propane stove. Emma had added a note: 'This flame will light your course.' They had put photos of themselves in the package. Cartier was sure he was still able to look at the photos, and to get strength from them. But it was an interminable wait.

Suddenly, it seemed as if Cartier's hope and confidence hadn't been misplaced after all. There was another miracle to add to this race's unlikely catalogue of survival. According to the Chilean search-and-rescue centre, an air force plane flying about one hundred miles to the north-west of Cape Horn reported that it had picked up a frag-mentary VHF-radio burst. The contact lasted only a few seconds, but the crew was definite: they had heard the words 'Groupe Lima Golf,' the international radio alphabet convention for *Groupe LG*. It all made sense. If Roufs had kept sailing at his normal speed, he would in fact have arrived in the vicinity of the Horn at just about that time – 17 January. It looked as if he had merely suffered a general communications-system failure after all. He had his hand-held VHF, and it could well have been the source of the radio message. In fact, by the time Jeantot received word of the contact, Roufs would have rounded the Horn. He would be heading for the four-hundred-mile-wide passage between Argentina and the Falklands, on his way out of the Southern Ocean. If the brief contact could be confirmed by another radio transmission or an actual sighting, then there would be no doubt that yet another Vendée Globe sailor had escaped the Great South by the skin of his teeth.

The Chileans flew planes in shifts for several days, in bad weather and poor visibility, but no one heard any thing more of Groupe Lima Golf on the radio. Still, Jeantot allowed himself to become cautiously optimistic. Laurent, sailing *Groupe LG Traitmat*, had been too far away from the Horn for the Chilean plane to have confused him with Roufs. Anyway, he reported that he hadn't used his VHF on that day. It didn't mean much that the Chileans hadn't been able to spot Roufs. He could easily have slipped through their net, even in the relatively small search zone. It just underlined how difficult it was to pick a boat out of the jumbled waste of waves. The visibility was seldom good enough to see very far anyway. The Argentine air force dispatched planes on the Atlantic side of the Horn. They sighted Autissier, but not Roufs. But he could have sailed past them unobserved as well. Jeantot's confidence in Roufs's survival grew. He believed that the communications breakdown theory best explained Roufs's silence, especially when the Chilean naval attaché in Paris and the French embassy in Santiago eventually confirmed the radio contact.

In fact, it was possible that no one would see Roufs until he approached Les Sables-d'Olonne sometime in late February. What a day that would be, even by the standards of this surprising edition of the race. The long-lost sailor, out of touch for six weeks, emerging out of the sea like a seaman of another century.

It had happened before, a boat slipping through nets of searchers. The racers tend to come in colours much like the ocean itself – white hulls and sails, perhaps blue anti-fouling paint on the bottom. *Groupe LG2* had a mauve hull and blue-green bottom paint, which was even more difficult to pick out of the sea's hues than white hulls.

Area or zone searches involving the hit-or-miss acuity of human eyes on planes or ships often fail in the vast and featureless steppes of the ocean.

In a recent example of a return from the fellowship of the dead in the Southern Ocean, an experienced sixty-eight-year-old English single-hander, Les Powles, left Whangarei, New Zealand, on 26 December 1995, in a thirty-four-foot cruising sailboat. He was bound around the Horn to the Falkland Islands, and eventually to England. He told his family and friends that he should arrive in the Falklands, or would make radio contact with the islands, in sixty days. Halfway to the Horn, he was capsized in a strong gale. His traditionally designed boat righted itself immediately, its rig intact. The sailor was badly injured, and all his communications equipment was destroyed. He gradually recovered from his wounds on a diet of painkillers and whisky, and kept sailing. But his progress was hampered by his injuries and unusual head winds.

When his predicted two months expired without word, Powles was declared missing and a widespread search got under way. Ships and planes across the Southern Ocean and the South Atlantic searched or kept an extra watch for weeks, but found nothing. He was declared presumed dead – lost at sea.

But Powles was all right, still sailing. By then, he had rounded the Horn without more trouble, but was blown away from the Falklands by gales. He decided to make for Brazil, but changed his mind because he thought his ship's papers might not satisfy corrupt port captains. He sailed for the Azores. Once there, though, he thought, What the hell, I might as well go home. And he kept going for England. In July 1996, two months after the search for him was called off, Powles sailed into a marina in Lymington, Hampshire, unaware that the world had looked for him for a month, and that he was officially a dead man.

The point is that, even today, with heavy ship traffic, coordinated searches, satellites, large and far-flung fishing fleets, a boat can still disappear for weeks or months at a time in the wide, wide ocean. Jeantot, and every other sailor, knew that. It was quite feasible to think that Roufs was still out there.

For the other skippers, the race had gone on as usual, as they contended with wind, waves and ice over virtually the whole stretch of the southern Pacific. But one was luckier than the rest. At four in the morning on 9 January, as the *Mass Enterprise* was beginning its search for Roufs, Auguin rounded the Horn after sixty-six days at sea. If he kept up his pace, not only would he break Lamazou's record of 109 days, he might get home in less than a hundred.

Auguin and his wife, Véronique, had agreed that they would try to rendezvous off the Horn, weather permitting. She flew to Punta Arenas and chartered a Chilean naval vessel to take her out to meet *Géodis*. The chances of meeting didn't look good the day before – the wind was blowing at fifty-five knots. But in the early morning of the ninth, it dropped. The unlikely rendezvous was suddenly possible. Auguin hove-to close off the Horn. He opened a bottle of champagne and, in the early morning austral summer light, toasted his milestone. He and Véronique waved and shouted back and forth to each other, the Chilean boat surging as close to the nearly stationary *Géodis* as was possible in the rough seas. Everyone on the visiting boat quickly became seasick. It turned back towards the shelter of the Chilean channels. On the radio, Auguin was sympathetic, but told Véronique that, to him, the ocean seemed almost flat. As *Géodis* faded astern, the now deathly ill visitors could see Auguin, oilskin-clad, thin and bearded, standing casually on deck in his seaboots, rolling with his boat's motion, still cheerfully swigging his champagne.

'It was very nice to have a little contact with civilisation at last,' he said. 'And I'm happy to have got out of these hellish seas unscathed – physically, at least – for the third time.'

Auguin had good reason to be happy. No one else was close to him. Barring bad luck, his win was assured, perhaps in record time. At the very least, he would gain a striking victory. He had avoided all of the traumatic, near-death experiences of some of his competitors. His boat had been absolutely solid, although it had suffered its share of minor gear failure, and the unavoidable stutterings and ghostly lapses of electronic instruments out of their dry and warm element. Auguin had excelled at that most important safety feature of ocean sailing: speed. He had got out of the Southern Ocean as fast as any single-hander ever had.

Five thousand miles behind the leader, and on the same day as Auguin rounded the Horn, Goss left Hobart, Tasmania. Goss was the last official competitor. While being rescued disqualified a sailor, carrying out a rescue did not; in fact, Goss received a 318-hour allowance for the time it took to save Dinelli and get him to Hobart. As always, sailing last was the worst position to be in. Especially across the southern Pacific. The tenuous lifeline offered to each sailor by fellow-racers was severed for the last boat. The devil might well take the hindmost. Like any lone single-hander sailing for the Horn, Goss was completely isolated.

He was also in bad shape. Emotionally and physically drained by the ordeal of Dinelli's rescue, Goss found getting back into the race one of the hardest things he had done in his life. He felt battered and bruised. His boat was a mess. Three vessels had been lost. Now Roufs was missing. As he sailed from Hobart, it looked as if he might get an early pasting from hurricane Evan, which was tracking down far to the south across his path.

'I've never been scared of the sea. I've had a healthy respect for it, which is a much better thing to have. But I was spooked when I left Hobart.'

He had to sit down and talk to himself, get back to basics. Why was he there? What was he trying to achieve? He knew what he was up against, but he'd survived the storm that had destroyed Dinelli. It was just a case of having a cup of tea and getting on with it, he told himself. But it was tough. He had lost the concentration he had had since the start. Sailing single-handed was largely a mind-game. You never knew what the next move would have to be. But every move could have dire consequences, because you were so vulnerable in the Southern Ocean. So when problems arose, your weapon was your mind. You had to sit down and think your way through them, make the best use of what you had on the boat, cobble things together. Somehow, he had to get back to that state of focused yet loose readiness. The Cape Horn sailor had to be centred, guts tranquil yet ready for battle, the mind empty of everything except the boat and the sea – Zen and the art of Southern Ocean sailing. 'I was a warrior in danger,' said Saint-Exupéry after a desert crash landing. That was the state of mind the Vendée Globe sailor had to cultivate too.

Goss struggled with his fear and depression for the next two weeks. Evan missed him, but then another big storm came through, almost identical to the one that nearly destroyed Dinelli – north wind, big pressure drop, quick wind switch to the south-west up to sixty knots or more. Jeantot, who was now taking an almost tender proprietary interest in Goss, faxed him a warning of the impending system. It was a worrying one, Jeantot added. And Goss thought, Shit, *they're* worried. They're on the other side of the bloody world.

But when the storm began its sweep over him, Goss was OK. It put him through the mincer – he even put his survival suit on during the night – but he felt much better afterwards, a renewed sense of achievement. 'All mental basically. Very interesting experience.'

As Goss sailed east, his radar failed, then his radio. He decided to stay north of fifty degrees to avoid the worst ice. Jeantot, as solicitous of his hero as ever, faxed Goss a series of satellite maps showing the main ice concentrations along his route.

The next boat to round the Horn after Auguin could have been Roufs, if everyone's hopeful theory was true. But Autissier did double the Cape on 17 January, for the third time in her life. She had done it while setting a speed record from New York to San Francisco and once during a BOC. Each time, Autissier said, she thought of all the dead men down there, somewhere under her feet. It was crazy doing what they had done – in their primitive ships, without proper clothing or food, going aloft in snow and wind to engage the heavy canvas hand to hand. It was amazing they had been able to do it. When you're there, she said, it's very emotional, you're deeply touched when you think of them – three centuries' worth of drowned sailors.

'*Methought what pain it was to drown!*' exclaims Clarence in *Richard III*. '*What dreadful noise of water in mine ears!/What sights of ugly death within mine eyes!*'

With all the near-catastrophes, the uncertainty about Roufs, her exhausting struggle to get back to him, Autissier felt pushed right to her limits. After all that, 'Cape Horn was a whooooooo!' She let out a loud, hooting sigh of relief and exaltation. 'You know, it was the first time I really felt that.'

The boats in the second group – Laurent, de Broc, Thiercelin and Dumont – which had held loosely together since the southern Atlantic – rounded the Horn in quick succession between 19 and 24 January. First was Laurent, precise and laconic. 'Done!' he radioed.

De Broc rounded the cape on 20 January. But he had serious problems. He was low on diesel fuel for his generator, and the propeller on his water-powered generator was jammed. Soon he would have no way of charging his batteries. More ominously, his floors – the structural supports in the hull-keel area – were damaged. The whole area of the critical hull-to-keel join was fragile. He couldn't tell how compromised it had become, but he wanted to take a good look at it while there was some land close by. He could have anchored precariously in some bay and tried to fix things himself –

dive down into the five-degree water to look at the propeller, slap fibre cloth and epoxy on his wobbly floors – but he suspected more extensive damage and decided to put in to the Argentine port of Ushuaia, on the Beagle Channel. Putting in to port would keep intact his dismal record; this would be his second disqualification in a Vendée Globe. He had been drummed out in the previous race after his forced stop in New Zealand – because of the unfounded fears of his architect and his sponsor about his boat's integrity. That had been the venerable *Groupe LG Traitmat*, now under Laurent's hand. At the time, de Broc's abandonment of the race had given Roufs his chance, when he was asked to bring the boat back from New Zealand to France. Next time, de Broc promised, it would be different. 'In 2000, I will come back with a war machine, to win!'

Thiercelin rounded the Horn later on the same day as de Broc, escorted by two dolphins and an albatross. When Knox-Johnston passed the great cape on his 313-day voyage, with few stores left except nineteenth-century beef, ship's biscuit, rice and beans, all he could do to celebrate was dream of a hot bath, a pint, a steak and sex, in that order. Thiercelin opened a bottle of champagne and ate some foie gras. He went on to emphasise how much long-distance sailing had changed in thirty years (or perhaps how much difference there had always been between French and English sailors) when he made a mushroom omelette out of fresh eggs that he had stored in wax for two and a half months, rehydrated dried mushrooms and various spices. He washed it down with a bottle of Bordeaux Médoc, to the accompaniment of a tape by The Who.

He was relieved to get out of the Southern Ocean for a more practical reason: in the pounding during his search for Roufs, the floors on his boat had also been damaged. He had noticed weaknesses in the hull near the bow. He had to slow down until he could wedge some wooden pillars into the area to shore it up. He could make more permanent repairs in the calmer Atlantic water. The next day, his first in the Atlantic, while he was sitting at his chart table happily singing along to a Platters tape and sailing at thirteen knots, the boat hit something and stopped almost dead. 'It mashed my lovely face straight into the chart table,' he said.

A huge piece of drifting rope was wrapped round his keel. Unlike Jeantot, who had been a commercial diver before going to sea, Thiercelin's only diving record had been set in his bathtub. He couldn't dive – his ear problems again – so he had to reef his sails right down and sail backwards and forwards for hours before he got clear of the entangling line. At least it hadn't been a container, he said. Soon he was moving again, sailing close-hauled at seventeen knots, bashing into the short, steep Atlantic waves, walking on the cabin sides as his boat heeled over.

While Thiercelin was munching his mushroom omelette, Dumont passed the Horn. He had a terrible time getting there. He experienced the worst weather of his life, with forty-foot waves, dangerously steeper than normal in the shallower water near the continent, and wind gusting to seventy knots. Once, he passed within a quarter-mile of a big berg. During the night, he put on his survival suit and made sure all his emergency equipment was in order. 'I had the scare of my life,' he said. 'The boat was knocked down several times, spreaders in the water.'

But then, the next night, he was at the Horn, the great, mythical cape, 'the end of the unknown land, the door to the path back'. After he rounded the Horn, like the square-rigger sailors who had survived it, he was entitled – and to hell with the laws of aerodynamics – to piss into the wind without getting wet. And to wear a gold earring in his left ear, the one towards the dread rock as you went around. When he got there, the wind dropped. He ghosted by in five knots, under a big moon as round as the earth, the snowy Chilean mountain tops gleaming behind the cape in the pale, austere light.

A few days later, the disqualified Parlier also passed the last of the three stormy capes. He made a fast southern Pacific passage since leaving Fremantle. At one point, he went far south, below sixty degrees, to avoid heavy weather. He also shortened the distance to the Horn, and he had made up a lot of time on the competitors ahead of him. He sailed by the Cape two miles off the sheer, wild cliffs. As he turned to the north, the long Southern Ocean swell, meeting land at last, died down and disappeared. It was like sailing on a lake in comparison. Parlier felt as if he was leaving a no-man's land, where humans had no place; as if he had climbed to the top of a mountain. Now he was starting back down again.

'I have sent a last message to the albatross, my faithful sailing companions for almost sixty days,' he reported. 'I salute you, but I'm leaving you for the north, for warm seas and my return to civilisation.'

As for Goss, he was having electrical, autopilot, sail-batten, radio and radar problems. Apart from that, everything was fine. Except his elbow. He'd damaged it more getting thrown about his cabin on the way back for Dinelli, and now it was getting worse, swelling up so that he couldn't use his arm at all. Truly single-handed sailing. During the last week of January, he was being slowed by calms and *Aqua Quorum* rolled abysmally, without wind, in the heavy swells.

'I can only drink tea, and wait,' Goss informed race headquarters. Goss's tea, the beginning of Dinelli's resurrection, was already an affectionate legend in France.

Twenty-five hundred miles back in the Southern Ocean, Chabaud continued her steady progress. She had settled down after the Christmas and New Year débâcles.

'I was traumatised by all the yachts that capsized,' she admitted. 'I didn't think it was possible for so many boats to go down like that. On the other hand, I was reassured by the efficiency and organisation of the rescues. I found this solidarity between seamen extraordinary. Surely people on land will learn a lesson from it. This Vendée Globe has taught me so much. We know when we leave how dangerous it is. But we take the risk upon ourselves lucidly, with open eyes. After seventy-nine days at sea, I can say that it's a very beautiful and a very difficult race. If I had known before I left how hard it would be, I'm not sure I would have gone. But now that I'm here, I'm very happy.'

Meanwhile, she missed her family and friends. She would give anything for a walk in the country. And another low-pressure system was on the way. Ten more days to the Horn.

After the race, Chabaud said: 'If you had asked me at the beginning of the race, How much chance would you give a sailor in those circumstances to be rescued, I would have said . . .' She hesitated.

'Not much,' I suggested.

'Not much,' she agreed. 'But three people came back.'

'It was amazing,' I said.

'It was beautiful,' said Chabaud.

For her, the true symbol of the Southern Ocean is the wandering albatross. When one of the birds began to keep company with her, south of the Cape of Good Hope, and then stayed with her boat for over a month in the southern Indian Ocean (she could recognise it by its distinctive white wing markings), she named the bird Bernard. She imagined it to be a reincarnation of Moitessier. Chabaud's feeling of kinship with Moitessier was particularly strong throughout the race. She had spent a lot of time reading *The Long Way* earlier on, when she was suffering a lot of technical problems with her gear. She discovered that even the great voyager had had to deal with the same sorts of bad times, had suffered fear and anxiety. It comforted her to realise that, if she wasn't the best at this Southern Ocean sailing game, she wasn't so bad at it either.

There's always been a strong symbolic connection between the Southern Ocean and the albatross. Like the Southern Ocean rollers, the bird continuously circles the earth south of the stormy capes. After its chickhood, and before it starts mating at seven or so, this biggest bird, with its twelve-foot wing-span, often spends two years at sea without ever touching land. It can live to be sixty or seventy years old. It sleeps on the wing, its flight an effortless ride on the sea-surface thermals and the updraughts of air generated by water-surface friction as the wind sweeps over it. Chabaud's naming of her bird seemed apt. Moitessier's spirit seems to drift, like the albatross, over the Southern Ocean. One followed him, too, for a long time on *Joshua*'s albatross-like, non-stop, one-and-a-half-times circum-navigation. The cindery-coloured bird glided around him in-differently, though – the boat and Moitessier existing only as a single, incomprehensible object in the sea.

On 25 January, the inconceivable happened. The precarious jocularity of the skippers leaving the Southern Ocean, increasingly shared by Jeantot as the days went by without incident, suddenly collapsed. The commander-in-chief of the third Chilean naval zone, based in Punta Arenas, announced in a press interview that neither the Chilean air force nor the navy had ever formally identified Roufs as the source of the 16 January, VHF-radio transmission. He outlined what the Chilean authorities now said had taken place. The pilot of the search plane had repeatedly transmitted the words 'Groupe Lima Golf'. on channel 16, the VHF international-calling channel, as the plane flew its search pattern. After an hour and a half, a boat had responded, 'Go ahead.' Asked for his position, the unidentified sailor had given latitude and longitude coordinates that put him almost one hundred miles north-west of Cape Horn (not north-west, as the initial communiqué from the Chilean maritime search-and-rescue station had said). The plane had been unable to see the boat because of heavy rain and strong wind, with low visibility. Back at his base, the Chilean pilot reported that the sailor had spoken English with a definite French accent. The completely bilingual Roufs spoke English with a Canadian accent, but without any trace of a French one. At no time, said the Chilean commandant, did the boat's skipper say the words 'Groupe Lima Golf'. The commandant offered no explanation for the conflicting reports. Nor could anyone else explain them.

Roufs's fate was suddenly up for grabs again. It was equally possible that he had collided disastrously with an iceberg, capsized and drowned, been lost overboard, or that he was adrift in a life-raft. He could be sailing under jury rig or with an intact mast, still in the race but without any working communication equipment. One hypothesis was as good as any other.

Joseph Conrad had complicated feelings about 'the destructive element'. Like all sailors, he had been purged of any illusions early on in his career afloat. The ocean fascinated and frightened him. He loved its purity and unspoilt nature, so different from the metastasising industrial blight ashore. The unbending aristocratic hierarchy of rank aboard ship was congenial to the intensely conservative exile. When he was separated from the sea, he pined for it like an addict. After he retired from life as a first mate to write, he kept going to sea as a yachtsman. He lived, with passionate nostalgia (like Joshua Slocum), through the period of the end of the age of sail; the cruel, graceful, widow-making ships and barques were fading away forever under the impact of coal, steam and ocean-linking canals. No more iron men, just iron ships. Even as he regarded the ocean as the earth's purest wilderness, the incarnation of Nature, Conrad had no doubts about its unequalled and malevolent power.

> *The ocean has the conscienceless temper of a savage autocrat spoiled by much adulation. He cannot brook the slightest appearance of defiance, and has remained the irreconcilable enemy of ships and men ever since ships and men had the unheard-of audacity to go afloat together in the face of his frown. From that day he has gone on swallowing up fleets and men without his resentment being glutted by the number of victims – by so many wrecked ships and wrecked lives . . . The most amazing wonder of the deep is its unfathomable cruelty.*

Not much has changed for sailboat sailors since Conrad's time. Fascination and fear are still the emotions the sea calls up. As always, the Southern Ocean on the way to Cape Horn provides the extreme version of the experience. The technology and ingenuity of our machines hasn't been enough to make a difference. But for Conrad and the Vendée Globe sailors alike, the danger of this vast and wild wilderness was an inescapable corollary of its attraction.

Bullimore knew as much as anyone about the hazards of the Southern Ocean. Yet it had a peaceful, 'untouched-by-man' serenity to it, he said. 'You know you really feel that you're out there in the wilderness, the wilderness of the sea.'

When you have spent time in the wilderness, Parlier said, it changes your idea of the earth and our existence on it. The experience puts things into perspective. Everyone needs that experience, although few can ever taste it. All of us have a need, which is a deep human need, to feed on virgin spaces, like the Southern Ocean, untouched by human civilisation, he said. 'It's really a no-man's land where humans have no place. It's the sea of the albatross and the other birds, and the whales.'

It's the part of earth where no one can say, 'This bit is mine.'

After the race, Laurent told me, he visited the Sahara for a week. He wanted to go to the real desert, the one made out of sand. 'It is the same, really the same,' he reported stolidly. 'Except the Southern Ocean is bigger.'

For Laurent, the engineer, remoteness was defined by the absence of technological interference. Humans found it unnecessary to concern themselves with the Southern Ocean. That was why the weather satellites provided only scrappy, almost accidental, data for that part of the planet.

The Vendée Globe skippers experience the Southern Ocean as a still-remote and untouched wilderness. For the sailor trying to stay afloat in a Southern Ocean low-pressure storm two thousand miles from the nearest land, the human link with nature feels intact – as intimate and primeval, as intricately engrossing as ever. Nature as it used to be, as Autissier called the Great South. But while it may be as close as anything on the planet's surface gets to primordial wildness, its seemingly impregnable naturalness has been breached. Because of the large-scale effects of human activity, which influence every part of the planet, the Southern Ocean, and the world's other remote areas, are no longer completely unchanged from their ancient state. Global warming, pollution, mass tourism, our own power to destroy everything with nuclear or biological weapons, all have had their effect on these remote regions, and on how we think about them.

The meaning of the last great wildernesses is most insidiously adulterated by people themselves, their drive to go to these places in increasing numbers. Yet the quality that draws people there is for ever elusive: it disappears at the moment people enter.

Many of the far regions left on the earth have turned out to be surprisingly fragile, more susceptible than we imagined to the effects of being visited. The risks involved in getting to them and staying there for any length of time should be enough to prevent them from becoming banal, exploited tourist sites. But cruise ships now sail regularly to southern Chilean and Argentine ports, to Antarctica, to the Falkland Islands and to the mythical cape itself, at least in the summer. Yachts periodically cruise the vicinity of the Horn – in the Strait of Magellan, the Beagle Channel and the Falkland and South Georgia islands. A handful even sail to Antarctica and anchor precariously in its deserted, icy bays. Few cruising sailors have the stomach for this. You still need to be a very tough and competent mariner to pilot a small boat near Cape Horn, and across the weather bellows of the Drake Passage between South America and Antarctica.

Nevertheless, their presence changes our idea of these places. Now there are people there in their little boats. The Horn is not quite as remote, harsh and untouchable a place as we once thought it was. When I see photographs in yachting magazines of cruising boats sailing to Cape Horn for pleasure, the cape and the hazardous seas and channels around it seem compromised. As they passed the cape, three of the Vendée Globe racers had rendezvous of sorts: Auguin with his wife Véronique, Autissier with three cruising yachts whose crews came out to meet and wave to her, and Goss with a small cruise ship whose passengers waved and shouted encouragement. All three sailors enjoyed these meetings. They were happy to see other human beings again after months alone at sea. Yet somehow, reading about them, I felt slightly let-down.

I wondered if these brief encounters meant that the Horn had lost some of the mystery and significance with which Moitessier, or my able-seaman great-grandfather for that matter, had invested it. People with the courage and skill to sail there, admirable as their achievements are, diminish it for all of us. Perhaps we feel something of the conqueror's inevitable discontent.

In the future, it's not hard to envisage Southern Ocean charter cruises – billed as one of the last great strenuous and extreme adventures – in big, fast multihulls or monohulls built or adapted for the purpose, making regular passages across the southern Indian or Pacific oceans. Just the thing for the jaded adventure-destination tourist with lots of money. That would certainly change our idea of this wilderness.

11

The Wounded Surgeon

> *I made companionship with what there*
> *was around me, sometimes with the*
> *universe and sometimes with my own*
> *insignificant self.*
>
> – Joshua Slocum, Sailing Alone Around the World
>
> *Who, if I cried, would hear me from the*
> *order of Angels?.*
>
> – Rainer Maria Rilke, The Drino Elegies

WHEN HE was about one thousand miles west of Cape Horn, sailing at eleven knots in relatively good conditions – a twenty-five-knot northerly wind with fifteen-foot seas – Pete Goss on *Aqua Quorum* strapped a flashlight to his head and a mirror to his knee, picked up a scalpel and began to slice open his own hugely swollen elbow.

The fluid sac on the joint had become infected months before, just after he crossed the equator on the outbound leg down the Atlantic. There was no particular reason for it. He just woke up one morning with a bloody sore elbow. On the advice of the race doctor, Jean-Yves Chauve, he treated it with antibiotics and analgesic cream from his medical kit. In bad weather, he had to wrap the elbow in protective strapping to try to prevent the intense pain he felt when he bumped it on cabin fittings or deck gear. He'd resigned himself to having good and bad days, and just living with it until the race was over.

But from the end of December, when he landed on the elbow while fighting back through storm-force winds to rescue Dinelli, it got steadily worse. For a month, he couldn't bend it at all. As he made his lone sail across the southern Pacific, the swelling increased, and he lost the use of his arm almost completely. He had to strap it to his body to stop it getting knocked about in bad weather. Unable to sleep because of the pain, he was almost literally sailing single-handed. He complained about how frustrating it was not being able to sail *Aqua Quorum* properly. It had been almost impossible to unfurl and trim his big genoa jib since he'd passed south of New Zealand. He had had to rely on his mainsail and the smaller staysail, and his speed was much below what his 'fabulous boat' was capable of doing. On 2 February, he reported spending a grim night beating into gale-force winds from the east instead of the usual westerlies. But in the peculiar relativism of the Southern Ocean, things were better now: the wind had gone into the west again, and he was running before a fifty-five-knot gale.

Then the big, crimson swelling ruptured. There were protruding hernias of soft tissue and 'a lovely gunge coming out'. An operation was the last resort, partly because the race doctor feared a potentially fatal post-operative infection, and partly because it's not easy, even for tough ex-Royal Marines, to blithely saw away at their own flesh. But there was no choice. Chauve decided that Goss should operate right away. There was less chance of infection in the cold Southern Ocean. And if one did set in, Goss could probably make it to the Falkland Islands in ten days or so for treatment. He would know by then whether the operation had been successful.

Goss followed Chauve's faxed instructions – sanitise the cabin, set out the instruments, put on gloves, sanitise the elbow and so on. He did a couple of dry runs to make sure he had everything in order. He had a cream anaesthetic, but he couldn't put it on the open flesh of the rupture. So he didn't bother with it and just began cutting.

'And once I started, it was as if I was working on someone else,' Goss said. 'Everyone wants to be a surgeon, don't they? And then it was just a farce because off I went, and the first thing that happened was blood dripped all over the mirror so I couldn't see what I was doing. So I'm cleaning the bloody mirror and I was cutting away and expecting quite a lot of fluid to come out, and none came out. I went deeper and deeper, and I thought, Shit, I'm going to cut a tendon or cut my arm off in a minute. So I put the scalpel in my teeth, and I had a cloth – the blood was dripping everywhere – and I'm faxing to Jean-Yves. I thought, Well before I go further, I'd like a bit of feedback.'

He had been faxing Chauve for two months without a problem. But at that moment, the doctor's fax machine broke down. Goss faxed race headquarters and asked them to ask Chauve what the hell he was supposed to do now. While he was waiting for an answer, he wiped up blood. Since he couldn't make a cup of tea and the sliced-up elbow was pretty sore, he decided to take some painkillers. The instructions were in French, which Goss couldn't read. But there were two 'bloody great tablets', which he swallowed.

'And as I'm doing all that, the wind picks up, and the boat heels and all the tools fall off the chart table. And the tablets turned out to be efflorescent and should have been dissolved in water, so now I'm frothing at the mouth, and it was quite funny really.'

Goss wasn't the first single-hander to act as his own surgeon. The Argentine circumnavigator Vito Dumas, a few days out of Montevideo in 1942 on his Southern Ocean circumnavigation, ran into a storm. Some of the seams in his small wooden ketch opened up. The twisting, torquing force of the waves had strained the timber and dislodged the caulking. To stay afloat, Dumas stuffed sailcloth and red lead into the hole. In the process, he cut his arm. The boat survived, but his arm turned septic. He developed blood poisoning and for days grew steadily weaker. All this time, Dumas had to handle his heavy gear and sails, and keep his boat going in the heavy weather of the roaring forties. Then the infected swelling burst, spewing pus. Dumas helped it along by cutting and gouging out the entire area of infected flesh with one of his ship's knives – no scalpels, anaesthetic, antibiotics or faxed instructions. His treatment seemed to turn the tide of the poison. He slowly recovered and continued on towards Cape Town.

As Goss sliced away at his own elbow, De Radiguès on *Afibel* was far behind with his familiar problems. He was stuck in Dunedin on the South Island of New Zealand, having entered the port to try one more time to get his electrical system sorted out. On the day of Goss's operation, while *Afibel* was being towed out to sea to resume the race, the towing line parted. The determined but unlucky de Radiguès found himself on the rocks near the harbour entrance. It would be weeks before he got going again.

Bringing up the official rear of the Vendée Globe fleet, Goss was almost six thousand miles behind Auguin, still the steady leader, and more than a thousand miles behind Chabaud, the next closest sailor. She was just a few days away from rounding Cape Horn. While Goss and Chabaud continued to wrestle with the Southern Ocean, all the other competitors, both official and disqualified, had rounded the last stormy cape. They were now dealing with a variety of conditions depending on their location within the complicated Atlantic weather systems. Seven competitors out of the original sixteen were still officially in the race. That number included Gerry Roufs, who had been silent for almost a month.

Even now, it was still possible that he was sailing on, his communications systems knocked out. But this storyline, with its eventual happy ending in Les Sables-d'Olonne, looked more and more like fiction. At race headquarters, and among the other sailors, doubts about Roufs's survival had grown very strong. In fact, most of the skippers had already come to their own private conclusions: the Canadian had been lost, flung irretrievably beyond the pale. Most likely, he died very soon after his ARGOS had stopped transmitting. The fact that he hadn't been able to activate any of his EPIRBs meant that the end had been quick and brutal. The general consensus was that *Groupe LG2* had probably run headlong into an iceberg, had broken up almost immediately, Roufs drowning quickly in the chaos – his protective frame ripped apart in seconds.

Laurent, who sailed by just to the south of the search zone a few days after Roufs's ARGOS went silent, recalled how much ice had been floating about the area. The *Mass Enterprise*, the freighter that had searched for Roufs for two days, saw lots of bergs and faxed their positions to the Vendée Globe boats. When the weather cleared, Laurent said, visibility returning to its normal mile or so, he saw ice every day.

Chabaud was succinct: 'An iceberg, I'm sure. It was quick.'

Parlier agreed. It was ice. Between the first shock and the swell breaking against the berg, Roufs's boat would have been quickly smashed to pieces.

Autissier, who struggled to get back to Roufs's position, and who hadn't been able to drive herself and her boat to do it, was more loquacious. When we spoke after the race, she circled the conversation around the subject of Roufs and his fate for several minutes. She seemed to be still coming to terms with it, thinking through how she felt as she continued to talk. She wanted me to understand how bad conditions had been, and how difficult it had been to go back when there was no position to aim for. It had seemed so hopeless from the start. Goss had rescued Dinelli because there had been a definite EPIRB position to drive his boat towards. But for her, there had been only a large, vague and always expanding area. She emphasised how much punishment she and her boat had taken in the same storm, how difficult it was to sail to windward without her mainsail.

Autissier more or less subscribed to the iceberg theory of Roufs's disappearance as well. She also speculated on the next most likely possibility: that he had gone overboard. In one of their last conversations, Roufs had told her that he was staying down below. But perhaps he had been obliged to go on deck for something, some problem. If he hadn't bothered to clip on his safety harness, a stumble on deck could have done the rest, or a big wave could easily have ripped the harness away from its attachment point. No material could resist the force of those hundreds of watery tons smashing into it at thirty knots.

Bullimore, who knew first-hand about the sudden shock of catastrophe in the Southern Ocean, acknowledged the usual scenarios. The boat could have capsized or pitchpoled with Roufs on deck; he could have gone overboard. But most likely, it had been the ice. A growler, Bullimore thought. *Groupe LG2* could have rolled right over one at twenty knots, the hull shredding like cheese on a grater, the boat's bottom disintegrating, the hull breaking up, filling, going down, Roufs never having a chance to flip a switch on one of his EPIRBs. No technology could save you from that.

The answers the skippers gave to my question of what they thought had happened to Roufs were thoughtful and as helpful as they could be under the unknown circumstances of the Canadian's disappearance. But it was the way they answered the question, the subtle tics and gestures of their body language, that was more interesting.

How to describe it? A flattening of tone, a slight, wary withdrawal, brief eye contact and then quick aversion, words carefully chosen, arms drawn protectively across the body, the body itself adjusted slightly away from me, from the abrupt intrusion of this question. I watched carefully each time I asked what had happened to Roufs. Each time, I saw the pain the question produced.

It was quite noticeable because there's a studied nonchalance in the way in which these people respond to queries about their work. In part, it's the practised manner of the professional who's been interviewed many times before. In part, these elite sailors have adopted a casual bravado as a protection against the dangers they face. Asking about Roufs punched through the shell.

Because he was a friend, and he died violently and young, it was difficult to talk about . But Roufs's disappearance and my questions about it provoked the anxiety of each lone sailor's terrible vulnerability in the wilderness of the Southern Ocean.

There could have been four dead in this race if not for the Australians, Goss, toughness and luck. This – the knowledge of Gerry's sudden and brutal disappearance from the face of the sea – would now be lodged in their brains, along with the knowledge of the other lost friends, every time they sailed the high latitudes.

Perhaps there was more, an unconscious level of self-protection. Like the members of any elite for whom the potential for sudden death is part of the deal, these sailors had a very strong sense of their own unusual ability. There was nothing exaggerated about it. They simply understood that they could do things with boats that very few other sailors could do; they were able to withstand physical and psychological pressures at sea that most other sailors could not deal with. Like Tom Wolfe's fighter-pilot jocks, they had the right stuff. Maybe the Vendée Globe sailors, like the pilots, lean on the same warped logic in the cause of self-preservation, a series of simple propositions. Roufs's death (assuming he was dead) occurred because he had failed. Indeed, his death *was* failure. Deep down, the sailors could say to themselves, there are no accidents. If you died at sea, it was because you screwed up, because you had the wrong stuff. The corollary was inevitable and was designed to be reassuring: if you have the right stuff – the true right stuff – you won't die.

The discomfort of the skippers when they had to think and talk about Roufs had complicated causes. Their feelings about his death, and its meaning for their own lives, must be complex, even confused. *Because if it happened to him, it could happen to me.* What a compulsion there must be for the skippers to deflect the implications of Roufs's death (or the deaths of Harry Mitchell, Jacques de Roux, Nigel Tetley, Mike Plant) away from themselves.

Michael Herr describes the reactions of some young soldiers in Vietnam riding in a big Chinook helicopter with a dozen filled body-bags. Confronted with their own possible future, they ridiculed the dead: 'What assholes! Look at 'em all. Buncha dumb, dead fuckers!' Their fault they were dead. Nothing to worry about really.

Until the first few days of February, Auguin had hopes of finishing the race in fewer than one hundred days – the latest in a string of round-numbered times that solo sailors aimed to beat. But suddenly, he ran out of the north-east trade winds into a fluky, light wind coming at him from the general direction of the finish line. One hundred days quickly became an impossible goal, but he still had a good chance of beating Lamazou's 109-day race record.

Beating into choppy seas near the Cape Verde Islands, one thousand miles off the coast of Africa, the only boat back in the northern hemisphere, Auguin lamented to race headquarters that the weather couldn't be worse. '*Géodis* and its man are suffering.'

Always a tiring and teeth-rattling point of sail, a beat was particularly gruelling in a Vendée Globe boat – the unhappiness of downwind surfers forced to pound into headseas. That night, Auguin had to change course to take the waves farther off the bow so that he could get some rest. The noise and vibration from the wave impacts were unbearable.

His weather forecasts predicted head winds until the north-west tip of Spain. That meant he had to tack. Each one took him forty-five minutes because there was so much to do each time: set up the running backstays, pump the water ballast over to the new windward side, swing the canting keel, adjust the attitude and area of the sails to the wind's varying strength. Often, after he had tacked to get the best possible angle, the wind changed direction again, and all his efforts were wasted. With the time lost in each tack, he needed three hours of stable wind to make the manoeuvre worthwhile. That wasn't happening. He was wasting miles and getting very tired.

The disqualified Autissier, fifteen hundred miles behind Auguin, worked her way through the doldrums. She would soon cross the equator. In spite of her enforced stop in Cape Town, she had over-taken everyone ahead of her when she rejoined the race, except the charmed Auguin. Like the other sailors who were out of the official running and the public eye, Autissier was relatively silent. Only the daily latitude and longitude position reports, and an occasional terse message to race headquarters, traced her gritty progress. It was so much more difficult for the disqualified sailors to endure the rough and frustrating going through the Atlantic weather maze knowing it wouldn't count in the race results. Officially, they had become almost invisible. But for the public following their progress and planning a trip to the Vendée to welcome the boats back, it didn't make much difference who was still official and who wasn't.

Anyway, there was still personal honour at stake: the individual goal to 'tie the knot', in the Anglo-Saxon phrase, of a circum-navigation, or *boucler la bouclé* (loop the loop), as the French put it.

Thiercelin and Laurent were sailing officially second and third, trailing Auguin by two thousand miles. Laurent's impressive per-formance in his older and relatively heavy boat had been consistent throughout. After the race, I spoke to him aboard *Groupe LG Traitmat*, which was docked at a nondescript marina in his home town of Lorient. Laurent's boat looked as if it had been through the wringer a few times but there had been no serious breakdowns of gear or rig. Perhaps the heavier materials and construction of the older boat made it less susceptible to damage; or maybe he had just been lucky. His tactics had helped as well, although they had put him in greater danger. When I asked him when he had felt particularly afraid during the race, he denied that he ever had. Then he paused. 'Well, yes, I was afraid of the icebergs because I had no radar; the antenna was broken.'

It had failed soon after the start, in the Bay of Biscay. Yet Laurent didn't let his fear stop him from going well south of the ice line to more than fifty-five degrees latitude – to shorten his route and make up for his boat's slower speed. He saw icebergs often; sometimes they were all around him as he sailed blindly on.

Otherwise, 'I was able to move at a steady speed, on a pretty short route, and without slowing down much when it was calm,' he said. 'I had a consistent and fluid race.'

In early February, Laurent was very tired, sailing in changeable and squally conditions, looking for the south-east trade winds to get him quickly to the equator and the doldrums. He was happy to have threaded his way successfully around the South Atlantic high-pressure system, without going unnecessarily far out of his way.

Thiercelin, sailing to the west and north of Laurent, was enduring violent squalls, but their westerly winds were helping him break away from his too-close proximity to the Brazilian coast. Thiercelin was keeping a close watch on Laurent, who, after twenty-four thousand miles, was only two hundred miles behind.

Thiercelin was more tired than usual because the day before, in spite of his ear problems and dizziness, he'd been obliged to climb his eighty-foot mast five times to make repairs. It was the emergency he had been waiting for, and fearing. Finally, he'd had no choice but to go aloft. And because it had been necessary, he found that he had been able to do it. That was one of the things about sailing, how it forced you sometimes to break through your fear. Heroism was really just a matter of doing something even though it scared you stiff. Sailing could draw out of you those sublime moments of transcendence, when your limits, for a while, no longer limited you. Every man or woman a hero.

Both de Broc, disqualified after his Chilean stop, and Eric Dumont, still officially in the race in fourth place, were working their slow way through the uncertain weather of the high-pressure southern horse latitudes. Dumont told race headquarters that his speedometer showed '00'. But that was just as well because he had broken his thumb two days before when his boat crashed violently into a wave. In the suddenly changing weather of the region, Dumont endured a force 9 or 10 storm (wind up to fifty-five knots). As he sailed under bare poles in heavy rain, the boat had been repeatedly knocked down. Beating into this sort of weather in the Atlantic wasn't like the Southern Ocean – not as much fear-inspiring as uncomfortable and tiring.

'The inside is full of water, and I jump four feet on every wave,' he reported.

Far behind Auguin and the others, still in the Southern Ocean wilderness, Catherine Chabaud continued her slow but steady progress. With the boats ahead of her beating to windward or sliding through light wind in the horse latitudes, she was the only racer sailing faster than ten knots. Just before she reached the Horn, sailing in her relatively conservative style, she hove-to for twenty-four hours to allow a violent storm-force front to pass over her. Race headquarters began to get concerned when Chabaud didn't report in by radio after the storm moved on. Jeantot could see how severe it was from his weatherfax satellite pictures. But to his relief – he would have been emotionally hard-pressed to handle another emergency – Chabaud briefly switched on her second ARGOS position beacon, the one with the GPS unit attached. This was the agreed-upon signal, in the event of radio problems, that all was well on board.

When she rounded the Horn the next day, in thirty-five to forty knot winds and the heavy seas left over from the depression, she opened a bottle of champagne. 'I'm happy to be part of the Cape Horners' brotherhood,' she said. 'I want to enjoy this beautiful landscape. The light is very beautiful [it was after 11:00 p.m. local time, but was still light in the high-latitude summer evening]. It's a magic time.'

Later, she told me: 'I had the feeling in front of Cape Horn that I was on top of Everest. I wanted to put a flag there.'

As for Goss, it turned out that his six-hour-long auto-operation was a success. His amateur sawboning provided almost immediate and tremendous relief. There were five worrying days while he carefully changed the dressing each day and watched for infection, but none developed. Five months after the operation, the elbow was still quite painful when he used his arm a lot, but it was slowly improving. The whole experience had been quite interesting, he said. 'At the end of the day, there's no one else to do it, so you get stuck into it yourself.'

12

————

The Sombre Season

With the great wisdom you have gained,
with so much experience,
you must surely have understood
by then what Ithacas mean.

– Constantine Cavafy, *Ithaca*

Separated we shall be
For ever, my friend
Like the wild geese
Lost in the clouds.

– Bashō, *The Narrow Road to the Deep North*

T HE ATLANTIC oceans, South and then North, were the final stages of the Vendée Globe. After the long crescendo of suspense and anxiety through the Southern Ocean, and the climax of the passage of the Horn, the prospect of the Atlantic had the feel of a long denouement – the last act in the drama begun a season ago. But while the tired sailors were released from the great dangers of the Southern Ocean, in place of its murderous simplicity – all you had to do was run hard to the east and stay in one right-side-up piece – they had to confront again the complexities of Atlantic weather systems and the dangers of heavy shipping. Rounding the last stormy cape after months at sea, in boats that often seemed to be disintegrating around them, they exchanged the fear and desolation of the South for the long, gruelling journey home.

They had got through the Atlantic on the way out, of course, in that intoxicating flight out from Les Sables-d'Olonne across Biscay, through the westerlies and the horse latitudes to the equator, and on to the South. The race and the sea had been fresh and exciting, the skippers finally released from the complicated confines of business and family ashore. Then they had sunk their teeth into the Vendée Globe with fierce determination, like predators on the hunt. On the way back, after the Southern Ocean and the Horn, with more than seven thousand miles still to go, it was different. They had been out on the edge for a long time. Tired veterans, they carefully conserved their strength and watched their boats anxiously for signs of decay.

Thiercelin seemed to have the most to worry about. By 12 February, trailing the leader, Auguin, by more than fifteen hundred miles, he had entered the belt of the north-east trade winds. Boats sailing in this predictable tropical wind system usually have a fine time – it's about as far removed from the Southern Ocean as it's possible to be. But the boat's heading in relation to the wind is always the crucial arbiter. Thiercelin was beating into the trades, trying to go in roughly the same direction from which the wind was blowing. It was worse in some ways than running before the average Southern Ocean storm. The boat rattled and banged, and the skipper had to suffer the anxiety of not being entirely sure it would hold together and get him to port.

'What hell this is!' he exclaimed. 'I have a wind of twenty-five to thirty knots with wave troughs ten to fifteen feet deep and no more than thirty feet between the crests. The boat lifts up on each wave and then falls into the trough behind it. It hurts!'

The short, steep waves, which would have been perfect to surf on if he had been running before them, west to the Caribbean, continuously swept the deck. Thiercelin double-reefed his mainsail and hoisted his small storm jib to reduce speed and diminish the wave impacts. Still, the harder collisions threw him right out of his berth. He had to wedge himself in the chair at his chart table to try to get some rest. The punishment would last for two or three days.

'I never thought that the way back through the trade winds, close-hauled at ten knots, could be so hard,' he lamented. 'Believe me, I prefer the storms of the Southern Ocean. But then, sailors always find something to complain about,' he added.

Thiercelin's real worry was the bow area he had shored up with cannibalised wood from the boat's interior fittings just after he had passed the Horn. Sure enough, it soon began to leak. He had to pump twenty-five gallons out of his bow compartment every hour; then forty gallons. His electric pump was taking care of it for now, but he was depending on one pump and an electrical system that was so often unreliable. If necessary, he could hand-pump the sea water out of the boat, at least for a while. It would be very difficult to keep it up until the finish, though, and the leak might get worse.

No one was having an easy time of it. Working his way through the northern horse latitudes, Auguin bashed excruciatingly into head-seas and wind one day, and nursed *Géodis* through frustrating calms the next. Although he was too far ahead to be caught, his lead had been reduced by the unusually light wind he had encountered. On his one-hundredth day of solitude, he spent the night flopping around in another calm. By mid-morning, however, the wind came back, and from the right direction. For the first time in months, he dragged his big light gennaker (a hybrid spinnaker and genoa jib) out of its sailbag and flew it with his mainsail. Under more than five thousand square feet of sail (an incredible amount; a much-heavier sixty-foot cruising boat might carry half that area), *Géodis* romped along at eleven knots. It was the fastest he'd gone in two weeks. The previous day, he saw a freighter, the first he had encountered since passing the Canaries on his outbound course the previous November. Like his rendezvous at the Horn, the sight of the ship pleased the gregarious Auguin.

'It was proof that there's still other life on earth. I've had enough of sailing alone. These three solo races took ten years of my life. That's enough. From now on, I'd like to sail with a crew – maybe a Whitbread. I'm trying not to think of the finishing line, but I really want to be back.'

He had been studying his weatherfax printouts and had decided to sail to the south of the Azores. In the prevailing weather system, he calculated that that route should give him an ideal north-west wind of fifteen to twenty-five knots as he closed with the French coast. He was trying not to push *Géodis* too hard. It would be a brutal disappointment to have something crucial break now. To be deprived of victory after leading the race by so much for so long would be like getting shot five minutes before the cease-fire. Just when he really needed it, in the heavy shipping lanes of the North Atlantic, his radar had broken down. He would have to keep a visual watch for freighters and fishing boats, and get even less sleep.

While Auguin was about a week away from the finish line, Goss rounded the Horn. In the previous Vendée Globe, the winner had crossed the line on the same day as the last boat cleared the cape. The gap wasn't so big this time. Officially, it would be reduced further because of Goss's 318-hour time allowance for rescuing Dinelli and getting him to Hobart. Goss was elated at sailing round the Horn, and he was also feeling better than he had in months. The wound on his self-doctored elbow was still draining, but there was no sign of infection. It was uncomfortable rather than painful, and for the first time in more than a month, he could actually use his left arm.

He passed by the Horn three miles off in perfect weather: a fifteen-knot westerly wind and sunshine. He had his rendezvous with the Antarctic tour ship, whose passengers shouted encouragement and took pictures. Naturally, he drank champagne. One of his deepest emotions, he said, was gratitude to his team for helping him experience one of the great moments of his life; it was their triumph as much as his.

Goss, the ex-soldier, valued his team, that enabling and life-preserving small group. Was his tribute also one of those nebulous characteristics we cavalierly describe as Anglo-Saxon, as opposed to French or Latin? None of the French sailors rounding the cape had mentioned their shore-based wizards and drudges. The Horn was for the sailor and the boat alone. Probably the more logical attitude. There was too much of a discrepancy between what the shore teams did and what the skippers accomplished. It was one thing to put together the boat and its gear. It was another thing to sail the Southern Ocean. Something else entirely to have chanced death to save another man's life, as Goss had done.

That night he had a meal to celebrate – food from Leclerc, his only French sponsor. Anglo-Saxons might be good with teams, but when you needed some celebratory grub, only the real French stuff would do. Goss's main problem now was that the cooling pump on his generator had given up the ghost. He adapted one of his hand-operated bilge pumps and that worked well. It was just that he had to sit and lever the handle back and forth for four hours each day to keep his generator cool and running and maintain his electrical power. He was Pete the pump, he said. It was very tiring and monotonous.

Between Auguin and Goss, the other boats stretched out across two hemispheres (excepting de Radiguès, still stuck in port in New Zealand). Some of the boats in the group that had coalesced behind the leaders months ago as the fleet cleared the southern horse latitudes – Thiercelin, Laurent, de Broc and Dumont – had separated under the pressure of Southern Ocean sailing. Thiercelin, in official second place and pumping his bow compartment hour by hour, was three hundred miles ahead of third-place Laurent, and eight hundred miles ahead of Dumont, in fourth. Dumont was still almost neck and neck with de Broc, sailing disqualified after his stop in Ushuaia. The two boats were only fifteen miles apart – another example of the close-quarters sailing that often occurred in these races. Before this Vendée Globe was over, there would be two unlikely close finishes as the boats raced for the line.

Laurent cleared the doldrums and began to beat into the north-east trade winds. *Groupe LG Traitmat* was showing its age and, like Thiercelin's boat, the strain of the race. Laurent could see the hull panels flex and deform as the boat hit the waves. Stress cracks like spiders' webs had appeared on the bulkheads. He could almost see them elongating. The hull-keel joint was leaking. Not much for now, but no sailor was happy to see the ocean trickling into his boat. On top of that, everything was turning red and getting gritty. Fine sand, sucked out of the Sahara desert by storms and blown a thousand miles out to sea, penetrated everywhere, on deck and down below. At least Laurent had fresh food. Flying fish landed on his deck overnight. Stranded there, they asphyxiated, and he cooked them for breakfast. One morning, he found twelve of them.

At the same time, Dumont crossed the equator. He had managed to carry the south-east trade winds unusually far north, right up to and across the line. He had run out of champagne, and instead poured a cup of his sponsor's coffee into the sea for Neptune and Aeolus. 'Now that I'm back in the northern hemisphere, I feel as if I'm in my own garden.'

He hit the doldrums and spent a day and a half rolling around in calms and fluky wind. He used his radar to locate the heavy rain showers that usually meant no wind. He zigzagged around them, sailing miles out of his way, but eventually creeping clear of the *pot au noir* and into the first tendrils of the north-east trades. Then he too

had to absorb their unexpectedly severe punishments. The so-called
Christmas Trades could be strong – up to thirty knots for weeks at a
time in late December and January. By February, however, they had
usually died down to the normal winter velocity of twenty knots or
so. This year, they were blowing harder for much longer than usual.
Once Dumont got into the established trades, he had to beat into
thirty-five-knot wind, with frequent rain squalls. He watched the
patched-up wounds on *Café Legal le Goût* anxiously. The spinnaker-
pole splint he had lashed to his boom in the middle of the southern
Pacific looked as if it could come apart at any time. He wrapped more
reinforcing lines around it as it flexed in the abrupt wave impacts. His
standing rigging was loose, but he couldn't tighten it because one of
the points of attachment (a chainplate) between the rigging and the
hull was damaged. He feared in equal measure tearing out the
chainplate if he tightened the rigging too much, and the unnerving
way both masts on his ketch-rigged boat whipped around because the
rigging was too loose.

Fifteen miles away, de Broc's course took him through almost
identical conditions. His compromised hull-keel joint seemed to be
bearing up well. There was no way of being sure, short of hauling the
boat out of the water, but at least it appeared to be upholding the first
rule of seamanship by keeping the ocean out of the boat. A potential
keel problem was always worrying, though, and in fact, it would turn
out that de Broc's adventures weren't quite over. His real problem for
now was a shortage of drinking water because of a weary and
faltering watermaker. He managed to collect rain water as he ghosted
through the doldrums – enough to last for another two weeks.

Parlier, like Autissier, out of the official running and relatively
silent, continued his catch-up drive north. He crossed the equator
two days after Dumont. He had climbed the mast the day before,
almost for the hell of it, and had discovered a worn genoa halyard,
which he replaced. Since the tune-up in Fremantle, Parlier had
reported no problems with the lightly constructed *Aquitaine
Innovations* similar to the ones that had dogged his outward-bound
course. It was probably another sign that a few months, or even
weeks, of extra preparation time before the start could have made all
the difference. Like many of the other sailors, he was already staking
out his ground for the next race. 'I'll be back in four years,' he faxed.
'When I have enough time to get ready, my boat will win.'

Meanwhile, Chabaud crossed the invisible border of the Southern

Ocean, out of the roaring forties. 'I won't miss them! I'm still being escorted by an albatross [not Bernard], and the petrels are every-where. Maybe I'll make it to Les Sables for March 21, the first day of spring.'

She continued to have problems with her electrical system. The diesel and wind generators were still *hors de combat*, and she was relying on solar panels to charge her batteries. With this intermittent source of power, her radio and fax were virtually unusable. *Whirlpool Europe 2* was doing all right otherwise. Just the usual hair-raising maintenance. She had been forced to climb her mast to replace the broken storm-jib halyard. Sailing fast in thirty-five-knot wind, she was still wearing her insulated clothes and foul-weather gear. She hadn't been able to shower in two weeks. Soon it would be warmer, and she would be able to face the icy, cleansing water.

Finally, one by one and two by two, they began to come home. They had begun the race in an autumn Bay of Biscay storm. Now they had to finish it sailing through the bay's late-winter and early-spring gales. All the time the boats had been off sailing the world, Biscay had been blustering away – its usual winter of discontent. It was a little easier heading back towards the Vendée coast than it had been leaving it, because the boats' generally north-east course brought the westerly winds of the winter lows farther behind the boats. They were able to reach rather than having to beat to windward. That reduced the apparent wind and, most helpfully, the impact of waves on the strained hulls.

When the skippers were in the Southern Ocean, it seemed as if no sea or ocean anywhere else in the world could test them, or scare them, the way the Great South did. They might complain that beating to windward through the north-east trade winds was worse than the Southern Ocean, but they didn't mean it. While it was very un-comfortable, and could damage the weakened Vendée Globe boats, it was over in a few days. The doldrums? A mere forty-eight hours or so of frustration. In reality, nothing was like the Southern Ocean, although the Bay of Biscay could come close to it in relatively short bursts.

Knox-Johnston describes a wild day in Biscay at the end of the catamaran *Enza*'s record-breaking, round-the-world sprint. The boat was overtaken by an intense late-March low-pressure system. As it headed across the bay towards the finish line off the Breton cape of

Ushant, the wind gusted above hurricane strength and the confused cross-seas rose forty to fifty feet high. Knox-Johnston tells how the crew rigged the boat as if it were sailing off Cape Horn. They streamed warps and chains off the sterns of the two hulls to slow the cat down and maintain some degree of control. Even so, he reckoned that the short, steep seas, lacking the rough majestic order of Southern Ocean rollers, were extremely dangerous. Sometimes the waves flung the half-ton of towed chain through the air. Several times, the catamaran surfed off the crest of a wave and fell into the trough ahead. As it crashed against the back of the next wave, its speed was instantaneously halved, or more, and crewmen were expelled from their bunks like pilots ejecting from the cockpits of crashing fighters. The helmsmen had to learn on the spot, and improvise the best way for the ninety-two-foot-long, forty-two-foot-wide *Enza* to negotiate the seas. Survival conditions on a spring day in the Bay of Biscay. 'It was a steep learning curve,' Knox-Johnston said.

Fortunately, Auguin didn't have to go through a storm like that as he approached Les Sables-d'Olonne, but he did have a complicated weather pattern to negotiate: two lows ranging across the bay in quick succession. He could ride on the back of the first one in thirty-five-knot wind from the west-north-west. A few hours after it moved off, the second system would overtake him with thirty-knot south-west wind, which would steadily increase over the ensuing twenty-four hours as the low passed by. Auguin had to control his speed so as to arrive off Les Sables close enough to high tide to allow *Géodis* to enter the harbour. His boat's keel was almost fifteen feet deep. Even though the port authorities had dredged the channel to accommodate the deep-draught Vendée Globe boats, the water was still too thin for them at low tide. The last thing Auguin wanted was to miss the tide and be obliged to heave-to off the harbour entrance, anticlimactically hanging around, waiting for the next high water.

In fact, he judged it nicely. He could have driven hard, sailed the last 335 miles in twenty-four hours and arrived on 16 February, his 104th day at sea. But he was still concerned about breaking something. He dreaded losing the race at the last moment by overtaxing his boat. With his defunct radar and the usual heavy shipping in Biscay (fishing boats especially), he was running on his last reserves of wakefulness. It would be easy to make a mistake. So he slowed down to delay his arrival until the next day.

'I have managed my race wisely up to now,' he said. 'I don't want to change my philosophy just for the last day. I won't risk losing the victory I've dreamed of for so long.'

On his next-to-last night at sea, he switched on all of *Géodis*'s lights to make the boat as visible as possible, and got a few hours' sleep, his last until the end of his race thirty hours later. The next day, a helicopter flew overhead and a fishing trawler steamed close by. Auguin was very happy to see them. There was none of the irritableness of Chichester, the reclusiveness of Moitessier when the outside world abruptly intruded on their hermetic lives at sea. Auguin would enjoy his last moments alone on his boat, but he was prepared to give up his solitude. He couldn't wait to see his family, his friends, eat good food again, experience all the things he had been deprived of at sea. Nevertheless, things wouldn't be quite the same. 'No one can come back from a Vendée Globe without being deeply changed. We don't come back intact from a race like this.'

Auguin crossed the finish line on 17 February just after nine thirty in the morning, in a swarm of spectator and media boats. He had been at sea for 105 days, 20 hours and 31 minutes, and had beaten Lamazou's record by just over three and a half days.

As soon as he crossed the line, he hauled down his mainsail and genoa. A race official handed him a headphone with a microphone attached. It was wired into dozens of loudspeakers on the quays of the port so that the eighty thousand people there to pay homage could hear Auguin's answers to journalists' questions in an instant press conference. On the Port Olona dock, Véronique and Erwan met him, together with a gang of media and political personalities. On the deck of his boat, Auguin picked up and held his son, and wouldn't put him down. At the dockside continuation of the press conference that had begun on the finish line, Auguin read a message of congratulations from the president of France, Jacques Chirac, and another from the minister of sport. A third message from the prime minister, Alain Juppé, celebrated nothing less than the existential power of Auguin's achievement, its deep moral significance.

'Your circumnavigation is one of those events which convinces people that they have the power to manage their own destinies. You are an example for a whole generation. I am sure that your victory will give hope to all those people in our society who are assailed by doubt, and who are looking for something to give meaning to their lives.'

Auguin, the redemptive hero, at risk for so long in the unknown zone beyond the pale, had returned safely home.

On 21 February, at one in the afternoon, four days after Auguin's arrival, Autissier sailed across the finish line, and into a short but nasty controversy. It had to do with Roufs. Officially, Jeantot was maintaining the line that Roufs might still be sailing. Things didn't look good, but there was a chance that he would be spotted any day now, perhaps pounding along through Biscay, closing with the Vendée coast. Unofficially, however, Jeantot agreed with the glum consensus reached by the other skippers, and by the media as well: Roufs had never rounded the Horn into the Atlantic; the confused Chilean reports about a radio message had been a false hope; the Canadian had died where his ARGOS had failed, or close by, in the most remote part of the Southern Ocean. However, this scenario begged the essential questions of what had actually happened to *Groupe LG2* at the height of the terrible storm, and how long it had taken Roufs to die. If it had been possible, for whatever period of time, to rescue him – if he had been inside his overturned boat or in his life-raft – had the rescue effort been adequate? That was where Autissier came in. She had been the prime searcher, the one closest to Roufs with the best chance of getting to him quickly.

After Autissier had finally given up her search and turned east for the Horn once again, there had been some murmurings in the French press that she hadn't tried hard enough. Goss – 'l'hero Pete Goss', as the media invariably called him – had found Dinelli. Why hadn't Autissier managed to get closer to Roufs's last ARGOS position? The weather in the area had eventually moderated to a wind of thirty or thirty-five knots, and she should have been able to make it to windward then, even without her mainsail. It was reported that Jeantot, exhausted and discouraged by the latest of this string of misfortunes, had said that he was disappointed in Autissier, that she gave up too soon. The day after these remarks, Jeantot told *Le Figaro* that his mouth had gotten ahead of his brain. But I recalled him talking about Goss's achievement. He said he wished that everyone in the race had the kind of determination and skill exhibited by the Englishman. Did he mean Autissier? Or Laurent and de Broc, who, in the face of a grim weather forecast, decided to keep running to the east without joining in the search? Jeantot wouldn't elaborate.

Autissier's welcome back was the usual ecstatic affair, with hundreds of spectator boats, shoreside crowds of tens of thousands, bands, champagne, flowers, the whole panoply of an official salute. She was overtly elated. She had lost so much weight that the first thing she jokingly asked for from the welcoming boats was a belt to keep her pants up. Her mother came on board *PRB* and the two had a joyful hug. As Autissier had said, the public didn't give a damn whether a skipper finished officially or not. Completing the course was enough for them.

Unfortunately for Autissier, the entire ceremony was over-shadowed by the issue of her search for Roufs. She found out about the media reports just three days before her finish. It was the first thing she talked about at her dockside press conference. She had been 'horrified' when she learned of Jeantot's insinuations.

'It is the most serious accusation that it's possible to make against a sailor. I would have thought that the race director would have better things to do at times like that than to call into question the honour of a competitor. This whole thing is so undignified. I absolutely refuse to get into an argument about it. I'm only going to say all this once.'

The two days she spent searching for Roufs were 'the most difficult of my life,' she said. 'I was in a state of shock because of the storm. I was exhausted, both physically and emotionally. My boat was in bad shape. I couldn't leave the search zone, but at the same time, I knew that I couldn't do anything useful. I was in no condition to make any decisions.'

She finally gave up and left the search area at the urging of the CROSS, which had told her to resume her course because prolonging the search was useless.

When Jeantot was questioned about his criticism, he blamed it on the press. Some reporters latched on to a few of his remarks and distorted them, he said. There wasn't the slightest coolness between himself and Autissier, for whom he had a great deal of admiration. And in fact, things appeared to be amicable between them as Jeantot joined the crowd at the dockside welcoming Autissier.

When I spoke to Roufs's wife, Michèle Cartier, in July 1997, she bitterly denounced all of the search efforts as inadequate. The search was called off prematurely, she said. Autissier gave up too soon. Laurent and de Broc should have joined the search. The CROSS should have done more. There was a dreadful aura of sorrow and grief in the big, airy house that Roufs and Cartier had shared. She had been obliged to wait a long time before she could be sure there was no more hope for Gerry – so many weeks of believing he must be sailing on, with only his communications system damaged. She endured the crushing disappointment of the Chilean reversal about the radio message. For her, it took him three months to die – Jeantot did not officially renounce all hope until 24 March. She kept her faith until then, months longer than anyone else. Her anger was understandable. Everyone else came back, why not Gerry? She couldn't blame him for being in the race in the first place. It was his life, and had been long before they met. She couldn't hold the Southern Ocean accountable. As Bullimore had said, it was merely being what it was. It was the other sailors, Jeantot, the CROSS, who must hold the key, who had, somehow, to be held responsible. Goss saved Dinelli. Bullimore and Dubois were rescued. Why hadn't someone saved Gerry? And it was terrible not knowing how it happened, how long it took.

While I listened to Cartier on that warm summer day, their eight-year-old daughter, Emma, was at a friend's house. Would I come with her, Cartier asked, to pick her up for lunch? I had another interview miles away later in the day. I had time to stay, but I used the interview as an excuse to leave. The sorrow in the house was overpowering. I couldn't face any more of it. I drove away down beautiful, tree-shaded Breton country roads to the autoroute to the south, and never met Emma.

When I described Cartier's comments to the Vendée Globe skippers I interviewed subsequently, they had almost identical reactions. They understood why Cartier would talk that way, but she didn't sail. She couldn't comprehend how difficult things were in the Southern Ocean in heavy weather, how even the simplest and most basic manoeuvres could be hurdles too high to leap. Occasionally, it was simply impossible to do something, even if you really wanted to and no matter how hard you tried. No one who had not been there could ever really know what it was like in a severe storm. It was hard to accept, but sometimes, in this dangerous game, as Moitessier had said, your number was up.

All this was true. And as understandable as Cartier's emotions were, she was wrong about the search. The most important aspect of Roufs's disappearance was that there had been no EPIRB signal. That made his silence equivocal – he might be all right – and it meant that there was no definite position to aim for, which was what really made

Autissier's task next to impossible. It was hard enough under good conditions to find a boat for which there were precise latitude and longitude coordinates. When a boat could be anywhere within an area of dozens, then hundreds and then thousands of square miles, in big seas, poor visibility and high wind and with no possibility of an air search, it was as good as gone forever.

Autissier's finish was unofficial. The race for second and third between Thiercelin and Laurent was still on. Thiercelin had a small card in his hand – a thirty-four-hour allowance for the time he spent searching for Roufs. It looked as if he might need it. Although he was three hundred miles ahead of Laurent on 12 February, a slight enough lead at the speed these boats could sail, by the time Auguin was drinking champagne in the channel at Les Sables-d'Olonne five days later, Thiercelin had fallen seventy miles behind. It was all a matter of getting around, or through, the North Atlantic High. Thiercelin elected to swing to the west of the high-pressure centre. This course was considerably longer than Laurent's direct route towards the finish, but Thiercelin hoped to get stronger and more favourable wind on the fringes of the high. The newer *Crédit Immobilier de France* was faster than Laurent's boat when running before the wind.

For his part, Laurent gambled that he would have enough wind to keep moving fast enough to take advantage of his shorter course, even if he ran into head winds as well. The venerable *Groupe LG Traitmat* was more efficient beating into the wind. Its narrower beam and heavier displacement helped it pierce the waves more easily as it met them head-on. There was less of the pounding that bedevilled the new beamy boats and slowed them down. Laurent had to endure a day of frustrating calms alternating with light breezes that often swung 180 degrees every half-hour. It went up to eighteen knots, then abruptly dropped to four from the opposite direction. Every time he tried to sleep, the wind changed and he had to go on deck to fiddle around with sheets and the autopilot. Without wind, the boat rolled like a barrel in the swells. The sails slatted and cracked as they swung from side to side; a day of no wind and swells could put more wear and tear on sailcloth than weeks of sailing time. Laurent managed to just about keep moving though and his strategy worked. By 22 February, he was still ahead of Thiercelin by thirty miles, both of them one thousand miles from Les Sables-d'Olonne.

Thiercelin continued to deal with his worrying leak. His electric pump had failed, and he had to move the water by hand. 'I can't identify the source of the leak,' he reported, 'but it seems to have stabilised at forty gallons an hour. So I pump, pump and pump.'

They cleared the horse latitudes and picked up the strong and favourable winds of the northern westerly wind belt. Now they were sprinting for the finish. Thiercelin had his best day's run of the race: 332 miles at an average speed of 13.8 knots. This was wild sailing in any ocean, and he suffered a knockdown in the heavier winds of a squall. The boat was undamaged, but the faster he went, the more it leaked. He had to spend even more time pumping to control the water in his forward compartment.

Laurent spent most of the day at the helm of *Groupe LG Traitmat*, trying to compensate for Thiercelin's greater natural speed with careful attention to the minutiae of each big wave, each gust of wind, working the sixty-footer like a dinghy. It was cold in these northern waters. He had to put on his fleece-lined polar clothes under foul-weather gear.

Then it was just a matter of getting through Biscay. After a few hours of near-calm, the two boats, never more than forty miles apart, were overtaken by a front with gale-force wind (Beaufort force 8 – 'moderately high waves of greater length; edges of crests begin to break into spindrift; foam is blown in well-marked streaks', the admiral noted dispassionately). For six hours, Thiercelin sailed and surfed at an average speed of almost seventeen knots, under a quadruple-reefed mainsail and storm jib. He was handling the boat, napping and pumping – no time for anything else. Laurent tried to sleep during the afternoon because he had had no chance the night before as the front crossed over him. But running before the wind, he had to stay up all day as well to keep an eye on the boat. Even a slight wind shift could force an accidental gybe and break something. More than anything else, Laurent said, he wanted to drink some clear, fresh water. For the last two months, his watermaker hadn't been able to get all the salt out of his drinking water. He was tired of its briny taste. He was also looking forward to eating sitting down, and not out of a pot. He thought he would start off with some pancakes.

During the heavy weather, Thiercelin reported that his leak had become much worse. The wave impacts damaged the watertight bulkhead between the boat's forward and main compartments. Water was now leaking into the cabin. He had almost a foot and a half of it around his chart table and engine, used only for charging the batteries. He had to slow down the boat, and he was using his main electric bilge pump, as well as the hand pump for the forward compartment. Luckily, he could keep his batteries charged because he had enough fuel to run his engine continuously. To stay afloat, he would need it until the end. 'In these conditions, the battle with Hervé becomes secondary. My objective now is just to get the boat across the finish line.'

Nevertheless, during their next-to-last night, in a fifty-knot Biscay gale, Thiercelin managed to keep going fast enough to pass Laurent. By dawn, after 113 days at sea, the two boats were eight miles apart. In better weather, they could have seen each other. (Two and a half months earlier, they had sailed eight to ten miles apart for several days in the southern Indian Ocean.) Over the final twenty-four hours, Thiercelin pulled farther ahead as the wind dropped and the sea calmed down. On 26 February, at seventy thirty in the morning, just before sunrise, in a light wind, *Crédit Immobilier de France* crossed the line in second place. Laurent arrived forty-seven minutes later. Thiercelin's official margin, however, was increased by the amount of his thirty-four-hour time allowance.

During their joint press conference, both skippers promised to be back for the 2000 Vendée Globe. Laurent was justifiably proud of a third-place finish in his old-stager boat. But next time, 'I hope to have a boat that will let me show what I'm capable of.'

Both sailors expressed hope that Roufs was somewhere nearby. Laurent said that he was haunted by Roufs's disappearance. For Thiercelin, the whole thing was still very difficult to talk about. 'I dedicate my second place to Gerry,' he said. 'For me, he is still here. He was ahead of me; I hope he's behind me now.'

Dumont crossed the line two days later. His entire electrical system had broken down and he had been without any power for several days. That meant no electronics and no radar. Without the latter, he missed being run down by a freighter in the Bay of Biscay by only fifty yards. He switched on his ARGOS unit with the GPS attached so that race headquarters could get a constant position fix on him and establish his arrival time. His autopilots were also a casualty of his electrical system failure, and, already very tired, he stayed awake to hand-steer throughout his last forty-eight hours at sea.

Even the relatively unknown fourth-place finisher rated a crowd of ten thousand to fifteen thousand people on the sea walls and docks of Les Sables-d'Olonne. Dumont provided a succinct personal race summary: the outcome had practically been decided the previous November as the boats skirted the fringe of the South Atlantic High on the way down to the Southern Ocean. That was when the leaders – Auguin, Autissier, Parlier, Roufs – jumped so far ahead of the second group. As for Thiercelin and Laurent, he stayed close to them until the Southern Ocean. But then they gained four hundred miles on him in two days, before he could get over his funk about the Southern Ocean waves. The Vendée Globe wasn't a race; it was an ordeal, a trial.

He had had technical problems with his boat, but they were nothing compared with the shock of Roufs's disappearance.

'I miss him like a brother,' said Dumont. 'I had been sending him two faxes every day. I kept sending them even though he didn't reply. I cried and I have never been so depressed in my life. I wasn't in the race any more. The boat was falling to pieces. I repaired it . . . but such a long silence; it made it hard to keep on living.'

Now, he would live, simply, and spend time with his children.

'I'm happy to be alive, to breathe, to walk. Everything is beautiful here when you've seen what it's like at the end of the world.'

On 27 February, the disqualified de Broc was sailing less than thirty miles behind Dumont in what looked to be another surprisingly close finish. Weather conditions were average for Biscay in February: a thirty-five-knot gale and steep seas. In a radio message to Jeantot, de Broc said how much he now regretted stopping in Ushuaia. It had been just like New Zealand during his first race, an unnecessary port call. Now here he was, a daysail from the finish line, and it wouldn't count. He would need a third Vendée Globe, he said. Otherwise, it was unfinished business.

A few hours later, with exquisitely ironic timing, the big bolts that secured the keel to the hull sheared off. The long, slender keel, with the three-and-a-half-ton bulb of lead ballast on its lower end, plummeted two thousand fathoms to the floor of the Bay of Biscay (de Broc was still in the deeper water to the west of the continental shelf). Like Bullimore's boat far away in the Southern Ocean, *Votre nom autour du monde* turned turtle in an instant. De Broc was only 280 miles from the finish line.

His rescue seemed like a run-of-the-mill affair after the distant heroics of the Southern Ocean. But there were no guarantees when it was a matter of picking up a distressed sailor in cold water and heavy weather. It took de Broc fifteen minutes to locate an EPIRB in the mess of the upside-down, waterlogged cabin. Fortunately, it was a SARSAT, which transmitted a quick, exact position to the search-and-rescue centre. But when he tried to wrestle his life-raft out of the cockpit, it suddenly inflated. Pinned against the cockpit floor, it was impossible to budge. Like Dubois, de Broc had no choice but to haul himself up on to the slick, overturned hull and hang on to a rudder (more accurately, he waited for a wave to wash him up on to the hull), with the boat rolling briskly in the cold, high waves. Within a few hours, a French naval helicopter homed in on the EPIRB position, lifted him off the wreck and deposited him on board the nearby tanker *La Durance*, bound for Brest.

De Broc was put ashore there the next day.

'It's completely crazy to lose your keel twenty-four hours away from the finish line,' he told reporters. 'But in spite of my stop in Argentina, I've had a good race. I got my quota of sea miles.'

His capsize could have been a lot worse, and he felt in good form.

'I feel well enough to run an Olympic race around the stadium this afternoon. But it's probably wiser to just go and see my friends in Les Sables-d'Olonne instead.'

De Broc began to work with the navy right away to make a salvage attempt. He wanted to get the boat, bring it ashore, fit a new keel, tow the boat out to where the keel fell off and then sail it across that damn finish line. The weather was bad though. The first tow cable broke, and *Votre nom autour du monde* drifted away into the Biscay shipping lanes, travelled by as many as 150 ships a day. There was a good chance it would be ploughed under by one of them. But a second salvage vessel managed to get the overturned hull into port on the Odet River, on the southern coast of the Brittany peninsula. Unfortunately, de Broc couldn't raise the money to re-fit his boat, and never did get it across the finish line.

By early evening on 1 March, Parlier finished, hugged his family, drank his champagne and gave his press conference. Forty thousand people cheered him into port. De Broc, a close friend, came out on a spectator boat and went aboard *Aquitaine Innovations*. The two men embraced and then sailed the last few miles together from the finish line to the harbour entrance. This was Parlier's second Vendée Globe,

and he joined only two other two-time Vendée Globe finishers: Alain
Gautier (who won the 1992–93 edition) and Jean-Luc Van den
Heede (whose boat Chabaud had chartered for this race). After their
second times, both Gautier and Van den Heede said emphatically
that that was it. They'd had more than enough of sailing alone in the
Southern Ocean. From now on, they would sail with crews and stick
to lower latitudes. But Parlier's hunger for the South, and the hard
life of solo competition there, had not abated. He confirmed what he
said earlier in the race: he would be back for the 2000 Vendée Globe
in a well-prepared and seasoned *Aquitaine Innovations*.

Now only two were left at sea. Goss was a thousand miles behind
Chabaud when he operated on his elbow on 4 February, but he had
gained on her steadily ever since he sailed from Hobart in mid-
January. By the beginning of March, he was only two hundred miles
astern. Both sailors, now four thousand miles from Les Sables-
d'Olonne, had communications problems: Goss's radio had been out
of commission for two months (to his secret relief), while Chabaud's
decrepit electrical system didn't permit contact of any kind. Jeantot
followed their progress by watching their ARGOS positions creep
across his plotting chart of the Atlantic Ocean.

Goss continued to gain on Chabaud and the two boats crossed the
equator on 4 March within minutes of each other, although, at
slightly different longitudes. There was a coincidental symmetry to
their race: on the outbound course, they crossed the equator less than
an hour apart.

'*Aqua Quorum* and all her equipment are very tired,' Goss reported. 'I've been working twenty hours a day on maintenance.'

His generator was acting up and he still had to pump by hand for
hours each day to keep cooling water running through it. He was also
practising the old sailor's art of stitching worn sails, pushing the
triangular-headed sail needle through the cloth with a low-tech
leather-and-bone sailmaker's palm – hour after hour of painstaking
work.

Goss passed Chabaud a couple of days after the equator. But then
she began to hold her own as the two boats nosed through the
doldrums and caught the north-east trades. These were beginning to
assume their spring and summer aspect and veered farther to the east.
The skippers could sail a direct course for the finish. For the next ten
days, Goss and Chabaud sailed as if they were in a regatta. He was

one hundred miles ahead, but hit a calm. She retook the lead by ten miles. He recovered and moved twenty miles ahead. After four months at sea, the boats remained steadily less than two hours apart.

For the first time in months, Chabaud made radio contact with the world – a VHF conversation with a freighter. The ship's captain passed along to race headquarters the message that she and her boat were in good condition.

Both skippers had to work their way through the Bay of Biscay, tacking wearily for two days in light and contrary winds, almost doubling the actual distance covered, staying awake to watch for shipping. They sailed the last few miles in a fifteen-knot westerly wind, on a calm sea. In the afternoon of 24 March, a sunny Sunday, they crossed the finish line – still separated by less than two hours – Goss first, flying his spinnaker, then Chabaud.

With their arrival, the 1996–97 Vendée Globe race was over. Their welcome had an air of a final and climactic celebration. As usual, there was a mob of boats around the finish line, and crowds of people onshore. It helped that it was a weekend, and that the weather was warm and sunny. But the numbers reflected how special this dual homecoming was. There were probably 120,000 spectators around the harbour and Port Olona, compared with the eighty thousand who welcomed Auguin. Many of the other skippers showed up as well, prominent members of what Jeantot called 'the great Vendée Globe family': Auguin, Autissier, Laurent, de Broc, and the unlucky Nandor Fa and Didier Munduteguy. The skippers and the big crowd were there partly because it was the last hurrah of this edition of the race. But the main reason for all this attention was Goss and Chabaud themselves.

It seemed odd to realise that after all the years Autissier had been racing alone around the world, the newcomer Chabaud turned out to be the first woman to succeed in doing it non-stop and without assistance. Her place in the elite single-handers' club, alongside Autissier, was secure. She sailed the race with a combination of tenacity and a kind of gracefulness that, so the media said, only a woman could bring to the whole enterprise. She was tough when she had to be – managing her boat in the Southern Ocean and bringing it through, slowly to be sure – but she realistically evaluated her abilities and stayed within them with a steady and hard-eyed determination.

Chabaud's romanticism also struck a chord with the public. The French responded warmly to her recognition of Moitessier (who had died just two years before the race) as a source of technical advice and inspiration, as well as her fancy that her accompanying albatross, Bernard, was a reincarnation of Moitessier, the perfect symbol of freedom and the wilderness, watching over her. Her evocation of him resonated in a country for whom he symbolised the charismatic and courageous outsider – the quintessential lone sailor. He had always been present in the story she herself was living, she said. Through him, she was brought to the great questions about life that only solitude allows a person to truly contemplate. Like the prime minister's claim of moral significance for Auguin's victory, Chabaud's experience confirmed what everyone believed about the Vendée Globe: it was far more than a harsh, manly bash around the world in the roaring forties. It was a spiritual journey.

'This is happiness!' she said as she stepped ashore for the first time in 140 days. 'My race was a good one, but very hard. I have a few regrets: I never did actually see an iceberg; I wasn't able to keep talking to Isabelle by fax or to Pete by radio. But Cape Horn! It was truly beautiful. The light was glorious. By then, I'd been in the Southern Ocean for sixty days. I had the feeling that it would never end. Finally, I really wanted the race to be over, to get off the boat. It lasted about a month too long for me.'

Chabaud told me she remembered thinking as she came ashore: 'I've followed my own road in my life. I've been true to myself. When you reach your objective, that's a great personal achievement. The feeling you have about that is one of the best things to have in your life, and that feeling will always be there.'

As big an attraction as Chabaud was, however, Goss was the real centre of attention. A small part of the crowd was English. They hopped across the Channel for a few days of cheering one of their own sailors, who had, like Bullimore, finally done something of note in one of these French-dominated races. It was a good day to be English in Les Sables-d'Olonne. Goss's rescue of Dinelli had become the great, pivotal event of this Vendée Globe. It seemed to symbolise the spirit of the race. A knowledgeable public and press had a good idea of what the Englishman endured to get back to the Frenchman. The exhaustive, and often sensational, media coverage of the rescue made sure of it. Everyone used the word *hero*, without the slightest irony or self-consciousness. When someone like Philippe Jeantot, with his great experience of the Southern Ocean, recommends Goss for the *Légion d'honneur*, then he has to be the real thing. His actions reverberated with so many antique and half-forgotten, or discredited, virtues. Goss acted like a knight: his great physical courage and strength deployed for days in the pure cause of saving another, one man against the dragon of the Southern Ocean. It was true that he had been obeying the law of the sea that mariners must risk themselves to save other sailors. It was an extreme demand, but the only one that made sense, or that had any honour, on the dangerous ocean. Still, no one could help feeling that Goss had done even more than that, something above and beyond his duty as a sailor. For the French, he was simply, *le courageux* – the brave one.

There was also something intensely romantic in the friendship that developed between Goss and Dinelli. Ironically, two solo sailors came back from a single-handed race friends for life – 'like brothers', Goss said. Amid the old national tensions and rivalries of Europe, it was sentimentally heart-warming that this had happened to a French-man and an Englishman. None of that mattered at sea anyway. The champagne that the nearly dead Dinelli brought with him on board *Aqua Quorum*, and the cup of tea with which Goss revived him, were such unlikely clichés that no one would have dared to make them up. This was why sailors went to the Southern Ocean: in that un-complicated, pure wilderness, usually corrupt humans were purified. Normal life – life ashore – was complex, compromised, full of ambiguity. In the Southern Ocean, it was simple and honourable. The path ahead was never safe, but it was always clear.

As Goss approached the finish line, he had no idea how big an event the rescue had become, or how big an item he was. Sixty miles out in benign wind and seas, he sat contentedly in the cockpit, drinking the inevitable cup of tea, and looking forward to the end, when the first aeroplane flew over.

'That was intrusive, but not a big problem,' he told me. 'Then, thirty miles out, the first helicopters came, and then, ten miles out, the first of the boats, hundreds of boats. What do you feel when you cross the finish line? Well, I couldn't find the bloody thing because of all those boats. Then, when I did get in, there were 120,000 people. It was extraordinary.

'People asked me, how did you adjust? Wouldn't it blow your socks off? Not a problem. I'd been by myself for four and a half

months. You couldn't shut me up. It was fantastic. It was very
organised. I remember being taken off the boat, surrounded by these
big, burly bodyguards, and then dragged off through thousands of
people. They were fighting the press off. And, you know, one minute
I'm by myself, and the next minute, I'm . . . Bloody hell! It was quite
funny. But you take it in your stride. Put down a few pops in the pub
and it was great.'

About his rescue of Dinelli, Goss told his press conference: 'They
were both the worst and the best moments of my life.'

On 14 February 1997, with the Vendée Globe still under way, Jean-
Pierre Champion, president of the French Federation of Sailing,
announced the formation of a committee to analyse the race and the
Open 60 designs, and to make recommendations for improved safety.
The members of the committee included Sir Robin Knox-Johnston,
Philippe Jeantot, Christophe Auguin, Nandor Fa and BOC sailors
Jean-Luc Van den Heede and Mark Schrader, who was also the
Around Alone race director. The most important of the committee's
recommendations, which apply to both the Vendée Globe and the
Around Alone, specify that boats must be self-righting after a knock-
down or capsize, and that the designer, builder and skipper must sign
a certificate to that effect.

The committee also reaffirmed the existing rules for three watertight bulkheads, but said that access through them should be
improved by the use of watertight doors. Two collision bulkheads
should be fitted, one located five per cent of the length from the bow
(some boats already had these), and one just forward of the rudder.
Masts must be secured on their steps (the reinforced base at the
mast's foot) so that they can't come free in a capsize and damage the
boat. Skippers must provide a written plan showing how they would
get in and out of an inverted boat, collect their 'panic bags' with
survival gear, and find and inflate a life-raft. Boat bottoms should be
painted with red or reflective anti-fouling, as should their topsides
over at least one-third of their surface, and the deck should be in day-
glo colours. No modifications to keel, mast, or water, fuel and ballast
tanks should be made without the agreement of the boat's original
naval architect, or another fully qualified designer if the original one
isn't available. Finally, Southern Ocean waypoints preventing boats
from going too far south should be set up to 'take full account of
known ice limits, weather patterns, and search and rescue capabilities

of the relevant national authorities, and other relevant safety factors.

*

On 28 March 1997, four days after Goss and Chabaud had finished and officially ended the Vendée Globe, Patrick de Radiguès finally left Dunedin, New Zealand. He sailed across the southern Pacific Ocean out-of-season. The southern hemisphere autumn weather had settled in, with more frequent and severe storms than in the summer. He was knocked down several times, suffered more damage, and had to put briefly into port again near Cape Horn. He arrived in Les Sables-d'Olonne on 9 June, battered and triumphant.

If the defining moment of inspiration and joy in this Vendée Globe was the rescue of Dinelli, its dark shadow was the absence of Gerry Roufs. His disappearance remained the cruel and veiled mystery of the race. The arrival of Goss and Chabaud marked the end of all hope for Roufs. By 24 March, only Michèle Cartier had maintained any faith that he would eventually sail into Les Sables-d'Olonne. And even her desperate optimism had withered, agonisingly, day by day. Jeantot made a formal announcement on the twenty-fourth that there was no longer any doubt that Roufs 'must be added to the long list of sailors lost at sea without explanation.

'It was possible to keep hoping until the arrival of the last competitor,' he said. 'It's difficult to accept, because there's no tangible proof of his disappearance. But after three months of silence, I'm now convinced that Gerry Roufs will never return.'

On 17 July 1997, ten days after I interviewed Cartier, a freighter sighted the wreckage of a yacht drifting approximately 260 miles off the coast of Chile. It notified the Chilean authorities. The next day, a naval aeroplane flew over the remains of the boat and videotaped it. The airmen could see an inverted hull with its intact thin keel attached, including the ballast bulb. With its blue-green bottom and mauve hull, the boat looked very much like a whale on the ocean's surface. Shortly afterwards, heavy weather developed in the area, lasting for four days. The wreckage disappeared, and a subsequent search by Chilean ships and planes was unsuccessful.

Five weeks later, the naval attaché in the Chilean embassy in Paris sent four photographs of the wreckage, extracted from the navy video, to Groupe LG. The photos were shown to Pascal Conq of Groupe Finot, and to Michèle Cartier. They formally identified the wreck as that of Roufs's boat, *Groupe LG2*. There was no doubt about it. The boat's name was clearly visible in the photos, as were its distinctive shape and paint colours.

Franck Oppermann, speaking for Groupe LG, said that if the wreckage was spotted again, a technical team would leave for Chile immediately to make a salvage attempt. Cartier, however, noted that the Chileans did not appear to be searching for the boat and had not responded to her request for information.

'It is regrettable that we were not told for more than a month about the discovery of the wreckage,' she said. 'If we had known about it in mid-July, we would have had the time to make preparations and get the necessary authorisation to go as soon as possible. We're waiting, always waiting, but for now, all we can do is wait and be ready to go.'

After her husband had been officially given up as lost, Cartier formed the Association on the Track of Gerry Roufs, which she ran from her home in Locmariaquer. She solicited donations for representations to the Chilean government to keep searching for *Groupe LG2*, and to distribute posters throughout the southern part of Chile asking vessels and people onshore to keep a lookout for wreckage. The association also set up a web site on which were posted the circumstances of Roufs's disappearance and news about the search. When I spoke to Cartier, she gave me a bundle of the posters, showing three photographs of Roufs aboard his boat, to pass along to the Vendée Globe skippers I had yet to interview. I did so, but I agreed with their view that the association was merely part of her attempt to deal with the dreadful grief. The quest was pointless, we agreed; *Groupe LG2* was long gone – most likely smashed to pieces by ice and sunk far out in the Southern Ocean. But we were wrong. Roufs's boat had survived intact and, against all odds, the freighter had stumbled on it.

The Chilean authorities never offered an explanation for delaying more than a month before they told anyone about sighting and filming the boat. In early June 1998, Cartier told me that a Chilean fisherman claimed to have spotted the remains of *Groupe LG2* somewhere along the desolate coast to the north-west of Cape Horn. He demanded money in return for disclosing the location of the wreck. Cartier refused to pay. On 16 September 1998, the Chilean armed forces reported that one of its patrol vessels had recovered pieces of Roufs's boat from the coast of one of the Atalaya Islands near the western entrance to the Strait of Magellan. The widely scattered and fragmented wreckage had been spotted on 24 August by a naval aeroplane, but bad weather had prevented salvage until two weeks later. There was no sign of Roufs's remains.

The identification of Roufs's boat doesn't answer most of the questions about what happened to him. It does, however, eliminate the possibility that many of the skippers thought had been most likely: that Roufs had run headlong into ice. In the Chilean photos taken in July 1997, the hull appeared to be intact. It was impossible to tell whether the boat's mast was still attached. If *Groupe LG2* remained upside down for all those months, it was likely that the mast was still in place, holding the boat stable and inverted against the righting force of the keel ballast. Although, in light of the behaviour of Dubois's *Pour Amnesty International*, it was always possible that *Groupe LG2* had remained capsized even after being dismasted.

There was no way of knowing which of the other explanations for Roufs's death was the most likely. It was possible that he went over-board, or that he was on deck when the boat went over. In either case, he would have quickly drowned. It was less likely that he was down below at the moment of capsize. With his hull intact, it's difficult to see why he would not have been able to activate one of his EPIRBs and find a way of getting it to the sea surface so it could transmit a signal – as Bullimore did – unless he was so badly injured in the violence of the roll-over that getting to an EPIRB, or releasing one to the surface, was impossible. A search of the wreck in July 1997 for Roufs's body would have settled that question. At the time of writing, no further attempts have been made by the Chileans to look for his remains among the scattered shards of *Groupe LG2*

In his last log entry, e-mailed the day before his ARGOS stopped, as the great Southern Ocean storm bore down on him, Roufs had written, 'It's high time to get to the Horn. You're always under stress in these waters. If you drag things out too long here, you're sure to come to grief.'

The Vendée Globe prize ceremony in Les Sables-d'Olonne on 3 May 1997 included a homage to Roufs. An image of him at the wheel of his boat was projected on two huge television screens. In the harbour, boats fired dozens of red flares. Flashing and pulsing, they filled the night sky. Over a loudspeaker, a woman's voice said: 'Look, Gerry, at all these lights in the bay. They're like our hearts beating for you.'

Epilogue

AFTER OUR sixteen-day passage from Charleston to the Virgin Islands, we cruised the Caribbean for nearly two years. We wandered up and down the chain of the Lesser Antilles from the Virgins to Grenada, and down to Venezuela to get out of the hurricane area during the worst months of the season between August and November. At the beginning of our long trip back north to Canada, we sailed through the Bahamas for three weeks. Near the end of that time, we motored for most of two days in a flat, muggy calm from Nassau to West End on Grand Bahama Island. It was the jumping-off spot for the trip back across the Strait of Florida to the United States. It can be a tricky crossing because of the Gulf Stream, constricted between the islands and the mainland, flowing at three or four knots to the north. Whether tidal, or one of these vast circulating rivers in the sea, currents always kick up potentially dangerous waves when even a moderate wind blows against them. If you picked your weather, though, it was a safe enough overnight passage.

On the afternoon of the second day, moving at five knots under diesel and autopilot, we were intercepted by a US, navy guided missile frigate, and were boarded by four armed coastguardsmen from a detachment on board the ship. They methodically but politely searched our boat for drugs. They had come over from the frigate in a small naval launch – a pinnace – which kept station ten yards off our starboard quarter. From it, a fifth coastguardsman kept his shotgun trained on us as we sat in the cockpit, keeping our hands still and in plain view, as we had been instructed. The frigate turned and followed us a few hundred yards off our other quarter. The big, missile-laden warship and our little sailboat motored along, incongruously but companionably, for an hour.

We were sure then that all the excitement was over, and that our last few days in the Bahamas would be pleasant and serene.

In the late afternoon, as we got closer to West End, a storm approached from the west. A wall of black and grey boiling cloud stretched across our entire horizon. Lightning flickered continuously throughout the cloud, which bore down on us majestically, taking its own sweet time. We changed course to try to get out of its way, but it was too big. We watched it coming for three hours. It hit us soon after dark. We handled the thirty-five knots of wind easily, motor-sailing under staysail. The rain was torrential and warm. But it was the lightning that terrified us. It was continuous for twenty minutes, the bolts flashing all around us. We spent more time lit up by them than not. Sometimes, the strikes were so close to the boat that we heard them coming – like artillery shells tracking in over our heads with a whizzing roar. They hit the water with cracking detonations. In the high-voltage light of their flashes, I saw several bolts hit within a hundred feet of us. We could smell the ozone. We huddled in the cockpit under the barrage, like infantrymen in a trench, trying not to touch any of the boat's metal parts. But we knew that if one of the big bolts hit us, it could kill us, or flash out our bronze through-hull openings and sink the boat. We felt like powerless palaeolithic humans bowed down, literally, under the weight of rain and the near-continuous blinding electrical flash, completely exposed to crushing Promethean elements.

Abruptly, the other wall of the huge squall passed over us and we were out of it. We could look astern and watch it moving away from us, flashing and booming, like a cloud of the apocalypse. There was a moderate breeze behind the storm. It had broken the muggy heat and calm. We got some more canvas up and sailed close-hauled under the clear, fresh sky and stars until morning.

There are no atheists in foxholes, goes the old saying. Nor in small boats in storms. We felt as if we had been visited, and spared, by the gods. I didn't believe in God, but I thanked somebody, or something, for letting us through that one.

Years later, sitting at the silent calm of my desk as I followed the clamorous Vendée Globe race on my computer screen, I thought that I was beginning to get a glimmer of an understanding of what the sailors were going through during their passage across the Southern Ocean. And that vague insight was later reinforced when I talked to the skippers themselves. Seeing their strength, yet glimpsing the shadow of the fear they felt when they were there, I thought I had a vicarious sense, although a slight and inadequate one, of what it was like in the Great South.

In those narrow, sheltered waters, the brief storm in the Bahamas gave us a premonitory suggestion of the Southern Ocean. It isn't necessary to sail there to get a taste of it, and of the unassailable power of nature. It could come on you just like that in the middle of a benign and populated tropical archipelago. Since then, I often think that that's what it must be like in the Southern Ocean – the power of nature beyond imagination, a lord of the earth just a tiny object in the huge wilderness of wind and waves, hanging on, hoping to come through.

Acknowledgements

I COULDN'T HAVE done it without the sailors. This book owes the most to the men and women with the courage to sail the Southern Ocean, and especially those who were so generous with their time in talking to me about it. Without exception, they told their stories with eloquence, honesty and humour. Most of their names are now familiar to the reader, but I'll mention them anyway. My warmest thanks to: David Adams, Christophe Auguin, Isabelle Autissier, Tony Bullimore, Catherine Chabaud, Raphaël Dinelli, Bruno Dubois, Yves Gélinas, Pete Goss, Philippe Jeantot, Sir Robin Knox-Johnston, Hervé Laurent, Yves Parlier and Mark Schrader. My thanks to Raphaël and Virginie for their hospitality in the house they had moved into just the day before.

Adrian Thompson and Jean-Marie Finot helped me understand how these beautiful boats are created. I received essential information and assistance from Caroline Adams, Mike Birch, Jim Cavers, Marie Gendron, Louis Hardy, Andrée Joffroy, John Kerr, Heather Ormerod, Philippe Ouhlen, and Michel Sacco. Vivien Lepper, Christine Mauro, Willie Walker and Eric Wredenhagen read the manuscript and set me straight about a number of facts and matters of style.

The suggestion that the Vendée Globe and the story of Gerry Roufs would make a good book came from Jack David. I'm indebted to him for that, and for his advice and encouragement over the last few years. No writer can fail to be grateful to the publisher who accepts a proposal, but Louise Dennys and Diane Martin at Knopf Canada also prodded and honed my outline from its rough beginnings into its ultimate form with incisive grace. Diane Martin's sensitive and skilful editing improved the manuscript immeasurably. Janice Weaver made further necessary amendments. I also want to thank Rachel Cugnoni of Yellow Jersey Press for her creative and thoughtful guidance in preparing the United Kingdom edition.

I'm most grateful to my wife Christine Mauro and my daughter Sarah Lundy for their love and support, and for their forbearance for all those missed weekends.

Finally, I thank Michèle Cartier for agreeing to an interview when her grief and despair were still so strong. As for Gerry, he knew that when you sail to the Great South, you take your chances, that mortal peril is the price for the beauty and exhilaration of sailing the edge of the world. Although we never met, I'll always remember him.

Grateful acknowledgement is made for permission to reprint excerpts from the following previously published material:

Chasing Liquid Mountains: Adventures of a Solo Yachtsman by David Adams (Pan Macmillan, Australia, 1997). Reprinted by permission of David and Caroline Adams.

The Dangerous Edge by Michael J. Apter (The Free Press, New York, 1992). Reprinted by permission of Michael J. Apter.

Beyond Endurance: Survival at the Extremes by Glin Bennet (Secker & Warburg Ltd London, 1983). Reprinted by permission of A M Heath & Co. Ltd.

The Hero with a Thousand Faces by Joseph Campbell. Copyright 1949 by Bollingen Foundation Inc., renewed 1976 by Princeton University Press. Reprinted by permission of Princeton University Press.

The Odyssey: A Modern Sequel by Nikos Kazantzakls, translated by Kimon Friar. English translation copyright © 1958 by Helene Kazantzakls and Kimon Friar, renewed 1986 by Martin Secker & Warburg Ltd. Reprinted by permission of Martin Secker & Warburg Ltd.

'Ithaca' in *The Complete Poems of Cavafy*. Copyright © 1961, renewed 1989 by Rae Dalven. Reprinted by permission of The Hogarth Press.

Heavy Weather Sailing, 4th edition, by K. Adlard Coles, revised by Peter Bruce (A&C Black Ltd, London, 1991). Reprinted by permission of A&C Black.

The Ocean Almanac, edited by Robert Hendrickson (Doubleday & Co. Inc., New York, 1984). Reprinted by permission of Doubleday & Co.

'Racing: Marathon Boats' by Bruce Kirby, in *SAIL*, May 1997, p 80 Reprinted by permission of SAIL Publications.

'Bagpipe Music' *in* The Collected Poems of Louis MacNeice (Faber and Faber, London, 1964). Reprinted by permission of David Higham Associates.

Tamata and the Alliance and *The Long Way* by Bernard Moitessier, translated by William Rodarmor (Sheridan House Inc., Dobbs Ferry, NY, 1995). Reprinted by permission of Sheridan House Inc.

Around the Big Blue Marble by Nigel Rowe (Aurum Press, London, 1995). Reprinted by permission of Aurum Press.

Saint-Exupéry by Stacy Schiff (Vintage Canada, Toronto, 1994). Reprinted by permission of Random House Inc.

'North Sea Off Carnoustie' by Anne Stevenson, in *The Oxford Book of the Sea*, edited by Jonathan Raban (Oxford University Press, Oxford, 1992). Reprinted by permission of Oxford University Press.

Illustration Credits

page
i   Map of the Vendée Globe race course reproduced courtesy of SAIL Publications © 1998.
x   Photo of a drawing by François Chevallier, reproduced by permission of Françoise Chevallier.
6   Map from *The Atlantic Crossing Guide* 3rd edition, by A. Hammick (International Marine, Rockport, ME, 1993). Reproduced courtesy of The McGraw-Hill Companies.

Every effort has been made to contact copyright holders. In the case of an inadvertent omission, please contact the publisher.